THE BASIC MINIMUM

A common presupposition in contemporary moral and political philosophy is that individuals should be provided with some basic threshold of goods, capabilities, or well-being. But if there is such a basic minimum, how should this be understood? Dale Dorsey offers an underexplored answer: that the basic minimum should be characterized not as the achievement of a set of capabilities, or as access to some specified bundle of resources, but as the maintenance of a minimal threshold of human welfare. In addition, Dorsey argues that, though political institutions should be committed to the promotion of this minimal threshold, we should reject approaches that seek to cast the basic minimum as a human right. His book will be important for all who are interested in theories of political morality.

DALE DORSEY is Assistant Professor of Philosophy at the University of Kansas.

THE BASIC MINIMUM

A Welfarist Approach

DALE DORSEY

University of Kansas

CAMBRIDGE
UNIVERSITY PRESS

CAMBRIDGE UNIVERSITY PRESS
Cambridge, New York, Melbourne, Madrid, Cape Town,
Singapore, São Paulo, Delhi, Tokyo, Mexico City

Cambridge University Press
The Edinburgh Building, Cambridge CB2 8RU, UK

Published in the United States of America by Cambridge University Press, New York

www.cambridge.org
Information on this title: www.cambridge.org/9781107017115

First published 2012

Printed in the United Kingdom at the University Press, Cambridge

A catalogue record for this publication is available from the British Library

Library of Congress Cataloguing in Publication data
Dorsey, Dale, 1976–
The basic minimum : a welfarist approach / Dale Dorsey.
p. cm.
Includes bibliographical references and index.
ISBN 978-1-107-01711-5 (hardback)
1. Political ethics. 2. Basic needs – Philosophy. 3. Political science – Philosophy.
I. Title.
JA79.D64 2012
172 – dc23 2011043832

ISBN 978-1-107-01711-5 Hardback

Contents

Preface

This book investigates the foundations of a basic minimum, with an eye toward developing a workable welfarist alternative to the dominant capabilities approach. However, I see the argument of this book at something of a subdisciplinary crossroads. Much of the most important work on the nature of a basic minimum, at least in the last half-century or so, has been conducted by focusing on the justice of political systems. This focus is certainly understandable. However, I hold that new avenues of inquiry can be opened by considering the *moral* fundamentals of alternative theories of the basic minimum, and bringing to bear concepts that generally appear in the normative ethical and metaethical literature: *moral reasons*, *welfare*, *impersonal versus personal value*, and so forth. Some thinkers interested in a basic minimum might find my methodology alienating, lacking engagement with the genuine problems of the world for which a basic minimum is a required normative tool. But I hold that if we articulate a welfarist basic minimum and its precise theory of moral reasons, etc., we find that a view that has been previously thought unworkable becomes comparatively attractive as a theory of political morality. I take this as progress.

However, credit for whatever progress this book makes on the topic of the basic minimum, or on any other topic for that matter, is not mine alone. As with any person who undertakes writing a book in philosophy, I have incurred many debts. I'd like to mention a few now. This book began life as one chapter of my Ph.D. dissertation at the University of California at San Diego. At UCSD, I learned a lot from the faculty and students with whom I interacted. I would especially like to mention David Brink, Jerry Doppelt, Sam Rickless, Nina Brewer-Davis, Matt Brown, Adam Streed, and Mike Tiboris.

I would also like to thank current and former colleagues at the University of Alberta and the University of Kansas. Jennifer Welchman, Phil Corkum, and Adam Morton at the University of Alberta were often helpful sounding boards as I was outlining the earliest version of this book. At the University of Kansas, Jack Bricke and Derrick Darby challenged me to address a number of important problems. In addition, Ben Eggleston read much of a previous draft of the manuscript, and offered very helpful and challenging comments. His reading led to a substantial revision and reorganization of the project. Nicole Hassoun read the entire manuscript (in one form or another). Her comments led to substantial changes in the first, second, and third chapters. Doug Portmore has been especially helpful at a number of stages, and has read several parts of the book in draft form. In addition, my work has also been improved by the helpful comments of people who are unknown to me. I thank in particular two anonymous reviewers for Cambridge University Press, along with a cavalcade of others who have commented on one or another piece of this book along the way.

Finally, I mention Richard Arneson. The dissertation Dick directed was a distant ancestor of the current book, but for those who know Dick's work, his influence must be obvious on every page. I have learned a lot not just from Dick's teaching, but also from his writing, including his proud embrace of a welfarist tradition in political thinking I seek to extend here. Dick was not only a great advisor, but is a great person, and a great philosopher. I cannot imagine what my life would be like without having the good fortune to study with him. Frankly, I'm glad I don't have to.

Some of the material in this book has appeared elsewhere. The second half of Chapter 1, and a few pages of Chapter 4, appeared in "Toward a Theory of The Basic Minimum" in *Politics, Philosophy, and Economics* 7 (2008), 423–45. §27 draws from "Three Arguments for Perfectionism" in *Noûs* 44 (2010), 59–79. Early sections of Chapter 3 appeared in "Preferences, Welfare, and the Status-Quo Bias" in *Australasian Journal of Philosophy* 88 (2010), 535–54. §4.5.1 appeared in "Headaches, Lives and Value" in *Utilitas* 21 (2009), 36–57. §§2.2–2.4 and §4.4 rework material from "First Steps in an Axiology of Goals" in *International Journal of Wellbeing* 1 (2011), 167–85. I am grateful to the publishers for permission to reprint and rework this material. I should also like to mention the institutional support I received while working on this book. In particular, I was the recipient of a 2009 New Faculty General Research Fund (NFGRF) award at the University of Kansas. I gratefully acknowledge this support from the University of Kansas.

Before I conclude the preface, I would like to acknowledge the influence, not just on this book, but on my life as a whole, of Erin Frykholm. Without her in my life this book would have been the work of a very different, and far less happy, person. I am, and will always be, grateful to her.

Introduction

O.I. QUESTIONS

In the *First Treatise of Government*, John Locke writes:

God the Lord and Father of all, has given no one of his Children such a Property, in his peculiar Portion of the things of this World, but that he has given his needy Brother a Right to the Surplusage of his Goods; so that it cannot justly be denyed him, when his pressing Wants call for it. And therefore no Man could ever have a just power over the Life of another, by Right of property in Land or Possessions; since 'twould always be a Sin in any Man of Estate, to let his Brother perish for want of affording him Relief out of his Plenty. As *Justice* gives every Man a Title to the product of his honest Industry, and the fair Acquisitions of his Ancestors descended to him; so *Charity* gives every Man a Title to so much out of another's Plenty, as will keep him from extream want, where he has no means to subsist otherwise.[1]

Though his account here is certainly underspecified, Locke seems to insist that any person has legitimate "Title" to enough of another person's goods sufficient for the avoidance of "extream want." In doing so, Locke appears to gesture at the plausibility of a *basic minimum*: no matter what else is true, no matter what one's own labor affords, or how resources are otherwise distributed, people, at the very least, have a moral right, or "title," to resources sufficient to *subsist*.[2]

Though I do not wish to enter into an exegetical discussion of Locke's great work, *if* Locke commits himself to something like a basic minimum, he is not alone. That individuals must be provided, at the very least, some basic threshold of goods, capabilities, or well-being is a popular view in contemporary moral and political philosophy. But though commitment to a basic threshold is common, and though much ink has been spilled on its policy implications, both global and domestic, two gaps in the literature have appeared. First, the moral fundamentals of a basic minimum have

[1] Locke (1689), para. 42. [2] See Sreenivasan (1995), 102–4.

rarely – with only a few notable exceptions – been explored in any great depth. By moral fundamentals, I mean to refer to the following general questions: what – in Locke's language – is the nature of "extream want"? What does it mean to "subsist"? In addition, Locke appears to grant that "charity" gives us a "Title" to whatever we need from another's "Surplusage" to subsist. But what counts as a surplus? What limits should we place on the demand that all be able to maintain the basic threshold? How important is the achievement of the basic minimum for any particular person? How important is it to promote the avoidance of "extream want" (whatever *that* is) in comparison to the promotion of other, valuable states of persons? These questions are difficult, and will require substantive investigation. A proper answer concerning the nature of "extream want," or the precise basic minimum threshold, will take (roughly speaking) the first three chapters of this book; a proper answer concerning the moral weight of the basic minimum will take the next two.

There is a second gap I wish to close here. Though it is assuredly natural, most have thought that a welfarist approach to the moral fundamentals of a basic minimum is a non-starter. Indeed, few have been content to defend welfarism on this score. I hope not just to give a welfarist approach a run for its money, but also to propose a basic minimum that is teleological in nature – compatible, even, with *act-utilitarianism*.

In this Introduction, I hope to gesture at the broader argument of the book, and to say a little about the limits of the current project. In particular, I stress the limits: I see this book as fitting in to a larger moral/political/philosophical exercise concerning our moral and social obligations to the worse-off. Insofar as this book is merely a part of this general project, there are many important questions I must leave out here.

0.2. ANSWERS

The argument of this book is contained within three broad *modules*. The first module is my particular understanding of the basic minimum itself: the basic minimum is the achievement of a sufficient threshold of well-being. My argument for this approach proceeds by process of elimination. In Chapter 1, I argue against its most important competitors: a *subsistence* approach, two *needs*-based approaches, a *primary goods* or *resourcist* approach, and the *capabilities* approach. I hope to show that each of these alternatives, combined with a very weak thesis concerning the moral importance of a basic minimum, fails.

In Chapters 2 and 3, I respond to three important *prima facie* challenges to a welfarist approach to the basic minimum: first, that a welfarist basic minimum must be arbitrary; second, that a welfarist approach is committed to the claim that a welfarist basic minimum implies that people should be forced to live lives that they do not value, or do not conform to their own conceptions of the good; third, that a welfarist approach is committed to a theory of well-being that succumbs to the problem of *adaptive preferences*. I show, in Chapter 2, that a welfarist basic minimum can (a) be plausibly, and non-arbitrarily, formulated and (b) needn't generate moral reasons to force individuals to live lives they don't value. I hold that the basic minimum is constituted by the achievement of a "valued project": the successful achievement of a long-term goal or project one endorses (in the right way, of course). In Chapter 3 I address the problem of adaptive preferences; I argue that this is a problem only for independently implausible theories of an individual's conception of the good, and hence a properly formulated account of a person's true conception of the good can and should avoid problematic forms of adaptation. Thus in avoiding problems that plague its competitors, and in solving its own unique challenges, there is reason to accept my welfarist approach to the basic minimum.

The second module concerns the relative intrinsic *value* of the basic minimum; in particular, how much the basic minimum is worth in comparison to other valuable states, states there is or may be moral reason to promote. To this question I devote Chapter 4. This inquiry is tricky, and requires us to consider, in relative detail, a number of depressing scenarios, i.e., how much the basic minimum is worth for one person in comparison to, say, minor benefits for individuals *below* the minimum, major benefits for individuals *just above* the minimum, and the like. Here I argue that the basic minimum lexically dominates welfare achievements below the basic minimum, and takes a form of weighted priority to welfare achievements above the basic minimum: this view in part relies on some general claims about well-being I make, and defend, in Chapter 2.

The third module broaches the topic of the general moral structure of the basic minimum: should we believe that individuals have a *right* to the basic minimum? Should we be consequentialists, and treat the basic minimum simply as one welfare achievement to be promoted among others? Chapter 5 argues that we should reject the idea that the basic minimum is the target of a human *right*, and instead argues that the moral reason to promote the basic minimum, and the weight of that reason, is derived only from the comparative intrinsic value of its promotion. In other words, we should accept what I call *The Teleological View*: there are no reasons to promote the basic minimum other than the general reason to promote overall goodness. However, or so I shall argue, this conclusion is not in tension with the robust moral importance of a basic minimum; in fact, given the relative intrinsic value of the basic minimum, we end up with a very strong basic minimum, indeed.

I stress the modularity of the current project. The arguments for each module are (at least most of the time) independent. One could, in principle, accept my particular account of the basic minimum while rejecting my account of the axiology of the basic minimum, or my claim that the morality of the basic minimum should be teleological in character. In addition, one could accept my account of the axiological weight of the basic minimum without accepting my claim that axiological weight determines moral weight. Though these modules are intended to be complementary, and though I hold that my own view works as a cohesive whole, one can accept or reject any particular module without doing substantive damage to the picture I support in the broadest sense. I present my view this way not because I lack confidence in the strength of any particular element, but rather because at least one purpose of this book is to provide skeptics with a reason to take a welfarist approach to the basic minimum more seriously than such an approach is generally taken. Hence it is a sensible strategy, in presenting my approach, not to let the controversial nature of one particular module get in the way of welfarism's broader virtues. Of course, there is a natural limit to such modularity; the independence of some parts of the book from the rest does not entail the complete independence of each part of the book from every other part. However, I have tried to show that a welfarist approach to the basic minimum can be plausibly rendered without accepting the *entirety* of my own view.

0.3. LIMITS

In defending himself from Francis Hutcheson's charge that he did not do enough, in a draft of the *Treatise of Human Nature*, to exhort individuals to moral behavior, David Hume famously insisted that there is a distinction in moral philosophical projects akin to the distinction between an *anatomist* and a *painter*.[3] The anatomist, so says Hume, is engaged in a detailed examination of the body, whereas the painter renders the human form beautiful, an object of wonder and delight. In moral theory, the "anatomist" deals only in the philosophical fundamentals: a complete account of our moral nature

[3] Hume (1739), 3.3.6.6.

and obligations. The task of endearing morality to those who might be skeptical of its charms is left to the "painter"; a task to which, incidentally, Hutcheson devoted the latter part of his own philosophical life.[4] Nevertheless, the task of the anatomist, according to Hume, is an essential part of the moral enterprise: an accurate account of the philosophical and psychological fundamentals of morality "may render" the work of the painter "more correct in its precepts, and more perswasive in its exhortations."

Like Hume, I do not see this book as the work of a "painter." My task in this book is not to render morality or a commitment to the basic minimum beautiful or endearing; it is not my task to motivate individuals to act in accordance with the moral principles for which I argue. However, there is a similar – vaguely Humean – distinction worth drawing here. Consider the distinction between an anatomist and a *surgeon*. The anatomist describes, in as much detail as possible, the human body and its inner workings. But the anatomist does not put that knowledge into practice, does not use this knowledge to reduce illness, or to increase the well-being of patients. This is the task of the surgeon. The surgeon uses his knowledge of anatomy to make correct incisions and to otherwise correct anatomical malfunctions. Of course, the surgeon and anatomist have a mutually dependent relationship; without the surgeon, the anatomist would be engaged in a project with no implications for human health. But without the anatomist, the surgeon wouldn't know where to cut.

My project is akin to the anatomist, not simply against the painter, but also against the surgeon. To put this point in a slightly less metaphorical way, this book is a work of *moral theory*. I aim to offer a theory of *moral reasons*, especially those that concern the existence of a basic minimum. I do not intend to engage in a discussion of the way in which the moral reasons for which I argue might best be fulfilled in practice. Given my task as I conceive it, the book I have written does not focus on the particular facts that are present in underdeveloped or poor nations, and does not seek to evaluate particular policies that are at least implicitly intended to achieve a basic social minimum (including, for instance, the United Nations "Millennium Development Goals," among others). My discussion is therefore abstracted from the conditions "on the ground." Nevertheless, an inquiry of this nature is important, even necessary. Our social policies should be informed by an inquiry into moral reasons, not the other way around. Without such abstraction, one offers a moral theory that is simply incorrect, and hence cannot be a worthwhile guide to policy.

[4] See, for instance, Hutcheson (1755), 1.

Some will dispute this. Some will hold, instead, that many political questions or questions of social policy are context-sensitive, that we cannot offer a more "general" theory of moral reasons that applies to all contexts, political, interpersonal, or otherwise. Political morality is formulated first and foremost *within* a given social context, and is informed by that social context; different political institutions may very well have different moral reasons depending on their context and moment in history. Thus any attempt to account for a basic minimum cannot simply rely on the idea of "moral reasons" without engaging with the very facts "on the ground" I proudly ignore. Of course, there may be some truth in a view like this. It could be that some obligations of justice cannot be separated from the concept of *institutions* of justice and the political and historical contexts in which they are situated. But how plausible is this view when it comes to the nature of a basic minimum? Not very. First, we should resist the claim that the idea of a basic minimum is grounded in individual political contexts. After all, we have a tendency to make use of the idea of a basic minimum *all the time* in our more general *non*-political moral thinking. Indeed, individual cases I discuss in the book bring this out explicitly (consider, for instance, *Famine*, introduced in Chapter 1; the fact that people are starving, or fall victim to "extream want," itself seems to provide sufficient moral reason to assist them whether or not political institutions should do so as well, or whether political institutions exist at all). So it seems to me, first, that there is a more general concept of the basic minimum that operates in a wide variety of moral contexts, political or otherwise. Second, and more importantly, though social *policy* will certainly vary with political context, and though the method by which a basic minimum will be put into practice will vary with political context, it seems entirely wrong to believe that the moral reasons to which any given political society must adhere are somehow relative or contextual in the way this objection would have us believe. If we believe that, say, the promotion of human needs or capabilities is important for some destitute person A, it seems to me wildly implausible to say that it is less important for some other person B, just as destitute, simply because A is in a different political or historical context than B. Third, though some such view may well be the truth, it is not compatible, as far as I can tell, with the guiding idea of a basic minimum. To say that a minimum threshold exists, but only within certain, highly contingent political or social contexts is to deny a guiding intuition that seems central to the implementation of the basic minimum: whatever else is true, the destitute must have their needs met. Of course, this intuition is underspecified and requires rigorous philosophical interpretation. But this interpretation is not dependent on individual facts of social context, but is necessarily abstracted from such facts.[5]

However, I do not claim that a philosophically informed inquiry into social policy is unnecessary or unwarranted. The surgeon has a role to play just as much as the anatomist. In medical practice, getting the anatomy right is step one; but without a surgeon no medical treatment will be possible. In moral philosophy, getting the account of our moral reasons is simply step one. Philosophically informed social policy is no less a necessary step. But (save for a few comments in §5.4 and §6.5) it is a task I leave for further study.

In addition to being "anotomical" rather than "surgeonistic," my book eschews a number of topics that might be approached with an anatomical gaze, but that are surely essential to any *full* account of our obligations to the disadvantaged. First, my project here is to clarify and argue for one particular account of the structure of a basic minimum and its comparative moral weight. But nowhere in this book will I argue that a basic minimum *should exist*. This book's audience is intended to be those who believe that a commitment to a basic minimum is plausible. I seek to argue for a palatable approach to the basic minimum, specifically a welfarist approach, and in so doing will assume that the general idea of a basic minimum is plausible overall. It may not be. Indeed, for some who are convinced of a failure of a welfarist approach, my critique of alternative views in Chapter 1 may provide reason to reject the idea of a basic minimum altogether. I do not engage such skepticism here; I take my task to be happily accomplished if my approach is considered the *best* of the basic minimum-favoring views, whether or not we should ultimately favor the existence or moral importance of such a minimum threshold.

Second, I do not wish to engage the interesting and important question of the *breadth* of moral obligations when it comes to the establishment of a basic minimum. Some hold, for instance, that we have moral obligations to provide the basic minimum not just for those within our own society or political context, but rather for all. Call this a "cosmopolitan" view. Others will hold that it is far more important, morally speaking, for ourselves and our political institutions to be directed to the task of promoting the basic minimum for those within our own social or political context. Call this a "non-cosmopolitan" view.

[5] Important to note is that this intuition does not necessarily rule out a *relativist* treatment of the basic minimum, of the sort I discuss in §1.5. It could very well be that the basic minimum, for all individuals, requires meeting some threshold of "social needs" or "social goods," though I argue strenuously against such a proposal in the next chapter.

My inquiry here does not concern the breadth of our moral obligations; I shall not broach the topic of *whose* achievement of the basic minimum we have reason to promote. Rather, this book is intended to outline the structure of a basic minimum and its moral importance *for those for whom we have a reason to promote the basic minimum*. My task is to show that whether one is a cosmopolitan, non-cosmopolitan, or whatever, one has reason to reject alternative approaches to the basic minimum and its relative moral importance, and to accept the view I defend here. Given this limitation, in speaking of the moral importance of the basic minimum, I will focus on moral agents, political institutions, schemes, or societies. I will not assume, however, that moral agents, political institutions, schemes, or societies must be morally interested only in those within, rather than without, their moral, political, or social borders.

0.4. POLITICS AND NEUTRALITY

One further note merits mention. In this book I offer an account of the basic minimum that indexes the obligations of political morality to a theory of the good life. In this way, my view violates the popular doctrine of *political neutrality*; my view implies that political morality is not neutral between competing theories of what makes a human life good versus bad, better rather than worse, etc.[6] I also identify the importance, for justice, of the basic minimum by means of an inquiry into substantive moral reasons (including moral reasons to promote the achievement of well-being). Hence I am committed to resting at least part of political morality on a "substantive ethical conception" of the sort that many neutralists and so-called "political liberals" eschew.

I flag this point here to lay it aside. I think there are decisive reasons against political neutrality about the good, and against refusing to treat moral reasons as an important factor in political justice.[7] But even if there

[6] Different writers will understand political neutrality, and the general concerns of political liberalism, differently. Some hold that political institutions should not be guided in any way by concerns about the goodness of lives (Barry (1992), 161–2). Some hold that political neutrality will allow reference to *some* conceptions of well-being, including "subjectivist" conceptions (see Arneson (1992)). Some political liberals believe that justice should not only be neutral with regard to the good, but also neutral with regard to substantive *ethical* or *moral* views (see Rawls, "Justice as Fairness: Political not Metaphysical" in Rawls (1999)). My own view violates the first and third conceptions of political neutrality, insofar as I believe that justice ought to take seriously substantive moral reasons, and that justice ought to take seriously at least a *roughly* subjectivist theory of the good life. Incidentally, however, I also leave open the possibility of an objective, preference-independent theory of well-being, and hence leave open a view that violates all three neutralist constraints.

[7] See, for instance, Sher (1997), Arneson (1997) and (2003).

are not decisive reasons against political neutrality, a version of political liberalism must take seriously the substantive ethical conception I offer here. I consider my view an *immanent* investigation into a particular substantive moral view: ours. I hope to show that considered judgments support a welfarist account of the basic minimum and its political importance. If this is right, any version of political liberalism – which insists that political reasons are not moral reasons, but are to be culled from an overlapping consensus of reasonable comprehensive doctrines – must accommodate the view I offer. A comprehensive doctrine that accepts the views I advocate here cannot plausibly be claimed to be unreasonable, or to be advocated only by those who "plan to engage in cooperative schemes but are unwilling to honor, or even to propose, except as a necessary public pretense, any general principles or standards for specifying fair terms of cooperation."[8] My view *is* a substantive ethical conception – one that I hope, by the end of the book, the reader will find reason to reasonably accept.

However, even *if* political neutrality should be accepted, and even *if* my account – drawing as it does on a substantive ethical conception – cannot be viewed as a feature of a reasonable political theory, there remains reason to take seriously my account of the basic minimum. Given that I seek to offer an account of the moral fundamentals of the minimum, any *moral*, as opposed to political, theory can embrace the basic minimum as I define it. Those who would reject the political appeal to the good life or substantive moral reasons are welcome to treat my view as limited to the moral, rather than political, domain.

With this in mind, I now turn my attention to the basic minimum itself. However, before we can assess competing theories of the basic minimum – including the welfarist approach I favor – we must understand, in at least general terms, what, exactly, a basic minimum is supposed to *be*. This topic begins the first chapter.

[8] Rawls (1995), 50.

CHAPTER I

On the concept (and some conceptions) of the basic minimum

Stated in the most general way, and leaving aside the nitty-gritty, that political morality should include a commitment to a *basic minimum* is plausible. Sentiments that point in this direction range from the following, by Ronald Dworkin: "it is important, from an objective point of view, that human lives be successful rather than wasted, and this is equally important, from that objective point of view, for each human life,"[1] to Martha Nussbaum: "moving all citizens above a basic threshold . . . should be taken as a central social goal,"[2] to Stuart White, who notes that there "is a widespread intuition that in a just society citizens must have access on reasonable terms to the resources necessary to meet their basic needs."[3] These sentiments are popular, and it is easy to see why. When any particular person fails to maintain a minimally decent life, or fails to obtain their basic needs, it is tempting to say that this fact *by itself* provides a moral reason for assistance. Political institutions should be concerned, it would appear, not just with equality, overall well-being, or the plight of the worst-off. They should *also* be concerned to see that people obtain a life that maintains a minimal, basic threshold.

Like all philosophical matters, however, the devil is in the details. How should a basic minimum be understood? What must a person fail to maintain to fail to maintain the basic minimum? What is the relative moral importance of a basic minimum against other social goals? The project of this book is to answer these questions in some detail and to support an underexplored welfarist answer to them. To this end, the first chapter sets the stage. First, I draw some conceptual blueprints – including what, at the most general level, a basic minimum *is*. In §1.1, I offer an account of the *concept* of a basic minimum: what any view must accept to qualify as a view that accepts a basic minimum. Very roughly, I conclude that a view

[1] Dworkin (2000), 5. [2] Nussbaum, "Women and Cultural Universals" in Nussbaum (1999), 43.
[3] White (2003), 131.

is committed to a basic minimum only insofar as this view is committed to the (at least) weak moral priority of a valuable absolute state of persons. With this conceptual groundwork laid, the second task of this chapter is to critically evaluate particular theories of the basic minimum. As it turns out, this chapter concludes on a down note (at least for those who find a basic minimum plausible). In §§1.2–1.8, I show that five accounts of the basic minimum fail, while a sixth faces a powerful dilemma.

1.1. THE CONCEPT OF A BASIC MINIMUM

So what is a basic minimum? It seems to me that the place to begin is by regimenting the intuitions that began this chapter and that, I hope, the reader will appreciate. As stated by Nussbaum and White, the basic minimum appears to be a particular state of persons that should be a "central social goal," or that is a demand of a "just society." Of course, different conceptions of the basic minimum will differ concerning which state forms this central goal. But for now, we might hold that any basic minimum-accepting political theory will conform to:

BM1: a basic minimum is a state of persons below which political institutions must not allow citizens to fall.

Is BM1 adequate to the concept of the basic minimum? Perhaps so. Consider, for instance, a case in which reference to a basic minimum has moral pull:

Famine: Group A and group B live in an extremely stratified society. Group A has very little access to material resources, and has fallen into a disastrous famine, leaving a substantial percentage of its members in conditions of severe starvation and malnutrition. Group B, on the other hand, though not living in the lap of luxury, is in no danger of falling into famine conditions. This society has the opportunity to promote the living standards of either group A or group B (but not both).

In *Famine*, and cases like it, it seems correct to say that political society, individual moral agents, etc., have a moral obligation to alleviate the starvation of group A rather than improving the living standards of group B. Offhand, this seems morally obvious. But why? Of course, one explanation for this might appeal to the fact that this society, on the whole, is *unequal*, or that this particular society fails to do all it can for *the least well-off*. But though these may be important reasons to assist group A rather than group B, an appeal to equality or to the moral priority of the worst-off doesn't seem to say it all. Rather, group A's interests seem to take moral priority here because the members of group A are *starving*. Any failure to correct the starvation of group A would seem to be a gross miscarriage of justice. Our considered judgment here seems to conform to BM1. The avoidance of starvation appears to be the sort of "state of persons" that many will find morally important to establish for all. But more than this: that its members are starving seemed to be sufficient reason, by itself, to require political institutions to address the needs of group A. Hence a basic minimum seems to be the sort of thing that, should anyone fall below it, political institutions have failed.

However, BM1 is inadequate for two reasons. First, BM1 seems to dictate, at a conceptual level, that the basic minimum will have a *very* strong connection to moral obligations of political institutions. In particular, it appears to indicate that the achievement of the basic minimum is a *requirement* of justice; when a citizen, indeed any citizen, fails the basic minimum, political institutions responsible have failed. But though the minimum will be *a* factor in determining the justice of social institutions (assuming such a minimum exists), the weight of this factor, at least at a conceptual level, is certainly up for grabs. Surely one might accept a basic minimum, but also believe that justice can obtain when some fail to meet this threshold. Achievement of the basic minimum is surely one among many social, political, and moral goals worth promoting. If and when such goals come into conflict, we need not insist that the basic minimum should take priority simply as a matter of *concept*.

Second, it is not clear that the interest in a basic minimum is confined to the political. Non-political morality need not be excluded from making moral use of a basic minimum. For instance, it might be the case that, even in the absence of political institutions, moral agents have reason to see to it that persons maintain some adequate "threshold" or achieve a basic level of "success." There may be strong moral reason to assist others to achieve a certain level of relief of suffering or maintenance of rational capacities or other valuable states simply because this particular state is morally significant.[4] In short, it's hard to see why the avoidance of starvation isn't just as significant for non-political agents in a position to assist groups A or B. Hence insofar as we're looking for a conceptual account of the basic minimum, it's best to avoid statements of the *concept* that apply only to political morality.

So the concept of a basic minimum should be broadened. Two things seem to me to characterize a view that accepts a basic minimum. First, views

[4] Such views are offered by, among others, Singer (1972) and Herman (1993).

that accept a basic minimum will include an *evaluative* element. To accept a basic minimum, one must hold that some particular *state* of persons, whether a welfare achievement or some level of resources or capabilities (e.g., the avoidance of starvation) is *of value*. However, it is important that this state be of a certain structure. States of persons can be either *relative* or *absolute*. An *absolute* state of persons is *non-comparative* (such as, for instance, "maintaining one's basic needs," or "possessing capabilities *x*, *y*, and *z*"); to determine whether an absolute state holds of a person, one need only look to that person. Relative states are essentially comparative; they are states that cannot hold of a person independently of a comparison between that person and others. Relative states include "being equal," or "being better-off," etc. Theories that accept a basic minimum will posit an *absolute*, non-comparative state and declare that this state is of special value. For example, though many views will hold that the state of "maintaining equality with others" is important for any person to achieve, such a state cannot constitute a basic minimum. A state of persons counts only as a basic minimum if that state could be possessed no matter one's place in the overall distribution, and no matter whether one has been made better- or worse-off over time, and no matter whether anyone else, or everyone else, also maintains that state.

The evaluative element of a basic minimum requires a further word of clarification. Some political theories will refuse to index obligations of justice to a vision of the good life. Such views generally hold that the political domain should remain neutral when it comes to theories of that which is intrinsically good for persons.[5] However, this form of neutrality need not disqualify a view from believing in a basic minimum, at least as I understand a basic minimum here. In particular, the basic minimum need not be, for instance, of value *because* it is valuable as a feature of the good life. One can believe that the avoidance of starvation is a valuable state of persons, but not as a *per se* feature of the good life. With this in mind, one might identify the basic minimum as some set of resources, capabilities, or primary goods that are not valuable as a matter of the good life, but are of value given that, e.g., every rational person has reason to desire them, or that they are the product of a reasonable overlapping consensus.[6]

The second feature runs as follows. Belief in a basic minimum has a moral, as well as evaluative, dimension. To believe in a basic minimum is to believe not just that a particular property of persons is of value, but

[5] There is a long and enduring list of liberal neutralists when it comes to the good. Among the *loci classici* are Rawls (1995) and Barry (1992).

[6] Rawls, "Justice as Fairness: Political not Metaphysical" in Rawls (1999), Nussbaum (2000), 76.

that this particular property of persons has a certain moral weight. A basic minimum is morally *special*.

One can put the moral dimension of a basic minimum somewhat more precisely as follows. It is common to make reference to the notion of a moral "reason," i.e., a consideration that counts in favor of a moral requirement to perform some action ϕ. However, moral reasons can be of differing weight or importance. Say that an action ϕ is "morally decisive with respect to" another action ψ if and only if the reason(s) to ϕ is/are stronger than the reason(s) to ψ. Say that ϕ-ing is *overriding* if ϕ-ing is morally decisive with respect to all alternative actions. With this terminology in mind, views that accept a basic minimum will hold that there is not just *pro tanto* reason to promote the achievement of the basic minimum, but rather that this reason has a particular weight or importance: to promote the basic minimum is *morally decisive* with respect to the promotion of other valuable states of persons. In this respect, the basic minimum – whatever it is – is morally special. This priority need not be overwhelming, or even particularly weighty. All that is required is what I call "weak moral priority":

Weak Moral Priority: For any two valuable states p and q, p is weakly morally prior to q if and only if, if ϕ is the action of promoting a single instance of p, and ψ is the action of promoting a single instance of q, ϕ-ing is morally decisive with respect to ψ-ing.[7]

p is weakly morally prior to q if and only if there is greater reason to promote p for A than there is to promote q for B, i.e., if there is greater reason to promote p than q in a one-to-one comparison. Given this terminology, it seems quite obvious that to be a basic minimum p must maintain *at least* weak moral priority to other valuable states of persons. In this way, we respect the moral "specialness" of the basic minimum. Of course, as specified, the requisite moral specialness is weak. Intuitions such as Nussbaum's and White's would point to a basic minimum of greater moral priority. Nevertheless, as a matter of concept, it seems right to say that any basic minimum p must take *at least* weak moral priority to any other valuable state of persons. If q maintains weak moral priority to p, p is no

7 I treat the notion of a "single instance" as primitive. In essence, what I mean is the achievement of a particular property for a single person. This is vague, however, given that different conceptions of the basic minimum will identify the locus of "achievement" differently. Some might hold that the achievement of the basic minimum for a person is the achievement of the basic minimum for a person over the course of that person's life. Others might believe that shorter time-periods are relevant, and hence a person can achieve the basic minimum at one time, but not at others. This, however, is a substantive matter that is rightly left aside in conceptual discussion of the basic minimum. I discuss this issue in the next chapter, §2.5. Thanks to an anonymous reviewer for calling this point to my attention.

basic minimum. This also holds of relative states. One might imagine the promotion of, say, equality, or the interests of the least well-off, tells in favor of ψ-ing rather than ϕ-ing. Though we may insist on the importance of the promotion of such valuable relative states, views that accept a *basic minimum* should insist that it takes at least *weak* priority to their promotion.[8] If equality, or priority for the least well-off, render ψ-ing morally decisive with respect to ϕ-ing, p is not a basic minimum, at least in the sense I discuss here. For p to be a basic minimum, an increase in equality, say, cannot be enough to morally outweigh p's promotion.

The weak moral priority of the basic minimum holds that the basic minimum should be, on a one-to-one basis, the most important social goal. However, this leaves open the possibility that the basic minimum might not conform to BM1: one might believe that the basic minimum takes moral priority to other valuable states, but not necessarily absolute or overriding priority. The basic minimum's moral priority – as a matter of concept, anyway – need only be weak.

A further feature of weak moral priority should be flagged. Consider the distinction, made famous by Philip Pettit, between different moral "stances" one might take toward morally relevant goods.[9] One might believe, for instance, that there is a moral reason to "honor" p, which would hold that there is reason to preserve it, not to harm or destroy it, etc. One might also believe that there is reason to promote p, where this entails a reason to increase the amount of p, to maximize the achievement of p, etc. My account of the priority of the basic minimum is limited to the priority one must grant to the basic minimum when it comes to the stance of promotion only: in a one-to-one comparison, there is stronger reason to promote the basic minimum than there is to promote other states. But this limitation is important. BM1 seems to hold that political societies are perfectly justified in stopping at *nothing* to secure the achievement of the basic minimum for all. However, one might believe that pursuit of the basic minimum can be limited by, for instance, a right not to be harmed. One might believe that there are reasons to "honor" some states of persons, reasons that are morally decisive with respect to the reason to promote the achievement

[8] This might sound a bit awkward: how do we promote only a single instance of, say, equality? If you, say, benefit one person for the sake of equality, doesn't that mean that two people now possess the comparative state of being equal? When it comes to weak moral priority to comparative states, I understand the idea (somewhat roughly) like this: promotion of the basic minimum is morally decisive with respect to benefiting one person *for reasons of the promotion of comparative states*, such as equality, improving the less well-off, etc. Though this language is admittedly awkward, the idea should be clear enough.

[9] Cf. Pettit (1997).

of the basic minimum. Hence, though it seems correct to claim that the basic minimum should have weak moral priority, it also seems correct not to rule out views that would restrict the promotion of the basic minimum in the face of moral rights not to be harmed, or reasons to "honor" other states.

As an improvement on BM1, then, we might consider:

BM2: p is a basic minimum if and only if *p* is a valuable absolute state of persons, which maintains at least weak moral priority to all other valuable states of persons.

BM2 seems to correct the deficiencies of BM1. BM2 accepts that an interest in the basic minimum is not confined to the political. Furthermore, BM2 allows that the basic minimum might not maintain overriding moral priority in all cases, avoiding a serious problem encountered by BM1.

Though BM2 seems to capture the basic conceptual structure of a basic minimum, I think one amendment is in order. BM2 seems to insist that, for any two people A and B, A's maintenance of the basic minimum must take weak moral priority to B's maintenance of any other valuable state *p*. But this might be too strong. We could imagine, for instance, conditions under which it is appropriate *not* to treat someone's basic minimum as weakly morally prior. For instance, one might imagine a view according to which the achievement of the basic minimum for cold-blooded murderers, or those who display some other form of negative moral responsibility, is less morally important than non-minimum states for others. On such a view, the basic minimum *for cold-blooded murderers* would not maintain weak moral priority. Hence given that such a view is possible (even plausible) it seems sensible to add a qualifier to the conceptual structure of the basic minimum:

BM3: p is a basic minimum if and only if *p* is a valuable absolute state of persons, which – in the general case – maintains at least weak moral priority to all other valuable states of persons.

My use of the term "in the general case" is meant to allow that the basic minimum for some might not maintain moral priority given some particular fact about *them* (being a cold-blooded murderer, for instance). However, for reasons already rehearsed, in the *general* case the basic minimum should take at least weak moral priority to all other states. For the purposes of this book, then, I accept BM3. The theories I consider, and the theory I offer, are intended to be conceptions of the concept identified therein. (I hereby abstract from the qualifier, which I discuss in more detail in §6.2.)

1.2. CONCEPTIONS

The conceptual structure of the basic minimum is now on the table. The remainder of this chapter will address the plausibility of various accounts of the basic minimum in light of the minimal requirements of BM3. Though there may be many more, in this chapter I discuss six such theories. First, I discuss the claim that the basic minimum is to be identified as the possession of a certain threshold level of primary goods or resources (§1.3). Second, I discuss the possibility – argued for by Henry Shue – that the basic minimum is the state of human *subsistence* (§1.4). As a third possibility, some have held that the concept of "poverty" (and, perhaps by extension, the concept of failing a basic minimum) should not be understood in abstraction from the various *social* needs of people in a given society or political context (§1.5). Fourth, one might adopt a suggestion, popular in development economics, that the basic minimum is best understood not as the fulfillment of social needs, but rather as the fulfillment of *basic human needs* (§1.6).[10] The fifth possibility has been strenuously defended by Martha Nussbaum. This view holds that the basic minimum should not be understood as the accumulation of primary goods, or the achievement of subsistence *per se*, but rather the maintenance of certain central *capabilities*.

The sixth and final option I consider is the option for which I shall ultimately argue. In contrast to the capabilities approach, a *welfarist* approach to the basic minimum holds that the achievement of the basic minimum is to be understood as *living a good life* to some threshold degree.

The remainder of this chapter discusses these options with a critical eye. I end on a down note. By the end of this chapter, I hope to have shown that there are very serious problems with each approach to the basic minimum. One might take this as evidence that no basic minimum exists. While this possibility may be tempting, I begin construction of a welfarist approach – one that can avoid the dilemma I pose – in Chapter 2.

1.3. GOODS AND RESOURCES

Take *Famine*. One might be tempted to claim that group A fails the basic minimum because group A fails to have sufficient primary goods (including food and purchasing power) from which to draw, resources that are available to group B. Hence, one might claim that the failure of a sufficient threshold of these basic resources provides reason to distribute to

[10] See, for instance, Streeten, et al., eds. (1981).

group A rather than B. If this thought is plausible, one might claim that the basic minimum should be expressed as a threshold level of such goods. Familiar from Rawls, primary goods include not just income and wealth, but also a range of other valuable resources. Rawls defines them as "things which it is supposed a rational man wants whatever else he wants."[11] Rawls distinguishes five kinds of primary goods, the most recent account of which runs as follows:

> (i) The basic rights and liberties: freedom of thought and liberty of conscience, and the rest. These rights and liberties are essential institutional conditions required for the adequate development and full and informed exercise of the two moral powers.
> (ii) Freedom of movement and free choice of occupation against a background of diverse opportunities, which opportunities allow the pursuit of a variety of ends and give effect to decisions to revise and alter them.
> (iii) Powers and prerogatives of offices and positions of authority and responsibility.
> (iv) Income and wealth, understood as all-purpose means (having an exchange value) generally needed to achieve a wide range of ends whatever they may be.
> (v) The social bases of self-respect, understood as those aspects of basic institutions normally essential if citizens are to have a lively sense of their worth as persons and to be able to advance their ends with self-confidence.[12]

A basic minimum composed of primary goods would presumably require some threshold set of each of these five types of primary good, perhaps weighing some more heavily than others, and perhaps allowing trade-offs among them. This view seems to adequately explain our reaction in *Famine*: because group A fails to possess adequate levels of resources (including income and food), there is stronger moral reason to assist group A rather than group B.[13]

But where is the threshold to be set? Two questions deserve answers. First: is the set of primary goods that constitutes the basic minimum to be understood to apply *universally* or *relatively*? A universal approach holds that a particular set of primary goods constitutes the basic minimum for all individuals within a given society. A relativist approach, by contrast, holds that for any particular person, the minimum threshold of primary

[11] Rawls (1971), 92. [12] Rawls (2001), 58–9.

[13] I here focus on Rawls's account rather than alternative "resourcist" or goods accounts offered by, e.g., Philippe van Parijs. Van Parijs claims that the basic minimum should be a "basic income" – specified as the highest possible unconditional income that can be granted to all (see van Parijs (1995), 34–5). However, van Parijs's view is only nominally a resourcist approach, insofar as he believes that this basic income is only morally resonant insofar as it allows people the "freedom to live as one might like to live" (ibid., 30). Hence, insofar as van Parijs insists on the maintenance of a basic minimum, this basic minimum seems to take the form of a capabilities approach: real freedom, real capabilities, to live as one might like to live. I argue against capabilities approaches in detail below.

goods will vary depending on factors such as that individual's abilities, disabilities, health, natural talents, etc. On this view, the basic minimum for A will be determined by whatever is required for A to maintain some *further* valuable, absolute state. But once we have identified whether a primary goods approach is universal or relative, we still must know what the proper threshold is. This, then, is the second question: if we define the basic minimum universally, what is the threshold of primary goods that counts as the basic minimum? If we define the basic minimum as relative between persons, to what *further* achievement do we index each person's threshold set of primary goods?

Take the first question. Is it plausible to establish some particular threshold of each category of primary goods that, taken jointly, could apply as the basic minimum for all persons? I think the answer is no. Take, for instance, a primary good such as the provision of health care. Presumably one might believe that the provision of health care is one institution that is "normally essential if citizens are to have a lively sense of their own worth as persons and to able to advance their ends with self-confidence," i.e., one of the social bases of self-respect. But what *level of access* to health care will count as essential for the basic minimum?

If we define the proper threshold universally at, say, level *h*, we are left with the following problem. Some individuals will not require level *h* to, say, "advance their ends with self-confidence." Others will require much more than *h*. Assume now that A is a healthy person, does not require any access to health care to maintain a life that A values to the fullest. Assume that B is extremely sickly, and has some illness that requires provision of health care in excess of *h* to advance his ends or goals. Now assume that providing level *h* for A will require providing *only h* for B. If the universalist primary goods approach is to declare that the basic minimum requires the provision of *h*, it must say that there is stronger moral reason to provide this level of health care access to A than there is to provide additional levels of health care access to B: the basic minimum, of course, is weakly morally prior to other valuable states of persons (including B's provision of additional health care access). But this is surely the wrong answer. A doesn't need *h*, while B requires more than *h*. Given BM3, a universalist primary goods approach cannot provide a plausible account of the basic minimum.[14]

[14] This is a classic objection to resourcist views about the nature of political distribution. It is made most famous by Sen, see (1993), (1980), (2009) 260–2.

So if we are going to accept a primary goods approach, we must accept a *relativist* approach: one that defines the primary goods that are to count as part of the basic minimum in a way that is sensitive to the distinction between individuals, including A's natural healthiness and B's natural sickliness. Indeed, this is Rawls's own approach. At various places, Rawls claims that one essential feature of political morality is the provision of primary goods sufficient for individuals to meet their *basic needs*. Rawls writes: "a social minimum providing for the basic needs of all citizens is . . . [a constitutional] essential."[15] Rawls also claims that the provision of individuals' basic needs may very well be the *first* principle of political morality: "[T]he first principle covering the equal basic rights and liberties may easily be preceded by a lexically prior principle requiring that citizens' basic needs be met, at least insofar as their being met is necessary for citizens to understand and to be able fruitfully to exercise those rights and liberties."[16] Rawls's own approach is relativist insofar as Rawls defines the basic minimum in terms of whatever primary goods are *sufficient to obtain one's basic needs*. This will allow variation when it comes to the particular level of primary goods constitutive of the basic minimum between persons.

If we accept that access to sufficient health care is a basic need, a relativist primary goods approach may be able to avoid the problem that plagued a universalist approach: because access to health care at level h is not one of A's basic needs, and access to health care at a level greater than h *is* one of B's basic needs, defining the basic minimum as "primary goods sufficient to meet one's basic needs" would appear to solve this problem. But a further problem must be obvious. In defining a primary goods approach to the basic minimum as whatever is required for an individual to maintain his or her basic needs, the primary goods approach is in danger of simply reducing to a basic needs approach: the basic minimum is defined not in terms of primary goods, but in terms of the maintenance of some set of important basic needs.[17]

15 Rawls (1995), 228. 16 Ibid., 7.

17 Of course, that Rawls's approach reduces to a basic needs approach is not strictly entailed by his own account. Rawls might insist that the basic minimum entitles a given individual *only* to the *primary goods* sufficient for the achievement of one's basic needs, and hence hold that the basic minimum does not include non-primary goods that might, for some people, be required for the maintenance of their basic needs. However, it seems to me that this position smacks of fetishism. If non-primary goods are essential for the ability to participate politically, and to exercise one's two moral powers, there is surely just as much reason to provide these non-primary goods as there is to provide the various primary goods. Indeed, this proposal seems to be internally unstable. It would appear that the moral force of *this particular level* of primary goods is given by the fact that it allows individuals to maintain their basic needs. But if the fact that doing so allows individuals to meet their basic needs forms the moral reason to distribute primary goods, why not also non-primary goods, as well?

This problem generalizes. A relativist primary goods approach must specify the appropriate level of primary goods in terms of some other index: primary goods sufficient *for p*, whether *p* is basic needs, subsistence, some level of capabilities or welfare, etc. But in so doing, the primary goods approach loses distinctiveness: the moral force of the basic minimum is determined not by the moral force of primary goods themselves, but by the moral force of *p*. Of course, a basic needs approach is important, and will be considered below, as will a number of other potential competitors for the role of *p*. But either the primary goods approach yields implausible verdicts in light of BM3 (on a universalist interpretation), or the primary goods approach loses distinctiveness (on a relativist interpretation).

1.4. SUBSISTENCE

Recall again *Famine*. Perhaps the fact that group A lacks adequate primary goods is not that which drives us to support group A's moral priority. Perhaps, rather, it is the fact that group A fails to *subsist*, for which food, resources, or purchasing power are essential (at least in this case). Surely, it might be claimed, if anything is a morally important state of persons, it is the achievement of subsistence. In weighing various reasons to promote particular achievements, it seems hard to believe that the promotion of human subsistence doesn't take at least weak moral priority to other distributive goals or valuable states of persons. Thus, if the failure of group A to subsist is morally resonant, we might be tempted to claim that subsistence constitutes the basic minimum.

Briefly suggested by Locke, the most important account of a basic minimum in terms of basic human subsistence is argued for by Henry Shue. For Shue, if any particular state of persons is to take moral priority, it must be subsistence:

> Why, then, according to the argument so far, are security and subsistence basic rights? Each is essential to a normal healthy life. Because the actual deprivation of either can be so very serious – potentially incapacitating, crippling, or fatal – even threatened deprivation of either can be a powerful weapon against anyone whose security and subsistence is not in fact socially guaranteed. People who cannot provide for their own security and subsistence and who lack social guarantees for both are very weak, possibly helpless, against any individual or institution in a position to deprive them of anything else they value by means of threatening their security or subsistence. A fundamental purpose of acknowledging any basic rights

at all is to prevent, or to eliminate, insofar as possible the degree of vulnerability that leaves people at the mercy of others. Social guarantees of security and subsistence would go a long way toward accomplishing this purpose.[18]

If Shue is correct, human subsistence clearly satisfies BM3 – it appears to uniquely satisfy his reasoning for a "social guarantee."[19] Offhand, Shue's claim is plausible. Shue notes that the lack of human subsistence entails an extreme cost (especially when it comes to resultant vulnerability). Subsistence, as Shue understands it, thus seems to be extremely important, morally speaking.

But a problem arises. "Human subsistence" sounds like a concept that itself stands in need of a theory. Defining a basic minimum in terms of human subsistence threatens emptiness without a plausible account of subsistence itself. However, Shue's own account is unsatisfactory:

By . . . subsistence, I mean unpolluted air, unpolluted water, adequate food, adequate clothing, adequate shelter, and minimal preventive public health care. Many complications about exactly how to specify the boundaries of what is necessary for subsistence would be interesting to explore. But the basic idea is to have available for consumption what is needed for a decent chance at a reasonably healthy and active life of more or less normal length, barring tragic interventions. This central idea is clear enough to work with, even though disputes can occur over exactly where to draw its outer boundaries.[20]

Shue's account is indeterminate. Shue writes that subsistence amounts to "adequate" food, "adequate" clothing, etc. But the problem with Shue's approach should be relatively obvious: how much is "adequate"? Adequate for what? One might be tempted to say that the basic minimum is maintained by A if and only if A has food adequate *for the maintenance of the basic minimum.* But Shue cannot avail himself of this response. This account of nutritional adequacy requires prior understanding of the basic minimum itself and hence would render an account of the basic minimum

[18] Shue (1981), 29–30.

[19] Importantly, Shue mentions a basic right to "security and subsistence." However, it would seem that, for the purposes of assigning a proper basic minimum, "security" is eliminable. Though I will argue for this in more depth in Chapter 6, a person who subsists, but whose subsistence is under threat, would not be said to fail the basic minimum. Rather, it would seem more appropriate to describe this person as maintaining the basic minimum, but in a way that is unsecured, or tenuous. Of course, there might be reasons to promote the security of persons, but not because security of persons is a valuable state *per se*, but rather because security is instrumental in achieving states that are genuinely valuable, including subsistence. Hence, it would seem most charitable to interpret Shue's suggestion as the claim that we have a basic right to the achievement of basic subsistence, to which security is an important means.

[20] Shue (1981), 23.

in terms of subsistence circular. But if we don't index food adequacy to the achievement of the basic minimum, to what do we index it?

The indeterminacy of Shue's approach could, in principle, be fixed in one of two ways. First, one could identify some particular set of calories, say, and hold that this constitutes "adequacy" when it comes to food. Call this a "universalist" approach. Or Shue could say that "adequate" food for any person A is food enough for A to maintain some other valuable state. Call this a "relativist" approach. But if these are the two options, a subsistence-based approach to the basic minimum is either (a) implausible, or (b) fails to be a distinctive account of moral reasons. The universalist approach fails for the same reasons that a universalist primary goods approach fails. Those with extremely fast metabolisms will starve; those with slow metabolisms will require much less. The achievement of a certain specified number of calories cannot maintain the weak moral priority required by BM3. The relativist strategy, as in the case of a relativist primary goods approach, lacks distinctiveness. One could, in principle, identify subsistence in terms of a range of possible *capabilities* for an agent. Here the basic minimum might be understood as "adequate" food for the ability, say, to be well-nourished, to live a life worth living, etc. However, on this account of subsistence, we have replaced the moral importance of subsistence with the moral importance of certain central *capabilities*. Such a view, of course, is an important and influential account of the basic minimum, which will be discussed here in due time. It might very well be that subsistence just *is* the achievement of certain basic human capabilities. But this would be to fail to adequately distinguish the subsistence approach from a capabilities approach.

One could, alternatively, understand "subsistence" in terms of what a person *achieves*, rather than in terms of what that person has the capability to achieve. For instance, one might suggest that "subsistence" is just *being* well-nourished, *being* free of diseases caused by dirty air and lack of shelter, etc. However, this view also appears to sap the motivation for a subsistence approach. What we have here is a "functioning" or "welfarist" approach. This possibility will be discussed in greater detail in §§1.7.3–1.8.

It is important to note that I do not regard the lack of distinctiveness as a substantive critique of Shue's approach. Shue offers an intentionally vague theory of the basic minimum, and it is easy to see any more substantive theory of the basic minimum being a reasonable candidate for the proper theory *of subsistence*. In such a case, Shue's theory is true, but only trivially. To better understand the basic minimum, we cannot simply understand it as basic subsistence.

1.5. SOCIAL NEEDS

In *Famine*, group A fails to meet a morally resonant threshold. But we have so far seen that this threshold cannot plausibly be identified as a set of primary goods, or as the maintenance of human subsistence (without some further theory of human subsistence). But one – *very* plausible – thought might be that whatever else is true of group A, its members seem to lack *what they need*. Of course, everyone has unfulfilled needs; for me to own my dream car, I need a substantially higher income. But there are two ways of understanding the needs that are central to the basic minimum that will be the topic of this, and of the next, section.

The first needs-based approach holds that the basic minimum is constituted (at least in part) by the fulfillment of certain important *social* needs, or needs that vary with social context. To see what I mean, consider the following. Assume that for a particular society, most people are expected to live rather poor lives – secondary education is rare, food rarely goes beyond what is required for survival, etc. It might seem that the basic minimum should not exceed what people in that society can or should expect to get in that particular set of social circumstances. Those who achieve that which their society can offer could not complain that they were somehow left behind: the basic minimum is indexed to their most basic life expectations. But contrast this society with one of rather less modest means. Imagine an extremely affluent society, call this place "Beverly Hills." Given the overall expectations that individuals have in Beverly Hills, it might be thought radically inappropriate to insist merely on the provision of primary education and nutritional adequacy. In Beverly Hills, for example, nutritional adequacy is surely a valuable state of persons, but the *basic minimum* ought to refer to a much higher standard of living, given the *social* needs of individuals that live in Beverly Hills. According to Peter Townsend, "people have needs which can only be defined by virtue of the obligations, associations and customs of . . . membership [in a given social context]."[21] Whether someone achieves the basic minimum will depend on whether that level is sufficient for the satisfaction of needs as understood to apply within that society, relative to their various practices, mores, and expectations.

Amartya Sen offers an account of just the sort of social need that might be central to the maintenance of the basic minimum:

[21] Townsend (1985), 662.

> [T]he absolute satisfaction of some . . . needs might depend on a person's relative position *vis-á-vis* others . . . The point was very well caught by Adam Smith when he was discussing the concept of necessaries in *The Wealth of Nations*:
>
> By necessaries I understand not only the commodities which are indispensably necessary for the support of life, but what ever the custom of the country renders it indecent for creditable people, even the lowest order, to be without . . . Custom . . . has rendered leather shoes a necessary of life in England. The poorest creditable person of either sex would be ashamed to appear in public without them.
>
> In this view to be able to avoid shame, an eighteenth century Englishman has to have leather shoes. It may be true that this situation has come to pass precisely because the typical members of a community happen to possess leather shoes, but the person in question needs leather shoes not so much to be less ashamed than others – that relative question is not even posed by Adam Smith – but simply not to be ashamed, which as an achievement is an absolute one.[22]

According to Sen, the avoidance of shame, or social stigma, is an absolute state of persons, and an important social need, that may very well form a part of the basic minimum.

However, the fulfillment of social needs is neither necessary nor sufficient when it comes to the basic minimum. First, they are not sufficient. Social needs do not appear to explain our considered judgment in *Famine*. After all, it would be very strange to say that we ought to distribute to group A simply because, otherwise, they may be ashamed, or may be subject to social stigma. This may very well be an important thing to avoid, but much more important is the avoidance of *starvation*, and starvation is important to avoid even if no one is stigmatized for starving, or if the avoidance of starvation is not a *social* need.

In addition, social needs are not necessary for the fulfillment of the basic minimum. Such a view cannot satisfy the moral dimension required by BM3. Surely it is not the case that the various social needs of people in very rich societies take weak moral priority to all other absolute states of persons. Consider Beverly Hills resident A in comparison to B, who resides in a comparatively poor social context. Assume that you are forced to choose between providing for A's Beverly Hills social needs (which include, imagine, a high-fashion wardrobe), or providing for B's basic nutrition, which is in fact *not* a social need, given the poverty that surrounds B. It seems clear that the right decision is to provide for B's nutrition. If so, the achievement of A's social needs, or A's ability to live without shame in Beverly Hills, clearly cannot be part of the basic minimum. The basic

[22] Sen (1983), 159. The Smith quotation Sen takes from Smith (1776), 351–2.

minimum has weak moral priority, which the social needs of Beverly Hills residents simply do not have. Hence social needs are neither necessary nor sufficient for the achievement of the basic minimum.

1.6. BASIC NEEDS

So social needs cannot constitute the basic minimum. But this does not exhaust the various need-based approaches. After all, it still seems plausible to say that the members of group A lack what they need. But what they need is surely not entirely relative to social context. To avoid starvation is not merely a social need (if a social need at all), but might be deemed a *basic* need. If so, one might characterize the morally resonant threshold in terms of the fulfillment of one's basic, rather than social, needs. On the importance of such needs, James Griffin writes:

> [B]asic needs . . . seem to have a quite special moral importance simply in virtue of being basic. For one thing, the presence of the notions of health, harm, and proper function make statements of basic need moral – in the proper, strict sense of the term that is not the contrary of "descriptive". They all involve a norm falling below which means malfunction, harm, or ailment. And that explains why basic needs have an especially strong link with obligation: my ailment makes a claim on others that my whims, hankerings, pleasures, and even happiness cannot. And these claims on others are of a strong sort; they depend not upon this or that person's particular wish or purpose, but upon something deeper and objective – human nature.[23]

Like "subsistence," however, the appeal to basic needs in defining a basic minimum appears to be rhetorically powerful, but theoretically thin. What is a basic need? According to Griffin, a basic need is a need that is somehow dependent on human nature. According to David Miller, some particular state of affairs or object p is adequately characterized as a basic need when p is required to achieve a minimally decent life.[24]

[23] Griffin (1989), 42.

[24] Miller (2007), 181. One further point is worth noting. Miller draws "a distinction between *basic needs* and *societal needs*, where the former are to be understood as the conditions for a decent human life in *any* society, and the latter as the more expansive set of requirements for a decent life in the particular society to which a person belongs" (ibid., 182). According to Miller, both sets of needs are relevant to the basic minimum, but only the former ground obligations that are reason-giving for all moral agents. The latter set of needs, however, are reason-giving only for those in one's societal context. Hence the basic needs approach, as outlined by Miller, is committed to defining the basic minimum in terms of that which is required for a person to live a minimally decent life, where this will include both basic needs and societal needs. Insofar as I have already argued against inserting such social needs into a theory of the basic minimum, for the purposes of charity, I propose to leave aside this feature of Miller's view.

Concentrate on Miller's view for the moment. Even if we understand what it means to live a minimally decent life, the basic needs approach is still indeterminate; the basic needs approach faces a set of questions similar in structure to the questions that faced previous approaches. To see this, consider the following. What is required for any *particular* person to achieve a minimally decent life is going to be wildly variable. Take the following case: A fails to maintain a minimally decent human life. But, given certain psychological facts about A, A cannot achieve a minimally decent life with the same basket of resources that everyone else can. However, assume that A *could* live a minimally decent life if A was given some particular good, *g*. Question: is *g* a basic need of A's?

The basic needs approach can offer two different responses to this question. The first is "no": *g* is not a basic need of A's despite the fact that A requires it to live a minimally decent life. Basic needs, on this view, just are the set of resources, calories, or other goods that *in the general case* are required to maintain a minimally decent life. This approach appears to simply define a set of basic needs without taking into account the possibility of interpersonal variation. But this approach has no plausibility. Such a view would appear to insist that there is more reason to provide these so-called "basic needs" to B, who does not require them to live a minimally decent life, at the expense of *g* for A, who requires *g* to live a minimally decent life. Such a view is unacceptable.

The better answer is "yes": *g is* a basic need of A's. Miller agrees. For Miller, basic needs are "the conditions that must be met for a person to have a decent life given the environmental conditions he faces."[25] But for A, this requires *g*. It would seem, then, that *g* is one of A's basic needs.

The problem here should be familiar. If *g* is a basic need for A just in case A requires *g* to live a minimally decent life, the basic needs approach is equivalent to a capabilities approach, viz., that a person should be given the capability to obtain a minimally decent human life. Here what is really central is not any particular set of goods, or the achievement of any particular valuable outcomes, but rather the ability, for A, to live a minimally decent life. If so, the most plausible understanding of a basic needs approach is just a version of the capabilities approach.[26]

Indeed, this result is on display in Rawls's (admittedly very brief) sketch of a basic needs approach. As Rawls writes, individuals must have their "basic needs . . . met, at least insofar as their being met is necessary for citizens to understand and to be able fruitfully to exercise [their] rights and

[25] Ibid., 184. [26] Sen, "Goods and People" in Sen (1984), 513–14.

liberties."[27] But in this case, Rawls explicitly ties the fulfillment of one's basic needs to the *capability* for individuals to "exercise" the various basic rights and political liberties that appear in Rawls's first principle of justice. Embellishing this view, Rawls later writes, with respect to medical care in particular, that "provision for medical care, as with primary goods generally, is to meet the needs and requirements of citizens as free and equal. Such care falls under the general means necessary to underwrite fair equality of opportunity and our capacity to take advantage of our basic rights and liberties, and thus to be normal and fully cooperating members of society over a complete life."[28] As seen here, Rawls identifies the primary goods approach as facilitating certain basic capabilities, including the "capacity" to take advantage of our equal basic rights and liberties and to be normal and cooperating members of a political endeavor. Hence, read literally, Rawls's own basic needs approach is simply coextensive with a capabilities approach.

The problem here is identical for *any* basic needs approach. A basic needs approach must answer the question: what are these basic needs *for*? But to properly answer this question, one must identify a particular goal, *p*, for which these basic needs are needed. One could avoid collapse by holding that the basic minimum is just that which *most* people need for *p*, or that which is needed for *p* in the general case. But this view is implausible. Hence A's basic needs must be those things that *A* requires to maintain the ability to achieve the set target *p*. In this way, it would appear that any basic needs approach that specifies a relevant target *p* is extensionally equivalent to a capabilities approach. Hence, for the purposes of charity, it seems sensible to describe the basic needs approach as one *form* of a capabilities approach (indeed, as some basic needs theorists readily admit).[29]

1.7. CAPABILITIES

Two possibilities remain. The first, and clearly most influential, defines the basic minimum in terms of a universally applicable set of basic capabilities. That capabilities should be an index of distributive justice has long been championed by Amartya Sen, and the capabilities approach has been used in the development of a basic minimum in more recent years by Martha Nussbaum.[30] The capabilities approach is important, and has justly received sustained philosophical attention.[31] The capabilities

27 Rawls (1995), 7. 28 Rawls (2001), 174. 29 See Streeten (1994).
30 See, for instance, Sen (1980), Nussbaum (2000) and (2006).
31 For a mere taste, consider Kaufman (2008).

approach, indeed, seems to provide a substantive core of other approaches already discussed here, including the basic needs approach.

Its plausibility is undeniable. Take *Famine*. In this case, it seems important that group A be given sufficient food, or resources with which to purchase food. But why? Surely at least part of the answer is that food or other fungible resources allow people the capability to live a life of sufficient length, to develop and live according to their interests, etc., etc. In other words, in caring about group A, and in choosing to assist group A rather than group B, we are interested not in the promotion of food access *per se*, not in resources *per se*, but rather in the promotion of the capability to live a flourishing life, which is already available for group B. Given its plausibility, I take the capabilities approach to be the chief competitor of the welfarist approach for which I will eventually argue.

According to Nussbaum, there are ten basic human capabilities, of which the achievement of each (or, more specifically, a threshold level of each) is required for a life worthy of human dignity, and which together form a primary obligation of political morality. Nussbaum has articulated many different versions of the list, which she maintains is a work in progress. As of this writing, the latest version is as follows (the parentheticals are paraphrased from Nussbaum's own descriptions):

1. Life (of normal length).
2. Bodily Health (adequate nourishment, shelter).
3. Bodily Integrity (freedom of movement, sexual satisfaction, freedom from assault).
4. Senses, Imagination, and Thought (literacy, education, religious exercise).
5. Emotions (emotional attachment and development not blighted by fear or anxiety).
6. Practical Reason (ability to form a conception of the good, engage in critical reflection).
7. Affiliation
   A. Being able to "live with and toward others."
   B. Having the social bases of self-respect.
8. Other Species (ability to live in a relationship with nature).
9. Play ("Being able to laugh, to play, to enjoy recreational activities.")
10. Control over One's Environment
    A. Political participation.
    B. Property and land-use rights.[32]

[32] Nussbaum (2006), 76–8.

Further questions can be asked of any member of this list (which Nussbaum fully admits). But the intuitive idea behind each facet is clear enough. To fulfill the basic minimum we are to have at least a threshold level of each basic capability. We do not need to have the maximal ability to, for instance, exercise our capacity for imagination, but we must be able to do so to at least some minimal degree, commensurate with a fully human life. In addition, Nussbaum believes that the obligation to provide for basic capabilities is an obligation of all governments, not simply of governments with reasonably abundant resources from which to draw.[33] Furthermore, in a way that corrects defects of the approaches of Townsend and Sen, Nussbaum does not rely on social needs to define the basic minimum.

Nussbaum's view is admittedly tentative, and open to revision based on circumstances, as it were, "on the ground." Nevertheless, this view contains four crucial elements that are important for our purposes here. The first element, *Capabilities Not Welfare*, is fairly self-explanatory, and contains the beating heart of every version of a capabilities approach. Nussbaum does not believe that to satisfy the basic minimum one must actually possess the functionings that make up a flourishing life (i.e., imagination, sexual fulfillment, and the like). Rather, it is enough that one has the threshold capability to do so. This is clearly plausible in the case of, say, sexual fulfillment. Though sexual fulfillment might be *good*, there appears to be no *per se* moral reason to ensure that everyone has had some threshold level of sexual satisfaction (including those who wish to remain celibate). In addition, however, Nussbaum believes that one should not insist on functioning, rather than capability, even for more basic elements of the list, such as life and bodily health. Those who wish to fast for religious or other purposes should be able to give up being adequately nourished if they so choose. The second element – call it *Expansive List* – is clear from Nussbaum's account of the basic minimum itself. Nussbaum does not merely suggest that some baseline of life and freedom from slavery, say, are required for the achievement of a basic minimum. She provides additional elements that she believes are essential to basic human dignity, and that are firmly rooted in a "global overlapping consensus," i.e., that are universal values found in every cultural tradition. She includes life and bodily integrity, but also political participation, recreation, affiliation with other species and the world of nature, etc.

Third is *No Trade-offs*. The threshold level of each capability is a discrete requirement for the achievement of the basic minimum. According

[33] Compare Baker (1992), 123. Nussbaum (2006), 401–2.

to Nussbaum, one cannot achieve the basic minimum by trading off a threshold level of one capability for the sake of additional gains in another element. It is not compatible with a concern for the basic minimum, according to Nussbaum, to refuse to grant the opportunity for play, but to make this up with a greater ability to form friendships, or to participate politically. "What the theory says is: all ten of these plural and diverse ends are minimum requirements of justice, at least up to the threshold level. In other words, the theory does not countenance intuitionistic balancing or trade-offs among them."[34] Again, "This account entails that the capabilities are radically nonfungible: lacks in one area cannot be made up simply by giving people a larger amount of another capability."[35]

One might break Nussbaum's elements into two categories: evaluative elements that define the structure of the basic minimum itself – such as *Capabilities Not Welfare*, *Expansive List*, and *No Trade-offs* – and moral elements, elements that form Nussbaum's account of the various reasons to promote the basic minimum and their strength. For our purposes here, there is but one relevant moral element: *Guarantee*. According to Nussbaum, justice requires that everyone have a crucial threshold level of basic capabilities. Nussbaum writes: "[I]n some form all are held to be part of a minimum account of social justice: a society that does not guarantee these to all its citizens, at some appropriate threshold level, falls short of being a fully just society, whatever its level of opulence."[36] Notice that Nussbaum does not suggest that a society that cannot avoid failures of the basic minimum for some fails to be the best society, or fails to be an ideal society. Rather, such a society is *unjust*. Somewhere along the line, if the ten basic capabilities are not granted to every citizen, political society has failed to conform to that which it has overriding moral reason to do. This is true even in extreme cases. "In desperate circumstances, it may not be possible for a nation to secure them all up to the threshold level, but then it becomes a purely practical question what to do next, not a question of justice. The question of justice is already answered: justice has not been fully done here."[37]

When put together, it is clear that the capabilities approach offers a genuine basic minimum. The ten basic capabilities are intended to be a valuable state of persons, and this absolute state clearly maintains the highest possible moral priority: it is a *guarantee* of justice.[38] Nussbaum's

[34] Nussbaum (2006), 175. [35] Ibid., 166–7. [36] Ibid., 75. [37] Ibid., 175.

[38] Of course, one might claim that a particular state is a guarantee of justice, but claim that this state does not take priority over other states. This could be possible if *p* and *q* are both guarantees

view is clear, powerful, and intuitive. However, it has grave defects, which I explore in the following sections.

One organizational note. Though it is useful to understand the whole of Nussbaum's view at the outset, the remainder of this section will discuss only Nussbaum's evaluative elements. I will presume that these elements are intended to form a basic minimum of moral strength at least sufficient to conform to BM3 (i.e., I will not assume *Guarantee* for the purposes of this discussion). I discuss *Guarantee* in more detail in Chapter 4.

1.7.1. No Trade-offs

Consider first *No Trade-offs*. Can it reasonably be held that a person who has substantial gains in one set of basic capabilities *cannot* obtain the basic minimum unless she has a threshold level of *all* basic capabilities? Initially, it seems plausible to say that a capability like political participation could be reasonably traded-off against gains in other areas, at least for a single person. Consider two choices: the first choice would allow one person, A, to develop the capacities and capabilities of Leonardo da Vinci, which A enjoys and exercises, but with no opportunity for political participation, which A does not value and use of which A would not make. The second alternative would allow A a threshold of each basic capability but just barely above the threshold level. It seems implausible to opt for the latter. And if that's right (given BM3), it seems wrong to say that these capabilities, in Nussbaum's terminology, should be radically nonfungible. Of course, Nussbaum has an account of basic human dignity that (she claims) supports the requirement of basic political participation, and hence supports *No Trade-offs*. I will say more about this in the next section, but for now I simply note that I find it very difficult to believe that a person living the life of da Vinci (*sans* opportunity for political participation) lacks *basic human dignity*. Of course, my point here should not be taken to mean that political participation is not a good thing, or that there is no moral reason to establish a right of political participation for all. Rather, I simply argue that one can maintain the basic minimum, or so it seems, without it: to grant a da Vinci-like character the opportunity for political participation cannot take the requisite moral priority.

of justice, and maintain equal moral importance. Though Nussbaum believes the basic minimum takes substantial priority over super-minimum states, Nussbaum is silent on whether the basic minimum, in a one-to-one comparison, takes priority over sub-minimum states (she believes that any such trade-off is simply unjust). This causes serious problems for Nussbaum's view, which I discuss in Chapter 4. For now, however, I'll assume that Nussbaum's basic minimum conforms to BM3.

No Trade-offs is thus implausible, but one caveat is worth mentioning. The implausibility of *No Trade-offs* is a consequence of the conjunction of *No Trade-offs* with *Expansive List*. Indeed, one might be tempted to accept *No Trade-offs* if the list of basic capabilities comprising the minimum is substantially shortened, a list composed of the capabilities to maintain, say, life and bodily integrity. It is worthwhile, then, to consider whether *Expansive List* has any independent support over such a restricted list, which may support *No Trade-offs* more plausibly.

1.7.2. Expansive List, *human dignity, and upward distribution*

A critic of *Expansive List* needn't claim that there are elements on the list of ten basic capabilities that are not valuable. It is perfectly open to someone who rejects *Expansive List* to declare that there is a moral reason to promote *all* basic capabilities. All one need deny is that the ten basic capabilities should form the basic minimum, i.e., that the conjunction of the ten basic capabilities satisfies BM3.

If so, to establish *Expansive List*, one must argue that *each* of the ten basic capabilities forms part of a morally important threshold as per the demands of BM3. According to Nussbaum, this is established by showing that *Expansive List* plausibly captures capabilities sufficient to maintain a life of *human dignity*. Nussbaum writes: "The basic intuitive idea of my version of the capabilities approach is that we begin with a conception of the dignity of the human being, and of a life that is worthy of that dignity – a life that has available in it 'truly human functioning'."[39]

The reference to human dignity here is certainly striking and rhetorically powerful. However, human dignity permits of interpretation. One might wonder whether political participation, or land-use rights, really is essential for a life comprised of "truly human functioning."[40] After all, "truly human functioning" is only sensible when considering its contrast class, i.e., less-than-human functioning, or functioning that doesn't go beyond that of non-human animals. But one needn't have political and material control over one's environment to avoid a life fit only for a non-human animal. Rather, one might think the elements of Nussbaum's list relevant for human functioning include, for instance, a threshold level of the use of practical

[39] Nussbaum (2006), 74. Nussbaum cites Marx as the inspiration for her understanding of truly human functioning, but it seems to me unclear that Marx's understanding of "rich human need," or the need of a "totality of human life-activities," need express itself in anything like Nussbaum's *Expansive List*.

[40] See Arneson (2000a), 48.

reason, or "senses, imagination, and thought." Such a view is not without precedent. Aristotle, in book 1 of the *Nicomachean Ethics*, identifies a truly human life as a life composed of "activity and actions of the soul that involve reason; hence the function of the excellent man is to do this well and finely."[41] Presumably, on an Aristotelian view of truly human functioning, one must develop at least a minimal capacity to exercise one's rationality; this will require some of the ten basic capabilities but not others.

Aristotle is not alone. Hurka, in developing a contemporary restatement of Aristotle's view, writes that "humans share with other animals certain bodily essential properties but are also essentially rational, in both the theoretical and practical senses of 'rational'. [This form of perfectionism has] three values: physical perfection, which develops our physical nature, and theoretical and practical perfection, which develop theoretical and practical rationality."[42] Hurka here is specifically referring to the human essence, the minimal instantiation of which is surely a reasonable account of "truly human functioning." On this view, some of the basic capabilities will be required for a life of truly human functioning, but others will not. (Though, again, this is not to say that a more fully developed human life would not require them.) Insofar as we are interested in "truly human functioning," which I discuss critically in the next chapter, Hurka's seems a better account. That the da Vinci-like life fails to maintain basic human dignity, or "truly human functioning," is not believable. If truly human functioning is to guide the choice of the basic capabilities, Nussbaum's list is too expansive.

Nussbaum might respond by suggesting that the operative term in "truly human functioning" is *truly*. In other words, though there might be some particularly minimal account of bare human functioning (as opposed to mere animal functioning), morally speaking we are interested in more than this. Thus "truly human functioning" is morally loaded: it should consist of elements that we find morally attractive or desirable; attractive enough to form the content of a basic minimum.[43] But I find it hard to assess this claim independently of particular considered judgments about the moral priority – the ability to conform to BM3 – of Nussbaum's basic minimum as opposed to a less expansive list. And in such a comparison, Nussbaum's list fails.

[41] Aristotle (1098a), 13–15. [42] Hurka (1993), 37.

[43] Nussbaum (2006), 181. This might be similar to a response often given to critics of Aristotle's account of the human function. For Aristotle, so the suggestion goes, the human function is morally loaded, i.e., constructed in such a way that the elements of the human function are intrinsically desirable of themselves. See, for instance, Whiting (1988), 38–9, Kraut (1989), 317–18, and Annas (1993), 216–17.

Consider two people, A and B. A is far below the basic minimum, with mere life and nutritional adequacy. B, however, possesses almost everything, except the land-use clause of number 10. Political society can either raise A to the level of B (i.e., by granting almost everything except land-use rights), or it can grant B land-use rights, but not both. If *Expansive List* captures the true account of the basic minimum *and* the achievement of the basic minimum is to maintain weak moral priority, the distribution should go to B. This simply follows from BM3 and from Nussbaum's *Expansive List.*[44] But this is implausible. Land-use rights, though perhaps important, are surely not of the same moral importance as the range of capabilities that could be granted to A. Land-use rights are not important enough to form a necessary feature of the basic minimum.

The above case illustrates an important dilemma for any view committed to a basic minimum. Call the occasional moral priority of the better-off to the worse-off "upward distribution." Upward distribution is a little-noted feature of views that accept a basic minimum, but it cannot be avoided. Any view respecting BM3 will imply it. Insofar as the promotion of the basic minimum must take weak moral priority to the promotion of all other valuable states (including comparative states), a single instance of the basic minimum must take priority to a single instance of the promotion of a valuable state for a worse-off person. Thus any view that posits a basic minimum must address it plausibly. Indeed, the stronger the minimum the more cases in which upward distribution is licensed. Thus any basic minimum must adequately negotiate the problem of upward distribution. In light of *Expansive List*, Nussbaum's basic minimum fails this test.

1.7.3. Capabilities Not Welfare

In this section, I criticize the essential feature of any view that defines the basic minimum in terms of capabilities: the rejection of a basic minimum in terms of the actual achievement of valued states (or, in Nussbaum and Sen's terminology: "functionings") in favor of a basic minimum defined in terms of the capabilities to achieve such valued states. My argument here will have two parts. First, I consider Nussbaum's arguments for a capabilities approach rather than a welfarist approach. As it turns out, I argue, Nussbaum's own considered judgments about the relationship between the

44 Alternatively, one could suggest that a sufficient improvement in some areas of the ten basic capabilities can render some elements of the list unnecessary in terms of the achievement of the basic minimum. But this would seem to deny *No Trade-offs*.

basic minimum and the capabilities approach are better explained by a welfarist approach. Second, I argue that any view that accepts *Capabilities Not Welfare* and posits a basic minimum (sufficient to satisfy BM3) is committed to absurd conclusions. This applies whether or not one accepts any of Nussbaum's other elements.

Why *Capabilities Not Welfare*? In the following passage, Nussbaum considers the possibility that a capabilities approach should be replaced by a welfarist approach that insists on the achievement of actual functionings, rather than capabilities:[45]

> I have spoken both of functioning and of capability. How are they related? Becoming clear about this is crucial to defining the relation of the "capabilities approach" both to Rawlsian liberalism and to our concerns about paternalism and pluralism. For if we were to take functioning in a single determinate matter, the liberal pluralist would rightly judge that we were precluding many choices that citizens may make in accordance with their own conceptions of the good, and perhaps violating their rights. A deeply religious person may prefer not to be well nourished, but to engage in strenuous fasting. Whether for religious or for other reasons, a person may prefer a celibate life to one containing sexual expression. A person may prefer to work with an intense dedication that precludes recreation and play.[46]

Nussbaum's motivation for a capabilities metric, then, involves concerns generally associated with political neutrality: people may desire to live a life that interferes with functionings that Nussbaum's approach declares important for truly human functioning. Of course, the central capabilities must be possessed by all – but there is no moral reason to insist that individuals develop particular functionings, lest we interfere with a form of liberal neutrality (or "pluralism") about the good life.

My view is that Nussbaum's point here, in broad outline, is surely right. We should not insist that persons achieve sexual satisfaction (or, perhaps,

[45] There is a reasonable question concerning whether all functionings-based approaches must also be welfarist approaches. In other words, must a theory of the basic minimum that insists on functionings also believe that these functionings are features of human well-being? Nussbaum herself seems ambivalent on this question (see Nussbaum (2000), 14). Though such a position is surely featured in logical space, it seems to me that a functionings-based approach that is not *also* a welfarist approach lacks plausibility, especially in the face of BM3. Assume that there are two valuable functionings that make up an approach to the basic minimum *p* and *q*, but that these functionings are not features of human well-being. Now consider A and B. A maintains *p* but not *q*, B maintains *q* but not *p*. In order to grant the basic minimum to A, however, you must disadvantage B in terms of well-being, and vice versa. Also assume that granting A *q* and granting B *p* will improve neither A's nor B's quality of life. I find the suggestion that one has a moral reason to disadvantage either A or B for the sake of these non-welfarist functionings morally absurd. Hence it appears to me rather clear that any *plausible* functionings-based approach will also commit to the welfare value of these functionings.

[46] Nussbaum (2000), 86–7.

other functionings they do not value). If a religious person is force-fed, for example, that person is to that extent living a life that does not reflect his conception of the good. But political institutions should refrain from forcing citizens to live lives they do not choose and do not value.[47] This tells in favor of a capabilities, rather than welfarist, approach: to insist on functionings precludes "many choices that citizens may make in accordance with their own conceptions of the good."

That which constitutes a person's true "conception of the good" (i.e., a person's set of genuine preferences, pro-attitudes, valuations, etc.) is a matter for substantive discussion – I will offer my own interpretation in Chapter 3. Leaving aside the details for the moment, however, it seems to me that a concern that institutions not undercut the ability of people to live lives they value is compatible with a moral concern, not for Nussbaum's ten basic capabilities, but for the achievement of conceptions of the good. It is a concern for what I shall call, admittedly somewhat awkwardly:

Proto-autonomy:[48] An individual is proto-autonomous if, and to the extent that, she fulfills those preferences, pro-attitudes, and evaluations that constitute her conception of the good.

An approach to the basic minimum organized around the achievement of proto-autonomy (rather than the functionings noted in Nussbaum's list) is compatible with Nussbaum's insistence that people should not be forced to live lives that they do not value.

Of course, compatibility is one thing, plausibility another. But an approach to the basic minimum in terms of the achievement of proto-autonomy also helps to explain and unify a number of Nussbaum's own considered judgments, upon which she relies in clarifying and defending her account of the basic capabilities. For instance, Nussbaum herself declares that functionings, rather than capabilities, should be enforced in a number of important cases. Nussbaum says that in children, functionings are crucial because they are required to produce adults who maintain the ten

47 Richard Arneson notes this implication of Nussbaum's examples in (2000a), 61. Arneson comes to a different conclusion, however, claiming that "freedom can be seen to be intrinsically, not just instrumentally, valuable. . . . But none of these perfectly reasonable claims is of the right type to justify the position that the fundamental concern of justice is to provide freedom and not achieved good." I claim that freedom *itself* is of no intrinsic value, merely the *achievement of conceptions of the good.* My defense of these claims, however, must wait.

48 I refer to this state as "proto-autonomy" rather than "autonomy" because I do not wish to commit to any particular theory of autonomy, or any particular theory concerning the relationship between the achievement of one's conception of the good and the achievement of autonomy. Though there may be some relation, even a strong relation, I simply remain neutral on its strength.

basic capabilities. Furthermore, even in adults, certain basic functionings are required because

> we may feel that some of the capabilities are so important, so crucial to the development or maintenance of all the others, that we are sometimes justified in promoting functioning rather than simply capability, within limits set by an appropriate concern for liberty. Thus most modern nations treat health and safety as things not to be left altogether to people's choices: building codes, regulation of food, medicine, and environmental contaminants, all these restrict liberty in a sense. They are understood to be justified because of the difficulty of making informed choices in all these areas, and the burden of inquiry such choices would impose on citizens, as well as by the thought that health and safety are simply too basic to be left entirely to people's choices.[49]

Nussbaum insists that some functionings should be enforced given an interest in the capabilities themselves. Choices that adversely affect important capabilities are prohibited. But, for Nussbaum, these proposals permit of *exceptions*. For instance, Nussbaum writes: "I do not favor policies that would make unhealthy activities such as boxing, unsafe sex, football, and smoking illegal, although education about risk seems to be highly appropriate, and the infliction of harm on others . . . could rightly be penalized."[50] Take Evel Knievel. Given the capabilities approach as stated by Nussbaum, it would be unjust for political institutions to enforce a safety norm against Knievel. For Knievel, jumping the Snake River Canyon is protected as an *exception* to the general edict to promote of functionings that are central to protecting the ten basic capabilities. But why?

Nussbaum's view strains in giving a coherent account of these exceptions. Where, say, food safety is concerned, the capabilities approach suggests that unsafe food is a hindrance to the development and maintenance of important capabilities. But then it is hard to understand her rejection of laws against smoking, unsafe sex, or general daredevilry. These things are just as harmful to one's overall capabilities. Nussbaum might suggest, given the rhetoric of the above-quoted paragraph, that regulation of building codes and food, etc., are vastly more important for the basic capabilities than, say, the avoidance of unsafe sex. But even if this "vastly" could be given a coherent interpretation, why should we imagine that it is true? Just as with unsafe buildings or unsafe food, the extent to which unsafe sex or risky motorcycle stunts are debilitating to one's capabilities seems to be a matter of luck; a bit of bad luck, and they are ultimately debilitating.

49 Nussbaum (2000), 91. 50 Nussbaum (2006), 171.

The best explanation of Nussbaum's exceptions, it seems to me, makes essential reference to the value of proto-autonomy itself. Though the exceptions Nussbaum allows do not straightforwardly serve the project of basic capability-promotion, they *do* serve the general purpose of *proto-autonomy*-promotion. Knievel is allowed to jeopardize his safety because in so doing he better achieves his conception of the good. General policies of food and drug regulation are acceptable given their importance to the proto-autonomy of individuals – rarely is eating unsafe food or living in unsafe buildings a part of anyone's conception of the good, and rarely will such policies interfere with anyone's conception of the good.[51]

Thus, it seems to me, Nussbaum's suggestions when it comes to enforcement of various types of behavior are best captured by an insistence not on the intrinsic importance of the ten basic capabilities for justice, but rather on the intrinsic importance of proto-autonomy. But if this is the case, Nussbaum's arguments for *Capabilities Not Welfare* appear to dissipate. While the importance of proto-autonomy rules out versions of a welfarist approach that insist upon the maintenance of, say, sexual functioning, it does not appear to rule out all welfarist approaches. Indeed, one might state a rough sketch of a welfarist approach as follows:

The Basic Minimum as Proto-autonomy: x achieves the basic minimum if and only if x is proto-autonomous to a sufficient degree.

Whether *The Basic Minimum as Proto-autonomy* can be plausibly sustained will be a matter for investigation in the remaining chapters. However, it is important to note that Nussbaum's own arguments for a capabilities approach and against a welfarist approach fail in the face of *The Basic Minimum as Proto-autonomy. The Basic Minimum as Proto-autonomy* can give precisely the answers Nussbaum requires: living a good life does not require sexual satisfaction if it is not part of a life one values living. Safe food is required because safe food is essential to the maintenance of a life one values living (in most cases, anyway; see note 51). From the point of view of proto-autonomy, forcing someone to achieve such satisfaction would be bad indeed. If *The Basic Minimum as Proto-autonomy* succeeds, Nussbaum's argument for a capabilities approach is deflated. (Chapters 2 and 3 are dedicated to defending a welfarist approach sufficient to capture

[51] What about someone who eats unsafe food proto-autonomously? Given everything that Nussbaum has said, it would seem that such a person should be allowed to do so; see, for instance, her suggestion that regulations should be justified "within limits set by an appropriate concern for liberty"; but given the effects of unsafe food on the general populace, purveyors are required to maintain safety standards. This is compatible with an emphasis on proto-autonomy rather than capabilities.

The Basic Minimum as Proto-autonomy. Suffice it to say that whether *The Basic Minimum as Proto-autonomy* can succeed is as yet undetermined.)

Though I have so far focused on Nussbaum's view, hers is not the only "capabilities approach." Different capabilities approaches will identify a different set of capabilities as the basic minimum, and will differ when it comes to the overall capabilities that one has reason to promote. But *no* version of a capabilities approach to the basic minimum could be plausibly motivated in the face of an acceptable welfarist alternative. The general problem is as follows. A capabilities approach is committed to the provision of capabilities even if these capabilities have no effect whatsoever on the lives of individuals whose capabilities they are, i.e., even if these capabilities are *never used*. But this is a seriously problematic result, especially in light of BM3. Take the following case, inspired by Nussbaum's view. Assume that A is missing, and could be granted, the capability for adequate nourishment. Assume B, however, maintains the basic minimum, but could be granted a number of additional capabilities. B values these additional capabilities and would make use of them. Nussbaum would insist that we favor granting the capability for adequate nourishment to A. This, I think, is a plausible result *only if* A values being adequately nourished and would make use of the capability to do so, as most would. But assume that he is a faster. A capabilities view would require that we grant the capability for adequate nourishment to A, who does not value being adequately nourished, and would not make use of such a capability, rather than granting additional capabilities to B, who does value them, and *would* make use of them. This implication is unacceptable. Insisting on the provision of a threshold level of capabilities, even when these capabilities would have no effect on the extent to which A might live a life he values living, is fetishistic, no matter which capabilities make up the basic minimum.

This point can be made in a slightly different way. Call a "mere capability" a capability that is not made use of. In the example above, the capability for adequate nourishment for A is a mere capability. Call a "substantive capability" a capability that is actually made use of to promote a given person's flourishing. B's potential non-minimum capabilities, in the example above, are substantive capabilities. Quite obviously, the capabilities approach cannot index moral reasons to substantive capabilities rather than mere capabilities: to do so would be, like the basic needs and primary goods approaches, to lack distinctiveness. Hence the capabilities approach can make no *moral* distinction between a mere capability and a substantive capability. But, of course, the capabilities approach to the basic minimum must respect BM3: it must claim that the basic minimum takes at least weak moral priority to other valuable states. If so, the capabilities approach is committed to requiring that moral agents favor the capabilities that make up the basic minimum in comparison to other states even if they are *mere* capabilities, capabilities that are *never used.* This cannot be the right answer. Though there may be some space for the moral importance of capabilities (see, for instance, §6.5), a capabilities approach cannot succeed as a proper theory of the basic minimum.

One further note is worth mentioning. Some insist on a capabilities approach rather than a welfarist approach on the grounds that only a capabilities approach can deliver the right verdicts when it comes to individuals who are in some way responsible for their own disadvantage. For instance, we might feel as though we have no further moral reason to assist an individual to whom we have granted the capability for a minimally decent human life, but who has culpably gambled away his necessary resources. We may feel as though granting capabilities is all that is required – those who are prudent will use them to achieve proto-autonomy, or well-being, or a "minimally decent life." But there is no moral reason to provide additional resources to those who are *not* similarly prudent, or who behave recklessly or irresponsibly. Hence, though Nussbaum's particular capabilities approach fails, it might seem more plausible to insist on some form of a capabilities approach rather than *The Basic Minimum as Proto-autonomy.*[52]

This motivation for a capabilities approach only succeeds if a welfarist approach cannot *also* deliver satisfying verdicts in response to cases of general negative responsibility or culpable behavior. I turn to this question in Chapter 6. In any event, that a capabilities approach is committed to the promotion of mere capabilities at the cost of substantive capabilities, which in turn lead to better, higher quality lives, seems to me to cause significant problems for such an approach, whatever the rationale.

1.8. THE WELFARIST'S DILEMMA

The problems that face a capabilities approach are significant. The obvious answer is to reject the capabilities approach in favor of a welfarist approach. A welfarist approach – like the previous approaches – adequately explains our gut moral reaction in *Famine.* One might claim that the moral reason to assist group A rather than group B just is the fact that the persons of group A fail to live *good lives.* We incline toward assisting group A not because we

[52] See Arneson (1989).

are interested in group A's capabilities, or basic needs, or primary goods, but rather because we are interested in group A's quality of life, full stop.

Though a welfarist approach seems plausible, at least initially, matters are not so simple. There appears to be a powerful dilemma facing any welfarist theory of the basic minimum. One might put the dilemma this way. A welfarist approach will either accept *The Basic Minimum as Proto-autonomy*, or it will not. Any welfarist theory that claims to take seriously *The Basic Minimum as Proto-autonomy* seems committed to claiming that the *preferences* or *values* of individuals have an important role to play in the construction of a basic minimum. But this gives rise to a familiar problem. As rational agents, we adapt our preferences and other pro-attitudes to our circumstances. On coming to realize I cannot achieve some goal of mine, *p*, I adopt an aversion to *p*, instead preferring that which I can actually achieve.[53] But if this is the case, people who would certainly be described under any reasonable criterion as failing the basic minimum might in fact come to value their current, awful, state of affairs. Nussbaum writes: "If one does not know what it is like to feel well nourished, it is especially easy to be content with the undernourished state in which one lives; if one has never learned to read and is told that education is not for women, it is very easy to internalize one's own second-class status and learn not to strive for, or even desire, what tradition has put out of reach."[54] She concludes that "A wise approach [will hold] that some existing preferences are actually bad bases for social policy."[55] If this is correct, we should reject *The Basic Minimum as Proto-autonomy*. Though this view would accommodate many of Nussbaum's concerns about the importance of capabilities rather than functionings, it appears *not* to accommodate Nussbaum's concern that the basic minimum (for anyone) not be defined by adaptive preferences.

In principle, a welfarist could reject *The Basic Minimum as Proto-Autonomy*. The basic minimum, on this view, might simply be the achievement of some objectively valuable welfare state (knowledge, flourishing, great achievement, etc.). But this view fails for a reason that must by now be familiar: this approach fails to accommodate Nussbaum's concern that individuals not be forced to live lives that are not compatible with their conceptions of the good. This view will declare that there is moral reason to insist that certain individuals adopt courses of action or embrace activities regardless of whether these states or activities are valued by them.

53 There are other important examples of this phenomenon. See Elster (1983), 111–24.

54 Nussbaum, "American Women: Preferences, Feminism, and Democracy" in Nussbaum (1999), 151.

55 Nussbaum (2000), 112.

Thus a welfarist basic minimum faces a dilemma. Any welfarist basic minimum must accommodate *The Basic Minimum as Proto-autonomy*. But any theory of the basic minimum that accommodates this thesis would seem to succumb to the problem of adaptive preferences, which is a death knell for any theory seeking to provide a plausible account of the basic minimum.[56]

1.9. CONCLUSION

To sum up, in this chapter I have specified a concept of the basic minimum to which any particular theories or conceptions of the basic minimum must live up: BM3. I have also argued that five important theories of the basic minimum (primary goods, subsistence, social needs, basic needs, capabilities) either fail to be distinctive approaches, or fail to posit a minimum threshold that meets the minimal moral priority insisted upon by BM3. In addition, I have argued that a welfarist approach faces a powerful dilemma. Offhand, the landscape looks rocky.

One might respond to the dilemma faced by welfarism in three ways. First, one might simply conclude that a basic minimum cannot be accepted. Indeed, this possibility appears to loom large: it would appear that no plausible conception of a basic minimum can be articulated. Second, one might accept a capabilities approach, warts and all. If the relevant alternative is to reject a basic minimum altogether some might find this an attractive option.

But there is a third possibility. One might try to show that a welfarist approach escapes the dilemma presented in the previous section. This is the possibility I embrace. I think a welfarist approach can avoid this dilemma – or, more accurately, I believe that it can be shown that there is no dilemma at all. To show this, however, I must first articulate a basic minimum that could plausibly accommodate *The Basic Minimum as Proto-autonomy* without seeming arbitrary. This is the topic of Chapter 2.

[56] Ibid., 117–18.

CHAPTER 2

A welfarist basic minimum

The previous chapter ended with a challenge to welfarist approaches to a basic minimum. These theories must avoid the horns of a powerful dilemma: either force people to live lives they do not value, or succumb to the problem of adaptive preferences.

This challenge cannot be met without offering a welfarist theory of the basic minimum. This chapter intends not just to do this, but to show how a welfarist approach can avoid arbitrariness *while* respecting the importance of an individual's conception of the good *while* remaining ecumenical between a wide range of theories of the human good. To this end, I offer and argue for an important distinction in welfare goods, beginning in §2.2. Once this distinction is in place, identifying the basic minimum becomes simple, even trivial. In §§2.6–2.7, I identify the basic minimum and defend my account from two important objections. This chapter intends to directly address only the first horn of the welfarist's dilemma; if this chapter succeeds, I will have shown that a non-arbitrary welfarist basic minimum can avoid forcing people to live lives they do not value. I proceed to the topic of adaptive preferences in Chapter 3.

2.1. THE DIVERSITY OF WELFARE

Much of this chapter and the next will be dedicated to discussion of human well-being in light of an interest in articulating a welfarist basic minimum. Though the need for such a discussion may seem obvious, a discussion of the nature of welfare itself has rarely graced the texts of those who seek to defeat a welfarist approach to the basic minimum, or to any other moral or political concept.

Opponents of a welfarist approach to the basic minimum, for instance, generally identify welfarism with a highly specific approach to the personal good: the fulfillment of preferences (a view I deem "Strong Strong Subjectivism," discussed in the conclusion of this chapter), or the experience of valuable mental states (most generally understood as a form of hedonism). For instance, Jonathan Wolff and Avner De-Shalit identify welfarism as "the theory of subjective preference satisfaction."[1] Sen claims that welfarists are interested in the promotion of "utilities,"[2] which he defines in terms of "mental satisfaction."[3] Even Nussbaum identifies welfarism as "subjective welfarism," which judges life quality solely on the basis of preference-fulfillment.[4] The identification of welfarism with an interest in the promotion of preference-fulfillment, or valuable mental states, appears to be entrenched in critical discussions of welfarism.[5] However, this identification is a mistake. Welfarism about any particular moral domain holds, simply speaking, that one's moral reasons in that domain are given by facts about human well-being. But different welfarists will accept different theories of well-being. Of course, it is quite true that many theories of welfare will take preference-satisfaction, or valuable mental states, as a primary index of life quality. But these views are controversial among welfarists.[6]

The diversity of theories of well-being offers two lessons. First, a lesson for welfarism's critics: critics of welfarism cannot simply rest on a rejection of a preference-based, or mental-state-based, account of welfare in seeking to depose a welfarist approach to the basic minimum, or any other moral concept. This point should be clear enough, but, unfortunately, is rarely grasped.[7] Second, a lesson for me: because any individual theory of well-being is bound to be controversial, it does a welfarist approach no favors to commit to any particular substantive account of the nature of well-being. So, in offering my account of a welfarist basic minimum, I offer a view that is ecumenical between a number of important theories of life quality. Of course, in this chapter and in others, I will commit to a number of positions concerning the nature of human well-being that will inevitably rule out conceptions of welfare that cannot accommodate them. But I hope to show that my own view needn't rule out a wide range of potential positions in the logical space of welfare theory.

1 Wolff and De-Shalit (2007), 21–2. 2 Sen (1999), 74.

3 Ibid., 19. See also Sen (1979), 473. Sen does not explicitly link welfarism with any substantive theory of welfare in Sen (1979), but his examples meant to show that welfarism is false rely on an implicit assumption of some form of preference-based or mental-state based-theory of well-being.

4 Nussbaum, however, does recognize some important distinctions. Despite the fact that she identifies "welfarism" with the claim that the fulfillment of preferences improves a given individual's well-being, she appears to claim that "welfarism" is not an adequate method by which to measure the quality of life. See, for instance, Nussbaum (2000), 116.

5 See also Dworkin (2000), 17–18.

6 See, for instance, Arneson (1999), Brink (2008), and Kraut (1994), for just a taste.

7 See, for instance, Arneson (2000b), 511–14.

2.2. A DISTINCTION IN GOODS

For a welfarist account of the basic minimum to be a plausible competitor, one must respond to the charge, leveled by Nussbaum, that such an approach would fail to respect individuals' own choices that reflect their conceptions of the good. But, as I noted in the previous chapter, one can respect the importance of the pursuit of a conception of the good by accepting *The Basic Minimum as Proto-autonomy*, which holds that one achieves the basic minimum by maintaining his or her conception of the good to a sufficient degree.

Of course, this proposal is fraught with ambiguity. On a welfarist approach, the basic minimum should be understood as some particularly important welfare achievement, or some particularly central or significant good. But how are we to understand the moral "specialness" of the basic minimum in terms of an individual's conception of the good? One can put this more pointedly. An essential feature of any basic minimum is that it is a "dividing line" between lives that maintain some morally or evaluatively important feature (such as human dignity, subsistence, basic needs, etc.) and lives that do not. But it is difficult to see how that "dividing line" might be established purely in terms of the maintenance of a person's conception of the good. It is not enough just to say that the achievement of the basic minimum is the achievement of a conception of the good to extent *e*. One had better show that lives that *fail e* are different, in a morally important way, than lives that are at or above *e*. But for any *e*, we could certainly imagine a person who maintains his or her conception of the good to an extent that is below *e* by a *very* slight amount. And if that's right, it would appear that there cannot be *that* much difference, at least in welfarist terms, between lives that maintain the minimum and lives that don't, rendering any basic minimum that satisfies *The Basic Minimum as Proto-autonomy* arbitrary.

I think this skepticism is misplaced. A welfarist basic minimum need not be arbitrary. One can specify a morally and evaluatively resonant *e* that is successful at drawing the crucial "dividing line" between those who maintain their conceptions of the good to a sufficient degree and those who do not. To see how this might be done, note that there is a distinction between *short-term* (or momentary) goods and *long-term* goals or projects that appears to play an important role in our thinking about the intrinsic good for a person.[8] We appear to treat welfare goods such as

[8] There are a number of terms for that which improves a person's well-being, among them "intrinsically good for," "good for," "prudentially good for," etc. I will use these terms interchangeably.

momentary hedonic satisfactions or the satisfaction of short-term desires as less significant when it comes to the evaluative quality of a life than some *longer-term* features of a life. Among these long-term goods are the goals we set for ourselves, or the valued states we maintain throughout the course of a life, that define and give meaning to our life's activities. Imagine, for instance, that I like lollypops, and I regard the pleasure I get from them as beneficial to me. However, imagine that I also value the achievement of a long-term goal: to be a successful novelist. It is surely true that a lollypop would improve my life. But the satisfaction of a lollypop, though I may want it *very much*, has an insignificant impact on my welfare in comparison to the impact of being a novelist.

Of course, in the normal case this is trivial. Most any person who sets themselves a goal of becoming a successful novelist will believe that this goal is more important to his well-being than the pleasure of a single lollypop. Intuitively, however, the achievement or fulfillment of such long-term goals or projects is more significant to a person's welfare, *even if this conclusion overrides a particular individual's preferences*. Generally, we would regard a person who prefers a lollypop to the achievement of a goal, like being a successful novelist, to have a prudentially mistaken preference. Though I do not insist that some particular achievement can improve someone's life if it is not *valued*, I do claim that valued long-term activities, states, goals, or projects form a crucial element of welfare in comparison to valued *short-term* goods, like the beneficial pleasure of a lollypop. In this way, such long-term projects are evaluatively "special": they form a distinct and central class of welfare goods.

Call a life-structuring activity, goal, or achievement a "global project." For instance, being a ballet dancer or professional trombone player are global projects, as are being a philosopher, climbing Mount Everest, being a cultivator of fine gardens, or a meditative monk. Call any global project *p* a "valued project" for A if and only if *p* is a global project and A *values* (in a sense to be explored in more detailed below) *p*. For lack of a better term, call goods that do not rise to the level of global projects "satisfactions." (I should note that different substantive theories of well-being will offer different accounts of the nature of satisfactions. I shan't commit to any one particular interpretation.) I desire a lollypop right now. To have it would surely benefit me. But having a lollypop is not a valued project, it is a *satisfaction*. In addition, I might have a goal to finally finish reading John Le Carré's *A Perfect Spy*. Though this might be a valued goal, it is a satisfaction, not a global project.

This distinction is *wildly* underspecified. However, leaving further refinements aside for the moment, I argue for the following claim:

Thesis: Valued projects are the primary element of human welfare, the success or failure of which is the most important determinant of the prudential quality of a life.

Though these views are importantly different, *Thesis* (or a relevantly similar proposal) is accepted by John Rawls,[9] T. M. Scanlon,[10] Simon Keller,[11] and others.[12] *Thesis* expresses what I take to be an initially plausible position. Valued projects are "special": they are the most important determinants of life quality. *Thesis* can explain the judgment elicited earlier: that my preference for a lollypop rather than to be a successful novelist is prudentially mistaken: in preferring the lollypop, I prefer something that is comparatively insignificant in terms of overall welfare value.

2.3. WHAT IS A PROJECT?[13]

To begin a defense of *Thesis*, it is important to say a little more about what it means to maintain a global project. It seems a fool's errand to attempt a precise account of the distinction, and so I will not attempt one here. Indeed, I doubt that a sharp distinction is possible; whether, in a given case, *p* is a global project or a satisfaction will require substantive investigation on the basis of our considered judgments. However, I do hope to clarify this distinction sufficiently for my purposes, although I leave open the possibility that further, perhaps better, accounts could be provided.

One thing should be made clear at the outset, however. Whatever account one provides, that there is such a distinction is plausible. A person who satisfies his preference to watch *American Idol* satisfies a *different sort* of preference than a person who fulfills his preference to be a good parent, or a loving spouse, or a great physicist, one with a very different impact on his welfare. Not all lives, even in their full description, will contain projects. Indeed, the distinction between a global project – or as Raz calls it, a "comprehensive goal" – and other more minor goods is an important feature of a number of theories of well-being. Hence though the precise

[9] Rawls (1971), 411: "If this conception of plans is sound, we should expect that the good things in life are, roughly speaking, those activities and relationships which have a major place in rational plans."
[10] Scanlon (1998), ch. 3. [11] Keller (2004). [12] Raz (1987), ch. 12.
[13] This section was heavily influenced by helpful conversations with Erin Frykholm.

distinction between global projects and satisfactions may be slippery, this does not mean that a distinction is not worth drawing.

A precise distinction is hard to draw in part because global projects can vary widely in structure. One variation seems especially worth noting. Some projects take the form of *goals*: a particular achievement someone works for over the course of a life. Consider, for instance, the global project of reaching the summit of K2, toward which a given individual may work for an extended period. This project may be valued based only on the final result: if I work tirelessly to climb K2, and don't, my tireless work may have been, at least from my perspective, a waste; prudentially valueless. Call these "goal-like" projects. On the other hand, some projects are "state-like." For instance, one might value the global project of "being a philosopher." In this case, there is no single identifiable goal that defines the project but rather a state a person maintains throughout a life, or at least a significant portion of a life.

What, then, unifies projects of disparate structure? I think there are three jointly necessary and sufficient conditions for project-hood. First, global projects help to narratively unify a person's life. To put this point in Vellemanian terms to be explored below, a global project is a primary element in an individual's *life story*; they form an essential part of the macro-level narrative of a person's life. For instance, if someone successfully achieves the project of reaching the summit of K2, we should expect that that project tells at least a very important part of the story of that person's life.[14] Of course, not all features of a person's life story are global projects. The second feature of global projects is that they must not just help to tell a person's life story, but must also narratively unify, in a broad sense, a person's *actions* and *decisions* and must be the *product* of such actions and decisions. For any person with a goal to reach the summit of K2, she will deliberate, make decisions, and act through the course of her life in a way that is explained by her maintenance of this goal-like project. Furthermore, any success at this project will be the product of her actions and decisions. In this way, global projects are not just any old feature of a person's life story, but are, literally, *projects* that a person might or might not choose to undertake. Third, global projects are "global" – the story they help to tell is that of a segment of a person's life of *significant temporal duration*. Though someone might "be a philosopher" for a day, to say that she maintains a

[14] Of course, this needn't be true of all individuals who climb K2. I'm assuming, however, that this particular goal is something that must be worked toward by the person involved not just for a little while but over the course of a life.

global project of being a philosopher, this project must structure her life and explain her activities for at least a substantial section of her life.

Some embellishment is in order. Take the first requirement. For a person to maintain a global project, it is not enough that some particular "story" of their life could be told. Rather, their lives must be narratively integrated. To see this requirement, consider the difference between two lives. The first person, A, spends long periods on college campuses, teaching courses and doing research, engaging with colleagues and traveling to conferences. A's life could be narratively integrated by the fact that she is an *academic*. The second person, B, acts in a different way. B attends school briefly, drops out, takes employment for short periods of time, spends time as a drifter, but establishes a permanent home for at least some extended periods, etc. Though B's life might be rife with satisfactions, it does not maintain a global project insofar as the activities of this life do not maintain any unifying thread. Of course, a story *could* be trivially told of this person's life. Such a story would simply consist in a list of this person's activities. But without a unifying thread, this life maintains no global projects.

One might ask further questions about what it means for a life to be narratively unified. Though I will not be able to provide any precise account of this generally intuitive idea, two points are worth noting. First, narrative unification requires *common explanation* of a substantial part of the events and activities in this life. For instance, A spends lots of time on college campuses, teaches courses, and goes to conferences. These activities permit of a common explanation: A is an academic. Second, narrative unification provides the events and activities of a life with a shared meaning. Again adapting a Vellemanian thought to be explored in more detail later, it seems to me that a life is narratively unified if the *meaning* of particular events (or at least a substantial amount throughout a life) cannot be properly understood in isolation. A narratively unified life will treat the moments or events of a life as not simply atomistic, but as having a meaning that is shaped by events prior and subsequent to the moment or event itself. For instance, imagine that A gives an academic talk at Big State University. This activity, for A, has a certain meaning: it is a natural part of an academic career, and, depending on her past research activities, may even be a highlight. The meaning of this event, in terms of A's life, is necessarily shaped by the longer-term project in which she is engaged: being an academic. However, we could imagine another person, C, who gives precisely the same sort of talk at Big State University. But if we imagine that C is a politician, rather than an academic, the meaning of this event will be quite different. This event will be an oddity, something unusual, perhaps an honorific capstone to a successful career in politics. The global project of being a politician will help to explain this event, but will also provide this event with a meaning distinct from the meaning of this event in A's life.[15]

Take, now, the second requirement. Global projects are the products of, and help to narratively unify, our *actions and decisions*. This feature of global projects helps to rule out certain things that may narratively unify a person's life, but that do not, intuitively at least, constitute global projects. Take a person whose life was entirely taken up by her brain being manipulated by electrodes for the purposes of eliciting certain pleasurable reactions. We might narratively integrate her life by saying that she was *hooked up to an experience machine*. Indeed, this will be a *central* part of her life story. But though this may be a narratively integrated life story, it is not integrated by means of a particular project. No narrative unification of this person's activities or decisions is possible, insofar as there are no such activities or decisions. This person's life is wholly passive, and hence does not maintain a global project.[16] Furthermore, some features of a person's life may well narratively unify his or her actions and decisions, but do not constitute global projects. For instance, one might say of a particular person that an essential part of his life story is being a member of a certain *race*. For instance, if A is born a Native American and spends virtually all of his life on a reservation, one can rightly say that a large section of his life is narratively integrated by the fact that he is a Native American. Indeed, the fact that A is a Native American will help to explain many of the actions and decisions he takes. But "being a Native American" is not a project in the sense I mean: whether he is a Native American or not is not the *product* of any actions or decisions on A's part.

Finally, the requirement that global projects be of substantial temporal duration is crucial: this element differentiates those mere momentary goals (such as to pour myself another cup of coffee), and those goals that form the major element of human welfare. But one qualifying note is in order. The global nature of such projects should be understood to require *long-term* narrative integration of one's actions and decisions, not *long-term* and *constant* narrative integration of one's actions and decisions. To be engaged in the project of "being a philosopher" or "reaching the summit of K2," one needn't be engaged in those characteristic activities at every moment during

[15] See, for instance, MacIntyre (2007), ch. 15.

[16] One might, quite accurately, say that "hooking one's self into an experience machine" is a goal-like project, insofar as this is a goal one might work toward, and that might narratively unify one's activities and decisions over the long term.

which they are valued. One can be a philosopher and spend a day or two reading Le Carré. However, we wouldn't say of a particular activity or goal that it is a global project if it doesn't provide a sufficient level of narrative integration in the long term. Consider, for instance, a state-like project of being a "Christmas churchgoer." This project consists of attending church once per year, on December 25. Though this might narratively unify some of a person's activities and decisions in the long term, it does not provide sufficient narrative unification: this state does not rise to the level of a global project. I take that to be the correct answer. This being said, the requirements of sufficient unification from project to project will likely vary substantially. Hence I won't be able to offer any precise account of "sufficient" narrative unification. Whether a particular project satisfies this constraint will require case-by-case inquiry.

Two further features of the achievement of global projects should be noted here. I have not insisted that for *p* to be a global project of A's, A must *know* that he is engaged in, or explicitly *decide* to maintain, this project. But this is the correct answer. One can successfully maintain a global project without ever fully knowing or deciding to do so. For instance, it might be that through a simple accident, and without ever planning to, A has maintained a successful career as an accountant. This project is still narratively unifying, despite the fact that *being a successful accountant* was never itself the product of deliberation on his part nor, perhaps, was it even known to him. We can live according to global projects in spite of our ignorance of so doing, or explicit decision to do so.[17] Sometimes we may just "fall into" global projects that may form the basis of an assessment of the quality of our lives. If that's the case, I see no reason to bar their value simply because the projects themselves, as opposed to the activities that constitute these projects, are not a matter of explicit intention.[18]

[17] In this way, my account of a global project differs slightly from Keller's. Keller writes:

> When we think of someone as having a goal, we think of her as *pursuing* it – as to some extent organizing her life, or intending to organize her life, around that goal. The extent to which something is a goal, or to which it is a strong goal, is in part a matter of the extent to which its bearer organizes her life around its pursuit. What's important here is that your taking on a goal involves taking an attitude towards *your* activities and *your* life (even if your reasons for forming that goal are entirely selfless). (Keller [2004], 32–3)

I do think, as noted here, that global projects are "organizers" – they organize and narratively unify the activities and decisions of our lives. But they can play this role without being the object of any conscious decision or active intention on the part of the person involved.

[18] Along the same lines, I do not regard a feature of such global projects as necessarily requiring any significant "self-sacrifice" on the part of the agent. In this way, my view differs from Douglas Portmore's. See Portmore (2007).

Furthermore, this account of global projects allows for a *very* wide range of potential projects, insofar as many things might narratively unify our actions and decisions.[19] Consider, for instance, the project of "being a reality TV watcher."[20] It might be that I live a life in which I watch reality TV, and that this particular "project" (state-like) in fact narratively integrates large sections of my life, my actions, and decisions (I plan, each day, to watch *n* reality shows before lunch, *m* before dinner, etc., etc.). I might also do this throughout the course of my life. It seems to me that there is very little reason to bar "being a reality TV-watcher" from being a global project in the sense I mean here. Of course, many will not value such a project. Furthermore, some might believe that such projects are not of sufficient "objective" value to constitute a project that would improve the quality of my life in a significant way (for further discussion of this point, see the conclusion of this chapter). Nevertheless, it seems to me that being a reality TV watcher might very well constitute a global project, and is certainly a *different sort of good* than the good of satisfying one's preference to, today, watch *The Next Iron Chef.* Somewhere along the line, engaging in these day-to-day activities shapes one's life story or narrative at a macro level, explains and unifies one's actions and decisions, and does so over the long term in a way that entails the maintenance of a global project.

This rough-and-ready account of the distinction between global projects and satisfactions is likely subject to counterexamples. Furthermore, my account of such projects uses *extremely* vague language ("significant temporal duration," and the like). A more thorough examination is surely required to account for the extent to which any particular welfare good is to constitute a global project rather than a satisfaction. Any general account will include a substantial amount of gray area. In any event, the intuitive idea is robust enough for my purposes here.

2.4. *THESIS*: TWO ARGUMENTS

This section contains two positive arguments for *Thesis*. First, I offer a simple appeal to intuition. Second, I advance a rationale for this view, independently of any direct appeal to considered judgment.

[19] One interesting possibility is that any such narrative unification might have to be within the bounds of recognized "social forms," as Raz urges. See Raz (1987), ch. 12. However, I shall not make this requirement explicit, though it does seem to me that any sensible narrative unification by a global project should at least be recognizable as such a project.

[20] Thanks to an anonymous reviewer for suggesting this case.

2.4.1. A bare intuition

The Penguin paperback edition of the rousing 1915 novel *The Thirty-Nine Steps* features this biography of its author, John Buchan:

John Buchan was born in Perth in 1875. His father was a minister of the Free Church of Scotland; and in 1876 the family moved to Fife, where John walked six miles a day to school. Later they moved to Glasgow and, when he went to Glasgow University, he published articles in periodicals. When at Brasenose College, Oxford, he published five books and many articles, and won several awards, including the Newdigate Prize for poetry. His career was diverse and successful, and despite ill health, he was a barrister and Member of Parliament, in addition to being a writer, soldier and publisher. He married, and had four children. He was created Baron Tweedsmuir of Elsfield in 1935 and became the Governor-General of Canada, until his death in 1940.

His first success as an author came with *Prester John* in 1910, and he went on to write a series of adventure thrillers, or "shockers" as he called them, all characterized by their authentically rendered backgrounds, romantic characters, their atmosphere of expectancy and world-wide conspiracies, and the author's own enthusiasm. His main heroes were Richard Hannay in *The Thirty-Nine Steps* and four other books, Dickson McCunn, the Glaswegian provision merchant with the soul of a romantic, and Edward Leithen, eminent lawyer. Buchan also established a reputation as an historical biographer with such works as *Montrose*, *Oliver Cromwell* and *Augustus*.[21]

In reading this biography, I am immediately overtaken by the feeling that Buchan's life was of tremendous quality. And this judgment has very little to do with any assessment of the merely momentary benefits he may have received. In particular, Buchan's life was so good not because of any momentary feelings of pleasure, say, but because he was successful in a number of widely varying pursuits throughout his life. Not only was he an accomplished novelist, biographer, and poet, he was also a startlingly successful politician, serving in Parliament, eventually taking the position of Governor-General of Canada. Of course, many politicians are also (or claim to be) writers, but Buchan's writing went beyond the normal subject-matter of politicos. Not only was he a historian, he was also the author of books that are meant, primarily, for fun and distraction: "shockers," or romantic thrillers told with distinctive panache. And at this endeavor he had perhaps his most lasting influence: *The Thirty-Nine Steps* has been filmed countless times, including once by Alfred Hitchcock, and has even been the subject-matter of a successful stage spoof, currently (as of this writing) playing off-Broadway.

[21] Buchan (1915), Author's Biography.

Reflection on Buchan's life, I think, supports *Thesis*. His life was of high quality, and we appear to maintain this conviction even in the absence of knowledge of his satisfactions, or mere momentary goods. If so, it would appear that Buchan's valued projects – being a writer, politician, etc. – and their success are the most important determinants of the quality of his life.

Those who would reject *Thesis* might argue that Buchan's life was extremely good not because of the projects he valued *per se*, but rather because these projects generated in him, say, pleasure, satisfied desires, or other momentary goods. But I think this is incorrect. Assume that he took less pleasure than other less successful men, or that his momentary desires might have been less satisfied than others. Does this alter our judgment of the broad quality of his life? It seems to me that the answer is surely *no*. One is tempted to judge Buchan's life of high quality not because it contained large amounts of pleasure (and indeed, his biography gives us very little information about Buchan's mental states, save for the fact that Buchan was never of robust health, and was probably more than a little annoyed at the six-mile-a-day walk to school). Beyond my assumption that Buchan seemed to value these projects, information about his mental states or preference structure seems unimportant to our judgment.[22] His long-term projects – *being* a historian, novelist, politician, etc. – seem to be the most important determinant of our assessment of his life as of very high quality. In light of these valued projects, the evaluative importance of potential satisfactions seems to fade into the background. Of course, few who maintain valued projects will reach Buchan's heights. But his case is illustrative, if only of the following point: Buchan's case shows that in assessing the quality of lives, we look, first and foremost, to the long-term projects that matter to the persons whose lives they are.[23]

This argument notes an intuitive reaction only, but this particular reaction seems to me sufficiently robust as to provide a reason, if only *pro tanto*, to accept *Thesis*. It simply seems right to say that judgments of life quality are dominated by the extent to which a person successfully maintains valued projects.

[22] When it comes to Buchan's well-being, we would certainly change our mind if we came to find out that he didn't really enjoy being a writer and didn't value it, or couldn't have cared less about his career in politics.

[23] One might complain that there is no evidence that Buchan actually valued any of the projects he maintained; but if we happen to discover, e.g., that he did not value being a politician or writer, etc., it seems to me that this would be good evidence to revise our judgment of the quality of his life downward. See note 22.

2.4.2. *Shape, meaning, and self-direction*

The above section noted an intuition I regard as robust. I hope the reader will agree. But it would be nice not to rely too heavily on it. In fact, I think that *Thesis* can be given a powerful independent rationale. Valued projects provide a life's activities with a long-term, self-directed *meaning*. To maintain a valued project is to be able to see one's life as more than simply the sum of its individual moments, but as tied together into a narrative whole. Maintenance of a valued project allows one to see one's life as organized around a central principle, which itself provides a shared and valued meaning to one's actions and decisions. This feature of valued projects explains, I think, their tremendous importance when it comes to overall judgments of life quality.

The importance of a life's self-directed meaning is on full display in the following insight by David Velleman. Velleman argues that well-being is not *additive*; in other words, the overall welfare value of two lives can differ even though these lives contain equal amounts of momentary well-being. Velleman's evidence for this claim is that the *shape* of a life (i.e., whether welfare benefits fall at earlier or later times) is itself important to well-being. Velleman writes:

> Consider two different lives that you might live. One life begins in the depths but takes an upward trend: a childhood of deprivation, a troubled youth, struggles and setbacks in early adulthood, followed finally by success and satisfaction in middle age and a peaceful retirement. Another life begins at the heights but slides downhill: a blissful childhood and youth, precocious triumphs and rewards in early adulthood, followed by a midlife strewn with disasters that lead to misery in old age. Surely, we can imagine two such lives as containing equal sums of momentary well-being . . . Yet even if we were to map each moment in one life onto a moment of equal well-being in the other, we would not have shown these lives to be equally good.[24]

Velleman contends that the former life is better than the latter, despite the fact that the sum-total of momentary benefits are identical in each case. Part of the explanation, according to Velleman, is the shape of one's life: an upward-sloping life is better than a downward-sloping life.

I think there is much in what Velleman claims. But we should be careful to avoid the claim that the *shape* of a life makes a *per se* difference to well-being.[25] For instance, imagine a person who is hooked up to an experience

[24] Velleman, "Well-Being and Time" in Velleman (2000), 58.

[25] Velleman, as I note below, avoids this claim. Frances Kamm, however, endorses it. See Kamm (2003), 223.

machine at an early age. This experience machine has imperfect software, so at an early age the person experiences pain as well as pleasure. Gradually (say, once per year) the software is updated, so that later in this person's life she experiences much more pleasure than earlier in life. This life is surely no better than the life of a person whose experience machine works perfectly in the beginning, and then slowly deteriorates. If this is correct, Velleman's intuition should be explained in a way other than by referring to the mere shape of a life; the shape itself does not, apparently, have the ability to alter the quality of one's life in all cases.

But Velleman quite rightly notes that later successes redeem earlier failures not because the shape of a life is *per se* valuable, but because there is an important *relationship* between the later successes and the prior failures:

> Why would a person care about the placement of momentary goods on the curve that maps his changing welfare? The answer, I believe, is that an event's place in the story of one's life lends it a meaning that isn't entirely determined by its impact on one's well-being at the time. A particular electoral victory, providing a particular boost to one's current welfare, can mean either that one's early frustrations were finally over or that one's subsequent failures were not yet foreshadowed, that one enjoyed either fleeting good luck or lasting success – all depending on its placement in the trend of one's well-being. And the event's meaning is what determines its contribution to the value of one's life.[26]

According to Velleman, the *meaning* of particular goods can be affected by events prior and subsequent to the achievement of a particular good itself. But later success can affect the meaning of earlier failures (and vice versa) only if these successes and failures are, in some sense, narratively unified across time.[27] The meaning of earlier events is affected by later events when these events concern the unified activities, goals, and projects in which one is engaged. Hence the variable meaning of these events is not best accounted for in terms of a downward or upward trend, but rather is better accounted for by the narrative structure of the longer-term projects of which these individual events are a part. If one has early electoral success, but a long downfall, it would appear that this early success, though perhaps pleasurable, was not a step along the way to success in the project of being a successful politician. In this way, the later events of one's life affect the "meaning of" prior events – not because they indicate a *per se* welfare-relevant trend, but because the meaning of these events is shaped by a narratively unified project, one that, in the case of the failed politician,

[26] Velleman (2000), 63. [27] Compare ibid., 63–4.

he is unlikely to value.[28] What I think Velleman's insight shows is that in judging the quality of a life as a whole, we are not *uninterested* in momentary achievements. But we are *most* interested in that which narratively unifies, and provides a shared meaning to, a life's activities and events in the long term. Velleman is right to declare that the "meaning" of a particular event helps to shape its importance to our welfare. But this claim itself implies the importance of valued projects, insofar as these projects are what *provide* such a meaning to the individual activities and decisions of our lives.

The importance of the sort of meaning provided by valued projects is also stressed by Bernard Williams. Williams notes that "A man may have, for a lot of his life or even just for some part of it, a *ground* project or set of projects which are closely related to his existence and which to a significant degree give a meaning to his life."[29] According to Williams, it would be "absurd to demand" of individuals that they give up such projects for the sake, e.g., of greater overall utility or conformity to the sort of impartiality required by Kantian moral theories.[30] And though I do not want to adjudicate between utilitarianism, Kantianism, and other moral theories at the moment, one reason that Williams's point is so resonant is the plausibility of *Thesis* itself: that the meaning provided by such projects is a dominant determinant of life quality. Being able to see my life and activities as participating in a shared meaning – a meaning I regard as valuable – is of great significance to the quality of my life as a whole. (This is true whether or not this project is a "ground" project in Williams's sense.[31])

The importance of global projects in providing for a life's "meaning" shouldn't be oversold. Global projects are not the only things that can narratively unify a life or large sections of a life. Hence it would be incorrect to say that global projects are required for any sort of long-term "meaning" at all. After all, in certain cases the events of a life may be narratively unified by things that, e.g., are not achievable by action, such as a person's born-into nationality or race. However, the meaning provided by global

[28] We can, of course, imagine a politician who did not seek to be successful in the long term, but who valued the project of being a politician even under circumstances of a tragic downfall. But in this case it does not seem plausible to believe that the shape of a person's life is *per se* important. I am tempted to believe that, given that this project is valued with full knowledge of its circumstances, it does not deserve to be placed lower on an overall ordinal rank merely for having a "downward" trajectory, as it were.

[29] Williams (1981), 12. See also (1974), §5.

[30] Williams (1974), 116.

[31] Williams (1981), 10. Williams, in his critique of utilitarianism, defines ground projects as: "projects and attitudes which in some cases he takes seriously at the deepest level, as what his life is about" (Williams (1974), 116).

projects, stressed by Velleman and Williams, is central in an important way. Because global projects are achievable in action, they provide for a shared, *self-directed* meaning to one's activities in the long term. A global project of mine captures the meaning of my life and activities that *I* help to shape. A nationality or race into which one is born does not.[32] But this supports the supreme welfare value of valued projects: we generally do not regard the sort of meaning provided by one's nationality or race as of intrinsic value, though it may naturally give rise to projects the satisfaction of which *is* intrinsically valuable.

Whether Velleman or Williams would agree with my gloss on their insights is beyond my purview here. However, their reflections ring true, and support the evaluative "specialness" of valued projects. Maintaining a valued project involves being able to see one's life and activities as participating in a shared, self-directed meaning – one that reveals one's life to be more than a simple collection of undirected activities. In light of the nature of valued projects, their evaluative dominance seems no more than commonsensical.

None of these arguments are knock-down. But *Thesis* is plausible, and is supported by further considerations about the essential connection between global projects and the shape and self-directed meaning of one's life. I have left until Chapter 4 the vexing topic of the precise evaluative relationship between valued projects and satisfactions. But the importance of valued projects to assessments of life quality, i.e., their evaluative "specialness," must now be clear.

2.5. WHAT IS A VALUED PROJECT?

Before I turn to my account of the basic minimum, one further element of *Thesis* must be clarified. *Thesis* insists on the evaluative dominance of *valued* projects rather than mere *global* projects. Indeed, it makes sense to do so. One would hardly accept that projects are evaluatively "special" as claimed by *Thesis* if they do not reflect the conception of the good of the person whose projects they are. But what, precisely, distinguishes a mere project from a valued project?

Two issues immediately arise. First, for a particular project *p* to be valued by A, A must take some sort of pro-attitude toward *p*. But which attitude is

[32] Though, of course, I may undertake any number of meaningful global projects in reaction to facts of my nationality or race. For instance, I might have as a global project of becoming a member of a new nationality, or a global project of advancing the outlook for members of my race, especially if I am a member of an oppressed racial minority.

this? One could understand this attitude as a belief, a particular conative or affective pro-attitude, or some other mental or intentional stance. Sorting out which psychological state one must take toward *p* to value *p* – especially if this sort of valuing is to reflect A's genuine conception of the good – is important, and my answer to this question will lay the groundwork for my response to the problem of adaptive preferences. I thus leave this problem aside until the following chapter. But there is a second problem that must be addressed here. The fact that I take a relevant pro-attitude toward a global project does not seem sufficient to render it the case that it is *valued* in the sense that would render it the most central element of a person's welfare. Take a simple example. I might take a pro-attitude toward *p*, but only as a result of a preference for *p* rather than *q*. But simply preferring something does not mean that I *value* it. For instance, I might prefer being a Grand Central Station janitor to being the king's food taster. (Indeed, I may even actively desire to be a Grand Central Station janitor insofar as I am currently the king's food taster.) But this certainly doesn't entail that, all-things-considered, I *value* being a janitor. All this might mean is that among the projects I do not value I hold that being a janitor at Grand Central Station is better than being the king's food-taster.

To take a pro-attitude toward a particular project is surely necessary for it to count as a valued project. But the pro-attitude must be of the right form. Now consider my stance toward being a Grand Central Station janitor in comparison to Glen, who *actually* values being a Grand Central Station janitor. What is the difference between Glen and myself? It would appear that though we both take at least some sort of pro-attitude toward this project (insofar as I prefer it to being the king's food taster), we differ along a crucial dimension. To value a project, one must not simply prefer it to some other project or welfare good. Rather, one must assess it as good in an *absolute* way. Glen, rather than myself, regards the project as being good rather than bad, of positive rather than negative value, as being "worth it" rather than not. Though I may prefer it to being the king's food taster, I still do not regard the project *itself* as being of positive value.

But how do we determine when a person regards a global project as good and not bad, "worth it" rather than not? Before I answer this question, I should add one complicating factor. I might value a particular project under some circumstances and not others. For instance, I might value the project of being a sailor on the assumption that my physical makeup is strong and robust. As I am (weak and sapless), I despise sailing: I regard it as tiresome and not worth the exertion. Do I value the project of being a sailor? Surely the answer is no. But if this is correct, whether I value this particular project will depend on *other* things in my life: my level of exertion, pain, seasickness, leisure, time off, advancement, etc., some elements of which are not properly regarded as part of the project itself. But it seems to me, then, that whether a particular project is *valued* is *context-sensitive*: to determine whether it is valued, we must view it in the context of the life in which that project is actually to be lived. Sometimes context will determine whether, within a particular life, a particular project will be valued rather than unvalued.

However, this feature of project valuation actually renders what it means to "value" a particular project less, rather than more, complicated. Because projects are valued, or not, in the context of an entire life, to value a particular project requires one to take the right kind of pro-attitude to the *life* in which that project is lived. But the question of whether a life has positive versus negative value, or has been "good rather than bad" is easier to understand: to assess a life as "worth it" rather than not, one must see it as *worth living*.[33]

The foregoing reflections might lead us to the following account of what it means for a global project to be a valued project: A values a global project *p* if and only if (a) *l* is the life in which *p* is actually lived, and (b) A regards *l* as worth living. (One point: it is important for the valuation of a given project that the presence and/or valuation of other projects not interfere. This is addressed by (c), below.)

Though this possibility is initially plausible, it is unsuccessful as stated. I might regard the life in which I am a Grand Central Station janitor as worth living, but in a way that does not entail that I value the project of being a Grand Central Station janitor. The explanation of my assessment that my life is worth living might be the product *simply* of non-project

[33] One might ask what it means for someone to assess a life as being "worth living." Though I shall not commit to any one particular method, one interesting proposal is offered by Campbell Brown (see Brown (MS)). Brown argues, very roughly, that the best way to understand the notion of "living a life worth living" is to compare one's actual lifetime well-being score to the well-being score one has in the life of shortest finite time. In other words, imagine a life that is .5 milliseconds long. One's life is worth living if and only if one's well-being is greater than the well-being one has in a life that is .5 milliseconds long (or whatever extremely short duration). A life of shortest possible duration has neither satisfactions nor projects. It has no welfare goods at all. It seems to me that Brown's suggestion can be adapted to my purposes here. On this view, one "values" a particular project only if one prefers a life that contains this project, and no other projects, to a life of shortest possible duration. On this view, if one prefers the life of shortest possible duration to all lives that maintain global projects, one values no such projects. (I do not wish to lean too heavily on Brown's proposal, though I myself find it attractive. There may be other ways of understanding what it means for a life to be "worth living," or what it means for someone to assess a life as worth living. In what follows, I shall rely specifically on the notion of a life worth living: the reader is welcome to substitute whatever analysis of that concept she prefers.)

contextual factors. Imagine that I am gaga for lollypops. I might regard a life in which I am a Grand Central Station janitor as worth living but only *because* I am able to obtain a threshold number of lollypops in that life, not *because* I maintain said global project. If so, to value the project means more than to regard the life in which that project is lived as worth living. One's judgment *that* such a life is worth living must be *explained* in the right way.

The fix is easy. To properly be said to find a global project valuable rather than valueless, good rather than bad, etc., it must be the case that one's assessment of one's life as worth living is – at least in part – *explained* by the global project this life maintains.[34] Though, when it comes to sailing, whether or not I view my life as worth living will crucially depend on non-project contextual factors (such as exertion, pain, etc.), if I am to value *being a sailor*, it must be that being a sailor *also* helps to explain why I regard my life as worth living. Glen sees his life as worth living in part *because* he engages in the project of being a Grand Central Station janitor. For me, though I take a pro-attitude toward this project, if I do happen to assess my life as worth living, this assessment is in spite of, rather than in part because of, this activity, which I do not value.

Putting all this together, A values a global project p if and only if (a) l is the life in which p is lived, (b) A regards l as worth living, and (c) A's assessment of l as worth living is at least in part explained by p. Though this account of the nature of valued, rather than global, projects is somewhat stipulative, it need not be inconsistent with *Thesis*. Quite the contrary: we would hardly say of a particular project that it is evaluatively special in the way suggested by *Thesis* if the life in which that project is lived is not seen as worth living, or that the project itself does not contribute to the worthiness of the life in question.

2.6. THE BASIC MINIMUM

In defining a welfarist basic minimum, we must offer an evaluatively special welfare achievement that could plausibly form a morally resonant threshold or "dividing line." Given *Thesis*, I submit that a plausible welfarist basic minimum can be formulated as follows:

Welfarist Basic Minimum (WBM): A achieves the basic minimum over the course of a life l if and only if A successfully achieves or maintains a valued project in l.

[34] I address the nature of such "explanation" in §3.3.2.

There is much to say for WBM. First, it is not arbitrary. Those who maintain a valued global project maintain a central, essential element of welfare. These lives have the sort of valued and self-directed "meaning" to which Velleman and Williams directed our attention. Those who fail to maintain such a project do not. Given the arguments detailed above, this is a substantial difference, and it hence forms a plausible "dividing line" between lives that fail the basic minimum and lives that do not. Furthermore, WBM is appropriate to the concept of a welfarist basic minimum. The central intuition behind the appeal of a welfarist approach is that individuals should live lives that are at least minimally decent, to cite a Millerian point from the previous chapter. But in maintaining a valued project, A lives a life that A judges not only to be *worth living*, but worth living given its long-term, narratively unified structure. When looking at individual lives strictly in welfarist terms, the maintenance of a valued project seems to entail a life of *at least* minimal decency.

Second, indexing the basic minimum to valued projects is itself plausible. Consider, for instance, the lives of two destitute sex workers A and B. Assume, however, that for A, her pimp grants her an unlimited supply of lollypops, which she finds delicious. In all other ways, these lives are identical. The lollypop-rich life of A, though better than B's life, does not achieve the basic minimum, we are tempted to say, no matter how many lollypops she gets. So what else must be achieved for a person to maintain the basic minimum? Lollypops are not enough, but why? In this case, we are likely to say that though A surely values the experience of such lollypops, the *major* element of her life, that which provides the basis for her life story, involves *being a destitute sex worker*. And it is *this* aspect of her life that most clearly drives the extent to which her life is awful. Few would see such a life as worth living, but even fewer would see this project as an active contributor to the worth of a life in which it is maintained. It is thus plausible to say that A's basic minimum is indexed not to momentary satisfactions, like the satisfaction of a delicious lollypop, but rather to the long-term elements of her life: the extent to which she maintains a valued project.

Third, WBM seems to correct important defects of its primary competitor. Recall that any basic minimum must be a valued state of persons with *at least* weak moral priority. But the capabilities approach would imply that capabilities for those who would make no use of them are morally prior to capabilities that are used, in fact, to enhance lives. But WBM does not make this error. Consider, for instance, a person who values a long-term, unifying project, but succeeds at this project without need of a particular capability. WBM rejects the claim that granting such a capability takes weak moral priority: this individual already maintains the basic minimum. Furthermore, Nussbaum's approach failed in part because her account could not support upward distribution. And though I discuss this point in more detail in Chapter 4, it seems correct to say that, at least on a one-to-one basis, the welfare goods that individuals might sustain without also sustaining a valued project (i.e., satisfactions, or unvalued projects) are insignificant enough to justify upward distribution for the sake of those who might obtain the most central element of human welfare: a valued project.

Finally, WBM successfully accommodates *The Basic Minimum as Proto-autonomy*. Because no one obtains the basic minimum without engaging in *valued* projects, there is no moral pressure, given WBM, to require someone to live a life that does not conform to his or her conception of the good. For WBM, as required by *The Basic Minimum as Proto-autonomy*, a given individual maintains the basic minimum if she achieves her conception of the good to a sufficient degree: if she maintains a valued project. Given these advantages, I conclude that WBM has much to say for itself.

One further point is worth making before I move on. WBM is a theory of the basic minimum across the whole of one's life. However, it appears sensible to ask, apart from the "whole-life" judgment offered by WBM, whether a given person does or does not maintain the basic minimum at a particular *time* within a life. Here WBM offers no guidance. However, WBM can be easily characterized in a time-relative manner:

Welfarist Basic Minimum (Time-Relative) (WBM):* A maintains the basic minimum at *t* if and only if A engages a successful valued project at *t*.

Of course, WBM* has a number of problems that must be cleared up. WBM* is a theory of what it is for a given individual to maintain the basic minimum at a time, but the definition of what it means for a given person to maintain the basic minimum at a time makes reference to the maintenance of valued projects at a particular time. But it would seem that this definition is appropriate only for *state-like* projects, such as "being a philosopher," for which the success conditions can hold of an individual at many different times, rather than *goal-like* projects, such as "reaching the summit of K2." If I will eventually succeed in my goal of reaching the summit of K2, but have not *yet* reached the summit of K2, is it the case that I fail the basic minimum (assuming that this is my only valued project)?

Intuitively, the answer to this question is no. But this point is easily accommodated. If, at *t*, my actions and decisions are narratively unified by a goal-like project, the success of which is determined at t_1 and, at t_1, this goal is successful, I maintained or participated in a successful project *at* t. The meaning of my actions at *t* are determined, at least in part, by participation in this activity. Hence, for some goal-like projects, it may not be obvious at *t* whether a given individual maintains the basic minimum at *t*. But this is the correct answer. If I work my entire life to climb K2, for the sole purpose of climbing it (such that I would not have valued the resulting narrative if I happen to fail), and, in fact, I fail to climb K2, I do not maintain a life of minimally decent quality; my life is a failure.

With the possibility of WBM* open, a further question arises. Which version of the basic minimum is the appropriate target of moral concern? If a person lives a life that maintains the basic minimum, but fails to maintain the minimum *now*, should we treat his or her state *now* as possessing (at least) weak moral priority to other states *now*? This question has been the topic of much discussion.[35] Rather than addressing this literature, however, I will assume here that the central moral question that concerns the basic minimum is the question of whether a given person maintains the basic minimum over the course of a whole life. I take my assumption as justified for the following reasons. First, this answer seems plausible. Though a person early or late in life might fail to maintain a valued project, they may very well have done so later or earlier in life: in this case, it seems wrong to treat their current state as maintaining the moral priority required by BM3. Second, nothing in this book rides on one particular answer to this question rather than another. Those who are more compelled to treat individual times as the locus of moral concern are free to replace WBM with WBM*; the arguments I offer will apply *mutatis mutandis*.

2.7. OBJECTION: DIGNITY AND CAPABILITIES[36]

WBM faces a number of objections. I will consider three in this chapter, more in Chapter 6. The first claims that a capabilities approach can accommodate an important claim unavailable to WBM. Nussbaum's capabilities approach, but not WBM, can accommodate the connection between the basic minimum and basic human dignity. According to Nussbaum, the capabilities approach draws support from its claim to link the basic minimum with a conception of truly human functioning.[37] However, WBM

[35] See, for instance, McKerlie (2001), Lippert-Rasmussen (2003), Temkin (2003).

[36] The argument of this section is developed in more detail in Dorsey (2010a).

[37] Nussbaum (2006), 74.

includes no constraints on the *sort* of projects that might be valued. In particular, we might consider a project that seems wholly incompatible with a life of human dignity, e.g., a life of a grass counter, or a life of total deprivation and destitution which by some strange occurrence allows the maintenance of a valued project. But, it might be said, without basic human dignity, or truly human functioning, one cannot maintain the basic minimum.

An easy response might be to claim that the basic minimum is indexed not just to the achievement of valued projects, but to the achievement of valued projects that maintain some connection to human dignity. Though any valued project might be valuable, this project cannot rise to the level of the *basic minimum* unless that project is reflective of the dignity of the person who lives it, or maintains some threshold level of preference-independent value. I consider this possibility in more detail in §3.5.

But though such a view might be sufficient to forestall the objection from human dignity, I think there is less to this objection than meets the eye. Two points. First, Nussbaum's own approach seems ill-designed to guarantee lives of basic human dignity, however this is understood. After all, Nussbaum's is a *capabilities* view. Because she does not grant moral importance to the *achievement* of human dignity, rather only to the capability for such achievement, the extent to which any given person actually maintains a life of minimal human dignity on Nussbaum's view is up for grabs. Any particular person could maintain the basic minimum while thoroughly lacking in achievements constitutive of basic human dignity or truly human functioning. In fact, the relationship between the achievement of basic human dignity and the achievement of the basic minimum on Nussbaum's approach appears to be fully dependent on people's conceptions of the good. My view says something similar: whether the basic minimum (as specified by WBM) requires a given person to maintain a life of human dignity depends on whether this person values dignified versus undignified lives.[38] Hence if a life of basic human dignity is a *requirement* for the basic minimum, a capabilities approach seems to fail.

[38] Although one might reasonably respond by claiming that *for some individuals*, Nussbaum's approach yields a life of greater dignity than the maintenance of a valued project would. Imagine that A values two projects, one of which is undignified, the other dignified. Granting A Nussbaum's ten capabilities would yield the opportunity to complete the dignified project as well as the undignified. For WBM, A need only complete the undignified project. While this is a possible scenario, I doubt it is common. More importantly, however, Nussbaum cannot very well reject a basic minimum on grounds that it fails to guarantee a life of dignity; whether or not Nussbaum's approach allows for *more* dignified lives, it certainly does not *guarantee* them.

Leaving aside this problem, however, there is a second, more fundamental, one. One must be careful in claiming advantage for any view on the basis of human dignity. There is a danger that the notion of human dignity is simply a placeholder for lives, activities, or projects we think are good enough to maintain the basic minimum. If basic human dignity is operating in this way, it is clearly table-pounding to claim advantage for Nussbaum's approach (or any other) on grounds of human dignity. To do so would be to simply assert what I deny, namely that some other approach to the basic minimum is more plausible than WBM.

Nussbaum might respond in the following way. Basic human dignity is not empty. One might understand basic minimum dignity in a *perfectionist* way. In other words, one might claim that a life of basic human dignity or "truly human functioning" involves the development of a certain conception of human *nature*.[39] On this view, dignity is to be given an interpretation that links truly human functioning with the characteristic or essential properties, activities, or traits of humans. If a person cannot obtain or achieve these activities to a sufficient extent, it might be claimed that this person does not maintain basic human dignity and hence cannot obtain the basic minimum.

However, the appeal to a perfectionist account of basic human dignity simply pushes the problem back a level. To see this, consider a classic objection to accounts of the good that treat human nature as morally significant, stated here by Bernard Williams:

> [A] palpable degree of evaluation has already gone into the selection of the distinguishing mark which is given [the role of human nature], such as rationality or creativity. If one approached without preconceptions the question of finding characteristics which differentiate men from other animals, one could as well, on these principles, end up with a morality which exhorted men to spend as much time as possible in making fire; or developing peculiarly human physical characteristics; or having sexual intercourse without regard to season; or despoiling the environment and upsetting the balance of nature; or killing things for fun.[40]

Williams's critique is important to take seriously. Thomas Hurka labels this the "wrong properties objection."[41] If "human nature" can explain the moral or evaluative resonance of certain properties that fall under its purview, it must be the case that we feel some requirement to treat "having sexual intercourse without regard to season" as morally or evaluatively important. But as this property is trivial, the appeal to human nature seems to imply the evaluative significance of the wrong properties, and

[39] See Nussbaum (2000), 71–2. [40] Williams (1993), 59. [41] Hurka (1993), 8.

hence fails as a morally or evaluatively important concept. Many qualities and characteristics separate humans from the non-human animal kingdom, not simply rationality, creativity, or any other element on Nussbaum's list. Some of what separates us from the animal kingdom is undesirable.

One might put the wrong properties objection in the form of a challenge. For an appeal to human nature to accomplish real work in rejecting WBM, it must avoid the problem that seems to plague a raw appeal to human dignity: lives that develop or exercise human nature are those, simply, that we think are good enough to maintain the basic minimum. This would render an appeal to human nature a simple table-pounding assertion that WBM is false. Instead, the appeal to human nature must itself *explain* why certain lives are better than others: human nature must itself be morally or evaluatively important, independently of whatever particular evaluative judgments it supports. But the wrong properties objection seems to shed doubt on the *per se* importance of human nature: we do not regard any old property as being important to an account of the basic minimum simply because it is a feature of human nature. If so, human nature does not maintain the requisite explanatory power.

Hurka offers an important response to this challenge.[42] His strategy is to provide a morally important concept of human nature that does not succumb to the wrong properties objection. For Hurka, the right way to rule out the undesirable traits noted by Williams is to provide an account of human nature in terms of the human *essence*, and to restrict evaluatively significant essential properties to those properties human beings possess necessarily and that are conditioned on their being living things, as opposed to things generally.[43] This rules out properties such as "upsetting the balance of nature."

But Hurka's move, I think, has the following problem. In narrowing our understanding of human nature to the *human essence* we appear to have simply chiseled out an understanding of nature that delivers the proper verdicts. The reason we have restricted our understanding of human nature, and not restricted it *further*, is that *this* account seems to yield verdicts we find plausible – *not* because there is anything intrinsically important about this, rather than any other, account of human nature. But if this is correct, claiming that a certain life fulfills human nature to a greater extent than

[42] I should note here that Hurka rejects perfectionism as an account of human welfare. But this is irrelevant for our purposes here. See ibid., 17–18, 194n17.

[43] Ibid., 15–17. Philip Kitcher argues that Hurka cannot, without imposing his own intuitions, derive a notion of goodness from human essence. I agree with Kitcher, but my argument will address a different point. See Kitcher (1999).

some other life is simply tantamount, once again, to a declaration of our confidence that this life is good (along relevant dimensions). An appeal to human nature or human dignity is simply eliminable, and, as an objection to WBM, reduces to table-pounding.

Hurka disputes this. Hurka agrees that in order to defend an appeal to human nature, it *must* be the case that human nature is a plausible ideal independently of whatever consequences it might entail: "A substantive defence of perfectionism must follow the same lines as a defence of morality. It must show that the theory coheres with our intuitive moral judgments at all levels of generality, or, in Rawls's phrase, is in 'reflective equilibrium' with all these judgments . . . It must show, first, that the general perfectionist ideal, that of developing human nature, is attractive when considered by itself as a potential foundation for morality."[44] But Hurka claims that human nature is itself an independently plausible ideal, and hence any "fine-tuning" of an account of human nature (i.e., accounting for human nature in terms of the human essence) in light of the wrong properties objection does not show that an appeal to perfectionist concepts performs no explanatory work.[45] After all, the concept is morally significant in itself, independent of any *particular* solution to the wrong properties objection.

But I think Hurka is mistaken. I deny that his strategy is simply fine-tuning of a *prima facie* plausible ideal. The appeal to human nature would not be plausible but for the fine-tuning in which Hurka is engaged. Without this fine-tuning, the appeal to nature, or essence, or any other perfectionist concept, would be a non-starter. And if this is correct, there is no evaluative work performed by an appeal to human nature, dignity, essence, or "truly human functioning"; appealing to a concept of human nature to defeat WBM is simply tantamount to asserting that WBM wrongly describes some lives as maintaining the basic minimum.

To see this, note that Hurka's claim that human nature is an independently plausible ideal is *testable*. One relevant test is *resistance to recalcitrance*. Consider the extent to which we are willing to revise our beliefs about value in light of a recalcitrant belief about what is part of human nature, even in Hurka's refined sense. If such an appeal is a plausible indicator of value, we should believe that this appeal has at least *some* power to override recalcitrant intuitions. For instance, let's imagine that we come to believe that a disposition to develop hypothermia under cold conditions is part of what is essential to humanity, conditioned on being living things. What pressure would there be to accept that property as morally significant or intrinsically

44 Hurka (1993), 31. 45 Ibid., 16, 32.

good? I contend: none whatsoever. Instead, the response (which models Hurka's own strategy) would be to revise that account of human nature further, such that the trivial property is avoided. For an appeal to human nature to play a role in a reflective equilibrium, it must have at least some resistance to recalcitrant beliefs. But it does not.

Consider *mortality*. Let's say that we come to believe that mortality is a valuable property of humanity, i.e., it's better not to live forever. Assume that this is a settled matter. However, on any plausible view, *length of life* is not valuable in and of itself; extended life is good or bad based solely on what that life contains. Length of life is surely only instrumentally good or bad. But suppose that we come to believe that mortality is part of human nature in Hurka's refined sense. (I'm uncommitted on this proposal.) On a perfectionist view, mortality would not simply be instrumentally good, but intrinsically good, good in itself. But are we prepared to make this change in our beliefs on the basis of a verdict about human nature? I find this far-fetched to say the least. A claim about human nature appears to have no power to influence the value of mortality one way or the other. But if so, human nature, the human essence, or other perfectionist concepts appear to be weak ideals, indeed.

Notice that in making this argument I'm not imagining that our nature or essence is different than it is. (As Hurka points out, one cannot evaluate a counterfactual involving essence.[46]) Rather, I'm imagining that we come to believe that our nature or essence contains mortality, which perhaps it may not. But this is the relevant test: if human nature is an independently plausible ideal, we ought to feel at least some pressure to revise our considered judgments about value in light of a contrary belief about human nature. If *we believe* that an appeal to nature comes along with a counter-intuitive verdict, we ought to feel some pressure to accept that verdict. But it appears we are prepared to accept *no* such verdicts. An appeal to human nature is only as plausible as its verdicts. But if this is correct, the appeal to human nature has no more force than a direct appeal to the verdicts it supports. It can play no *per se* moral or evaluative role.

We should be reluctant to believe that an account of the basic minimum should take as crucial an appeal to "truly human functioning," "human dignity," or various other quasi-perfectionist notions as important in defining the basic minimum. By way of an objection to WBM, an appeal to human dignity (however it is understood) has no greater force than merely insisting that some lives that maintain the basic minimum according to

[46] Ibid., 21–2.

WBM are not worthy of the basic minimum. And while there is a powerful objection of this form on the horizon – that WBM allows insufficiently good lives to maintain the basic minimum – WBM is not threatened by any objection that derives its force from an appeal to human nature, human dignity, or "truly human functioning."

2.8. OBJECTION: AUTONOMY

Though an appeal to human dignity cannot motivate an objection to WBM, there may still be some hesitation to accept it, given that it includes no reference whatever to *autonomy*. Some have held that autonomy is essential to the basic minimum.[47] Indeed, in the abstract, such a view is plausible. A slave, or a destitute sex worker, would seem – no matter how well their lives are otherwise going – not to possess the basic minimum simply because they fail to exercise a proper degree of autonomous control over their lives.

Take, for instance, the following case:

Sarah: Sarah is a slave. She is forced, under threat of death, to perform tasks, some offensive to her, for the benefit of others. Though she never escapes slavery, Sarah develops and maintains a long-term love relationship with another slave. Sarah values this relationship and maintains it for much of her life.

The problem presented by Sarah appears to be this. If Sarah's love relationship with another slave is a valued project, WBM must hold that Sarah maintains the basic minimum. But this is *wildly* implausible. The partisan of WBM might respond that Sarah's love relationship is not a *global* project, but this seems difficult to motivate insofar as her relationship might very well be life-structuring, narratively unifying, and of significant temporal duration, i.e., might display the various necessary features of a global project as identified in §2.3. But, contrary to WBM, for Sarah to maintain the basic minimum she must not be a slave. She must be (to at least some extent) autonomous.

One might reasonably ask why Sarah lacks autonomy in the relevant sense. After all, she seems able to choose a love relationship that she values. Why is she not, then, autonomous? Or, at least, autonomous enough for the basic minimum? To answer this question, it is important to note that the sense of autonomy important to the basic minimum – according to those who insist on its importance – is more robust than that which Sarah

[47] See, for instance, Hassoun (2008).

maintains. Consider, for instance, the account of autonomy proposed by James Griffin. Griffin writes that to be autonomous, one must "choose one's own path through life – that is, not be dominated or controlled by someone or something else."[48] This view is expressed forcefully by John Stuart Mill, in a crucial passage from *On Liberty*:

> He who lets the world, or his own portion of it, choose his plan of life for him has no need of any other faculty than the ape-like one of imitation. He who chooses his plan for himself employs all his faculties. He must use observation to see, reasoning and judgment to foresee, activity to gather materials for decision, discrimination to decide, and when he has decided, firmness and self-control to hold to his deliberate decision. And these qualities he requires and exercises exactly in proportion as the part of his conduct which he determines according to his own judgment and feelings is a large one. It is possible that he might be guided in some good path, and kept out of harm's way, without any of these things. But what will be his comparative worth as a human being?[49]

The ideas pointed to by Griffin and Mill might plausibly be grouped under the heading of "agency." On this view, to live an autonomous life, one must life the life of an *agent*. To live the life of an agent, one must do more than simply live a life that *to some degree* reflects one's values, or that was chosen in some minimal way. One must deliberate practically about one's life and decisions, and act on the result of this deliberation. In this way, Griffin and Mill seem to have the power to plausibly account for our reticence to describe Sarah as fully autonomous, and to describe the extent to which Sarah fails the basic minimum as the extent to which Sarah is *not* fully autonomous. Though Sarah's life might pass the test of the basic minimum laid down by WBM, she certainly does not choose her own path through life; she is under the thumb of her captors, despite achieving a long-term project she values.

However, I resist the claim that one must deliberate or engage one's practical rationality or agency to maintain the basic minimum. Take, for instance, the following character.

> *Han:* Han is a soldier of fortune. He has no plan of life, and does not deliberate according to his own activities. He acts in short-term ways; he engages his rational capacities only insofar as these capacities are required to obtain sustenance. His life is not in his deliberative control. In performing a particular action or in engaging in a certain activity, Han decides solely on whim – how he is feeling in that particular moment. Han never has any desire, nor performs any action, that is sustained by deliberation. Hence Han does not choose his own path through life. However, he

[48] Griffin (2007), 33. [49] Mill (1859), III, 4.

does value the project of "being a soldier of fortune" (which unifies and explains a large chunk of Han's decisions and actions despite his lack of agency) under the conditions under which his life is actually lived.

Han does not reason practically about his life, but rather conducts his life on the basis of whim, caprice. He chooses on the basis of mere fleeting inclinations. He does not adopt plans. According to WBM, Han maintains the basic minimum. As you will recall, one can "fall into" valued projects, as Han has done here. Though he does not deliberate, does not exercise his agency, and is controlled by the winds of fortune, he obtains the basic minimum because the life he ends up leading is narratively structured by a project he values, i.e., being the sort of person who eschews the agency in question. But this verdict is not embarrassing; it seems to me quite wrong to say that Han does not, pretheoretically anyway, conform to the basic minimum. If so, agency is not required.

Those who insist on the importance of autonomy will object that Han clearly has something that Sarah does not, viz., the absence of external control. Han, were he to so choose, *could* reason, deliberate, etc., about the projects and activities of his life. Sarah, on the other hand, is forced to live a particular kind of life, a life that is beyond her control. Perhaps, as a compromise position, one might insist that the basic minimum needn't require substantial agency, but – given Sarah's condition – it *must* require *options*, different ways one might live one's life.

Two problems arise. First, the original problem comes up again: why does Sarah lack options? After all, one might claim that Sarah does have *certain* options, viz., Sarah has the option to either engage in a love relationship or refrain, about which she might or might not choose to exercise her deliberative agency. Furthermore, Sarah might have her choice of possible partners, and may even use her capacity to deliberate and reason practically to determine which possible partner would provide her the most fulfillment.

Of course, the obvious response is that Sarah does not have the right *kind* of choices or options about the structure of her life. To maintain the correct kind of autonomy, Sarah must also be able to deliberate about and choose her life in a *broad* sense, viz., must have options that are more all-encompassing than the choice between one or two particular projects. But leaving aside the vagueness of this suggestion, it is difficult to see how any person could have control over such all-encompassing options over the direction of his or her life. The extent to which any particular life is open to someone will depend on many things, including intelligence, talents, upbringing, etc. Almost every person will have certain significant possibilities for life closed by the forces of happenstance and the choices of others. Hence substantive options in a broad sense – however this is understood – do not seem necessary to the achievement of the basic minimum.

A further case sheds light.

Rex: Rex is king. His status as such comes along with great privilege and high social esteem. Furthermore, being a good king (a task at which he succeeds) is for Rex a valued project. However, were Rex to abdicate his throne, this would cause his nation to be thrown into chaos, and would result in Rex being executed by a neo-facist revolutionary front.

In a very real sense, Rex has no ability to alter the long-term, all-encompassing nature of his life. He is either king, or abdicates his throne, leading to capture and execution. But I am strongly inclined to believe that Rex, as king, does not fail the basic minimum. Further, it seems plausible to say that Rex's life goes well beyond the basic minimum: Rex lives a life that is a rousing success. But this is compatible with saying that Rex, like Sarah, has no reasonable options. Thus the basic minimum does not require options, agency, or autonomy.

2.9. OBJECTION: TOO LOW, PART ONE

A final objection to WBM must be dealt with here. WBM seems *too low*. Leaving aside dignity, autonomy, or agency, WBM seems to allow lives that are substantially awful to obtain the basic minimum. One need look no further than Sarah.

This is an important objection; it will require careful examination. Indeed, one can read the suggestion that WBM sets the minimum too low in (at least) two ways. First, one might say that according to WBM the basic minimum can be achieved without some of the central paradigmatic elements of a basic minimum, viz., medical care, shelter, decent food, basic needs, etc. If that is correct, WBM is not responsive to the initial intuitions that motivate the acceptance of a basic minimum. I consider this in the following section. A far more serious challenge, however, is that WBM implies that – leaving aside agency, autonomy, options, resources, capabilities, etc. – someone could maintain the basic minimum without living a life of minimal decency. In discussing this objection, I focus again on Sarah. The problem with Sarah, as we have so far discovered, is not that she lacks autonomy, options, or other non-welfarist goods. Rather, she simply lives a life that is not good enough to describe as maintaining any reasonable basic minimum. I discuss this problem in §2.9.2.

2.9.1. WBM, basic needs, and basic capabilities

WBM seems to set a basic minimum that is *far lower* than competitor conceptions. To see what I mean, consider Shue's account of subsistence: "unpolluted air, unpolluted water, adequate food, adequate clothing, adequate shelter, and minimal preventive public health care . . . the basic idea is to have available for consumption what is needed for a decent chance at a reasonably healthy and active life of more or less normal length, barring tragic interventions."[50] WBM guarantees none of these things. Furthermore, one might consider WBM in relation to Nussbaum's approach. Nussbaum's list is too expansive, but one might even consider the most basic elements of the capabilities approach: nourishment, basic security, etc. If, to maintain the basic minimum, one need only maintain a valued project, surely some sort of achievement of the basic minimum is possible to eke out without even the most central of Nussbaum's capabilities. This is especially true if – pursuant to my conception of valued projects – to achieve the basic minimum one need only *barely* regard the life one leads as worth living.

Of course, to argue against WBM on the ground that it does not guarantee some particular level of food, basic needs, or other non-welfare good will beg the question against any welfarist approach: no welfarist approaches will guarantee that those who obtain the basic minimum will obtain some set of *non*-welfarist goods or resources. But the problem here might be stated in a different way. Even among welfarist views, WBM is uniquely problematic. If we set the basic minimum at a *higher* level of welfare, we may be able to insist that the basic minimum in at least most cases guarantees more of the paradigmatic basic needs or commodities that generate the intuitive pull of any basic minimum. After all, if the basic minimum does not guarantee, to at least most people, "unpolluted air, unpolluted water, adequate food," etc., who cares about a basic minimum, anyway?

In response to this problem, it is important not to lose sight of the fact that the basic minimum does not constitute simply the achievement of some welfare good or other, or any old life that is preferred to the shortest possible. Rather, it requires a valued global project. WBM requires that one live a life that is narratively unified, the activities of which maintain a

[50] Shue (1981), 23.

shared meaning, such that this particular meaning is part of an explanation of one's own assessment of that life as worth living. But if this is correct, two points are important to keep in mind. First, engaging in valued projects requires a life to have a certain narrative thread – something that explains and unifies one's life in the long term and is, at least in part, constituted by one's actions and decisions. And although such a narrative thread can be sustained without agency in some cases, as in Han's, most lives that maintain such unity must do so as a result of the agency of the person involved: effort to stick to a particular track, agency to make the relevant decisions, practical reasoning sufficient to be successful.[51] In short, the achievement of a global project, for most people anyway, will require autonomy or agency just in the sense Griffin describes. If that's correct, and if this sort of agency requires a sufficient degree of education, shelter, food, freedom from disease, the achievement of a valued project will require these things (for most people anyway).[52] I find it very difficult to believe that any global project of this sort could be successfully maintained in the long term if a person lacks access to adequate food, shelter, medical care, and the absence of violations of a person's body in the form of violence and coercion. Without these things, few could engage in the unified activities and deliberations that are constitutive of a long-term global project.

This point permits of an easy response. As noted above, global projects just *are* narrative unifiers. Any such unifier, if it successfully explains, is in part constituted by, and provides a shared meaning to one's activities and decisions in the long term, will count as a global project. But if that is correct, any number of lives that lack basic needs, or even a moderate set of capabilities, etc., could be described as maintaining long-term projects: "being a destitute sex worker" could in principle unify and be constituted by one's activities across the course of a life. But surely this project cannot be sufficient to capture the intuitive concept of a basic minimum, insofar as this individual will not maintain virtually any basic needs, or even the most central elements of Nussbaum's capabilities approach.

Of course, this is correct. Any number of wildly poor long-term states or activities could count as global projects in my sense. But – and this is the second point – even if some people might be able to engage global projects while lacking access to adequate food, shelter, medical care, and the absence of violations in the form of violence and coercion, virtually no one will *value* the achievement of a global project *under such conditions*. Though I may be able to complete a global project of being a destitute sex

[51] Rawls (1971), 423–4. [52] Cf. Hassoun (2008).

worker, I will not *value* this project. Insofar as my life is worth living at all, any explanation of my assessment of it as worth living will surely *not* appeal to the fact that I am a destitute sex worker. If that is correct, though *some* global projects might be achievable without the central basic needs, or central capabilities, virtually none will be valued.

Of course, the key phrase in the preceding paragraphs is "virtually none" rather than "none." But to insist on a basic minimum that requires *all* persons to maintain, e.g., Shue's basic needs or Nussbaum's capabilities is simply to beg the question against any welfarist approach. However, I have shown that *most* people will require such basic needs, and a stiff helping of Nussbaum's capabilities, to be able to engage in any project, let alone a *valued* project. And that is all that is required to defend WBM from the objection at hand. Any approach to the basic minimum that insists on the further provision of needs, capabilities, etc., to those who do not need them to maintain the central element of human welfare will display a problematic fetishism of needs, resources, or capabilities that we have already uncovered in rival conceptions.

2.9.2. Reconsidering Sarah

So WBM captures the most intuitively significant of the paradigmatic basic needs or basic capabilities. I take this to be substantial evidence that WBM is not too low for our considered judgments. However, there remains skepticism not about the ability of WBM to capture the requirements of other theories of the basic minimum, but rather to be compatible with the driving force behind a *welfarist* basic minimum, i.e., that those who maintain the basic minimum should live lives of minimal decency. In short, the problem is Sarah. Sarah's life seems bad enough as described. But let's embellish. Though Sarah maintains a valued project, and thus must see her life as worth living, we can assume that as far as Sarah is concerned, her love relationship renders her life only *barely* worth living. Thus, given that she is a slave, and given that she *barely* regards her life as worth living, can we legitimately say that she lives a good enough life to maintain the basic minimum? Surely the answer is no.

I must admit that this intuition is powerful. I won't waste my time arguing that this considered judgment is not robust. But even if this is correct, I think the balance of reasons tells in favor of Sarah's achievement of the basic minimum. This is a bullet-biting response. But it seems to me that to embrace Sarah's basic minimum is in fact a *strength* of my approach. I offer two arguments to this effect. The first is an argument from within

Sarah's perspective. I claim that if we recognize the nature of global projects and what it takes for them to be valued, it is less implausible to believe that Sarah's life is good enough to maintain the basic minimum. The second argument, however, appeals to the nature of any basic minimum. The basic minimum *by nature* picks out a very low threshold. If so, any view that suggests that Sarah *does not* maintain the basic minimum is, as a theory of the basic minimum if not as a theory of desirable social goals, false.

First, when looking at Sarah, it is tempting to declare that her slavery itself renders her life insufficiently good to exceed the minimum threshold. (For someone who achieves a valued project and is not a slave, we wouldn't have the same hesitation to declare that she maintains the basic minimum.) But this intuition should be discarded. It seems to me incorrect to believe that no one could possibly maintain the basic minimum or live a life of minimal decency under conditions of slavery. Surely whether a slave can meet the minimum threshold depends on the sort of life one lives *as* a slave. We could imagine a slave treated with a reasonable degree of respect (beyond the obvious violation), provided a thorough education, left physically unharmed, allowed and encouraged to pursue projects and interests, etc. Though there may be very good moral reasons to condemn this sort of slavery despite this person's overall level of welfare (see below), these reasons surely do not result from an interest in the basic minimum. But if that's right, cases in the midst of slavery, and other typically awful conditions, must be considered case-by-case.

What about Sarah? I think the most telling evaluative aspect of Sarah's life is the attitude she takes to her love relationship. Recall that any valued project must be valued in context; it must be lived within a life seen as worth living, and must help to explain why that life is seen as worth living. However, under slavery conditions virtually *no* global project would be valued because virtually no one would regard such a life as worth living. Of course, this is only in the normal case. We have assumed that even under conditions of slavery, Sarah values the maintenance of a successful love relationship with a fellow slave. Even considering the conditions *as* a slave, Sarah regards the life in which she maintains this love relationship as having been worth living. To put this another way, Sarah values her love relationship *enough* to accept slavery as a condition of obtaining it. Her achievement of this project helps to explain why she regards her life, even under the otherwise horrible conditions of slavery, as good rather than bad, "worth it" rather than not, of positive rather than negative value. If this is correct, I find it difficult to see why her life shouldn't be good enough to maintain the basic minimum even under conditions of slavery. (One might be tempted to claim that Sarah's preferences might have been shaped by her slavery, and that for this reason these preferences are not to be trusted. This is certainly possible, but this critique falls under the general heading of adaptive preferences, and will be discussed in more detail in the next chapter.)

I find the foregoing suggestions convincing, but I confess that the contrary judgment is powerful. My second argument for biting this bullet runs as follows. Recall the *concept* of a basic minimum. BM3 declares that when it comes to the reasons to promote valuable states, including welfare states, the reason to promote the basic minimum will be stronger, on a one-to-one basis, than the reason to promote any other valuable state. Given this, any basic minimum must occasionally allow upward distribution: moral priority for the better-off. Nussbaum's capabilities approach failed in light of this feature of a basic minimum: *Expansive List* was too expansive to plausibly support upward distribution. Hence we should be hesitant to set the basic minimum too high. If that is right, the *conceptual nature* of the basic minimum drives its appropriate level downward.

Indeed, as I shall now argue, WBM supports this form of upward distribution, and basic minimums that could avoid Sarah's case *do not*. Consider Mary:

Mary: Like Sarah, Mary is a slave, but fails to maintain any valued projects whatever; if she obtains any welfare benefits at all, they are mere satisfactions.

Imagine that one has a choice between granting Mary a valued project (while a slave), and allowing Sarah to escape slavery (which would, assume, improve Sarah's life). Which is to take priority? Such a choice is obviously tragic, and is difficult to intuitively evaluate. But I cannot allow myself to believe that, in this case, Sarah's escape from slavery is to take moral priority to Mary's achievement of a life of valued, self-directed meaning, a life she regards as worth living in part because of the meaning she helps to shape. But if Sarah's escape from slavery does not take weak moral priority to Mary's valued project, Sarah's escape from slavery *cannot* be an essential part of her achievement of the basic minimum. Whatever the basic minimum is, it must be compatible with its achievement while a slave. Any view with a contrary verdict seems to imply an implausible degree of upward distribution. Of course, virtually no one will value a project in such circumstances. But this does not alter the general point: we should not treat Sarah's case as a counterexample to WBM. Rather, WBM gets a feature of the basic minimum *exactly right*. WBM is not barred from plausibly accommodating the requirement of upward distribution.

Take a different example.

Glen and Jerry: Glen fails to maintain any valued project, but could become a Grand Central Station janitor, a project he barely values. Jerry is a Grand Central Station janitor, which he also barely values. However, Jerry could be promoted to a Grand Central Station ticket-taker, a project he values more strongly.

Is there greater reason to grant Glen the life of a Grand Central Station janitor, or to grant Jerry the job as a ticket-taker? Plausibly, Glen ought to take moral priority. Jerry's life already contains a long-term, narratively unified, and self-directed meaning, which Jerry regards as helping to explain why his life is worth living. Insofar as Glen does not obtain this central element of welfare, it seems to me that his potential project takes priority to Jerry's promotion. If that's right, then the conceptual requirements of any basic minimum support WBM rather than some "higher" minimum.

A critic might accuse me of cheating. So far I have compared Sarah to Mary, Glen to Jerry. But let's compare Glen to Sarah. Insofar as Glen does not, but Sarah does, maintain a valued project, WBM must hold that Glen's (barely) valued project takes moral priority to Sarah's escape from slavery. But this, one might think, is absurd. *Surely* Glen's valued project is less morally significant than Sarah's freedom from slavery. Glen has something very important going for him: he is not a slave. If that is correct, it cannot be that Sarah's valued project constitutes her achievement of the basic minimum.

For what it's worth, I do not share the foregoing judgment. Given Sarah's interest in her valued project, which includes a willingness to regard a life of slavery itself as worth living *because* of it, I do not find the mere fact of her slavery compelling reason to believe that her freedom takes moral priority to Glen's valued project. But I shan't rest much on my considered judgment, as I recognize that I may very well be in the vast minority. Assume, for the moment, that Glen's valued project *does not* take moral priority to Sarah's freedom from slavery. Even if we accept that Sarah already maintains the basic minimum, Sarah's moral priority to Glen *is perfectly compatible with WBM*.

Recall the difference between BM1 and BM3. BM1, which I rejected as too strong, holds that political institutions must not allow anyone to fail the basic minimum; in this sense, the basic minimum is the dominant, overriding, priority of justice. If we accept BM1, we had better not say that the basic minimum is constituted by the achievement of a valued project. If the basic minimum is of overriding moral importance, and if WBM is true, Glen's valued project must take moral priority. But BM3 – the correct account of the concept of a basic minimum – differs in two ways. First, the basic minimum need only take weak priority: priority on a one-to-one basis. Of course, this does nothing to alleviate the problem in this case. But notice that BM3 also claims that the basic minimum must take weak priority only when it comes to reasons to promote the achievement of valuable states of persons. But there may be other important moral reasons that go beyond reasons to promote valuable states. For instance, it might be that there is a blanket moral prohibition on slavery, and that a reason to free someone from slavery takes moral priority to the promotion of any valuable states in non-slaves (including Glen's basic minimum). Furthermore, we might believe that to honor the rights of individuals (such as Sarah) not to be enslaved is morally decisive with respect to the promotion of valuable states for others. Freeing Sarah from slavery is surely the promotion of a valuable state; and viewed strictly in terms of the promotion of valuable states, Glen's project takes priority. But this does not entail that there are not other, perhaps very strong, moral reasons to free Sarah from slavery, including reasons that have nothing to do with the promotion of valuable states. Hence those who are convinced that Glen's valued project cannot take moral priority to Sarah's freedom from slavery needn't believe that Sarah's freedom from slavery is an essential element of Sarah's basic minimum. All such a person need believe is that there is more to morality than the promotion of valuable states of persons.

To sum up, there is good reason to believe that the achievement of a valued project, as I define "valuing," is not too low to constitute the basic minimum. It's "lowness" is precisely one of its strengths given the nature of any basic minimum (a strength that evades accounts of the minimum like Nussbaum's). While I recognize that there are strong considered judgments that tell against Sarah's maintenance of the basic minimum, many of these judgments can, in fact, be accepted by WBM: it is perfectly in keeping with WBM to declare that though Sarah maintains the basic minimum, her rescue from slavery should take moral priority (given reasons other than the promotion of valuable states) to benefits for non-slaves. I should note here, however, that the objection that WBM is too low will *rise again*.

2.10. CONCLUSION AND THEORIES OF WELL-BEING

This chapter has argued that reflection on the importance of valued projects in assessments of life quality leads naturally into a welfarist theory of the basic minimum. WBM is plausible in its own right. WBM is able to fix the defects of previous approaches. Furthermore, WBM has resources to avoid three substantial objections. Hence, it seems to me, there is good reason to give WBM a very serious look.

By way of a conclusion, I want to make good on a promissory note. In the first section of this chapter, I said that my version of a welfarist basic minimum is compatible with a number of substantive theories of well-being. To show this, it is helpful to note an important distinction in welfare theories. The logical space of theories of well-being is entirely covered by the distinction between *subjective* theories which, in the words of L. W. Sumner, treat "my having a favourable attitude toward something as a necessary condition of the thing being beneficial to me";[53] and *objective* theories, which hold that "something can be (directly and immediately) good for me though I do not regard it favourably, and my life can be going well despite my failing to have any positive attitude toward it."[54] To put this a little more precisely, subjectivism about well-being holds that *p* is valuable for A only if A takes a pro-attitude toward *p*. Objectivism holds that it is not the case that *p* is valuable for A only if A takes a pro-attitude toward *p*. These views are mutually exhaustive and exclusive.

Though not every theory of well-being can accept WBM, a wide range of objective and subjective theories can. I begin with subjectivism. Subjectivism encompasses a wide range of theories of well-being, including desire-satisfaction theories, "life satisfaction" theories, and various other views. But there are distinctions to be made when it comes to the broad structure of subjectivism, and the relationship between a given individual's valuing attitude and that person's good. First, consider:

Weak Subjectivism: p is intrinsically good for A (at *t*) only if *p* is valued by A (at *t*).

Weak Subjectivism insists on a weak connection between a person's well-being and a person's conception of the good. Weak Subjectivism leaves it open that A might endorse, or take a pro-attitude toward, some particular *p*, but that, because of some independent fact about *p*, *p* is not good for A. For Weak Subjectivism, ratification by A's conception of the good is a necessary, but not sufficient, condition of genuine prudential goods for A. However, some subjectivists will hold that the connection between well-being and one's own conception of the good is considerably stronger. There are two versions of a strong subjectivism that are worth distinguishing here. Consider:

Weak Strong Subjectivism: p is intrinsically good for A (at *t*) if and only if *p* is valued by A (at *t*).

[53] Sumner (1996), 38. [54] Ibid.

According to Weak Strong Subjectivism, that *p* is intrinsically good for A is simply determined by whether A endorses *p*. However, Weak Strong Subjectivism still leaves it open that there may be facts about A's well-being that are independent of A's conception of the good. In particular, Weak Strong Subjectivism allows that though *p* and *q* might both be endorsed by A, and hence both improve A's well-being, the comparative value of *p* and *q* could, in principle, be determined not by A's preferences among *p* and *q*, but rather by some other facts about *p* and *q* that are independent of A's conception of the good. With this in mind, the strongest version of subjectivism is:

Strong Strong Subjectivism: p is intrinsically good for A (at *t*) if and only if, and to the extent that, *p* is valued by A (at *t*).

Strong Strong Subjectivism, as opposed to Weak Strong Subjectivism, holds that not only is A's endorsement of *p* a necessary and sufficient condition for *p*'s prudential value for A, but that *how valuable for A p is* is determined by A's conception of the good. A might, for instance, maintain a preference for *p* over *q*, which would then entail that *p* is better for A than *q*.

Strong Strong Subjectivism is incompatible with *Thesis*. One might imagine some individual A who prefers some particular satisfaction *p* to some particular valued project *q*. In this case, Strong Strong Subjectivism would entail that *p* makes a bigger prudential splash for A than *q*, violating *Thesis*.

Of course, there is nothing internal to Strong Strong Subjectivism that prevents it from claiming that the achievement of some valued project or other is that which constitutes the basic minimum. Nevertheless, in denying *Thesis*, Strong Strong Subjectivism lacks a crucial rationale for WBM.[55] Weak Strong Subjectivism (not to mention Weak Subjectivism) can declare that the achievement of valued projects is evaluatively *special* when it comes to individual well-being in a way that Strong Strong Subjectivism cannot. For Strong Strong Subjectivism, the achievement of a valued project is just one preferred good among many. Hence, without being able to

[55] Take, for instance, two individuals A and B. A prefers all valued satisfactions to all projects. B prefers all projects to all satisfactions. A and B prefer their preferred objects with the same intensity, or to the same extent. Assume that each person A and B satisfy their preferences to degree *x*. Strong Strong Subjectivism claims that A and B must life lives of equivalent quality, though WBM declares that A – because A prefers satisfactions – does not maintain the basic minimum. This seems to violate the basic guiding principle of any welfarist basic minimum, i.e., that the basic minimum should be some evaluatively special welfare achievement, that the life of a person who fails the basic minimum should, at the very least, be *worse* than the life of a person who maintains the basic minimum.

accommodate *Thesis*, it would appear that Strong Strong Subjectivism is ruled out as accommodating WBM.

I take this result to be a problem for Strong Strong Subjectivism, not for WBM. Insofar as there are independent reasons to accept *Thesis*, there are very strong reasons, or so it seems to me, to reject Strong Strong Subjectivism. However, this does not mean that subjectivism on the wholesale is prevented from accommodating WBM. Weak Subjectivism and Weak Strong Subjectivism can support *Thesis*. Because they allow that certain preference-independent facts about particular welfare goods can alter the overall rank-ordering of welfare goods, Weak and Weak Strong Subjectivisms can claim that *q* is a more significant determinant of A's welfare than *p* despite the fact that *p* may be preferred by A to *q*. Hence, WBM can be supported by subjectivist theories, if only two of the three distinguishable versions.

Objective theories hold that for *p* to be intrinsically good for A, A need not endorse, or take a pro-attitude toward, *p*. In other words, a view is objective if it holds that so much as one particular welfare good *p* is good for one particular person A without A taking a pro-attitude toward *p*.

The most famous version of an objective theory is the so-called "objective list." The objective list view is simply a list of items that benefit individuals. The items on the list need not share any individual unifying thread. For instance, an objective list view could identify the maintenance and fulfillment of a valued project as one entry – indeed, a very important entry – on the list. Other items on the list could include hedonic satisfaction, the fulfillment of momentary desires, knowledge, virtue, etc.[56] Hence it is perfectly open for an objective list view to declare that the fulfillment of a valued project is evaluatively special, and hence to accept *Thesis*, along with WBM.

Some might object. After all, the basic minimum as defined by WBM is importantly subjective: whether I maintain the basic minimum depends only on whether I achieve a valued project, which is in turn defined relative to my own conception of the good. Nothing in this definition of the basic minimum makes any reference to preference-independent or "objective" value at all. However, it is important here to distinguish between *subjectively defined welfare goods* and *subjective theories of welfare*.[57] One might suggest

[56] For the best defense of the objective list view, see Arneson (1999).

[57] Thanks to an anonymous reviewer for calling this ambiguity to my attention.

that the achievement of a valued project is a subjectively defined welfare good in the sense that such a good is defined relative to an individual's subjective pro-attitudes, including their own assessment of their lives as worth living, and the contribution of a particular project to that assessment. But to suggest that a subjectively defined basic minimum is an important aspect of human well-being is not to be committed to a subjective *theory of welfare*. Subjective theories of welfare treat A's pro-attitude toward *p* as a necessary condition for *p*'s intrinsic value for A. Objective theories of welfare do not. Objective theories are perfectly licensed to accept that some welfare goods can be subjectively defined. Indeed, it is sensible for them to do so. Sometimes things can be good for me simply because I value them: some nights I just prefer Spanish plonk. The value of this may very well depend simply on its being the object of some preference of mine. But objective theories can accommodate this: sometimes the satisfaction of a subjective attitude *as such* improves one's life.

Objectivism is thus extremely flexible. Whether an objective theory should accept the achievement of a valued project as prudentially special thus depends on the substantive arguments I offer in favor of *Thesis*. I hope that the arguments in this chapter have convinced readers – including objectivists – that it should be so regarded. It is worth noting here, however, that some objectivists will see an important "dividing line" not just along the dimension of those lives that maintain valued projects and those that do not, but along the dimension of those lives that maintain valued projects *of sufficient preference-independent value* and those that do not. Whether this "dividing line," or the one identified by WBM, is the proper basic minimum I leave until §3.5.

Of course, not all objective views are compatible with *Thesis*. One such objective view, at least as I identify the taxonomy between objective and subjective, is *hedonism*. Hedonism holds that pleasure is the only welfare benefit. But given that pleasure cannot plausibly be described as a valued project (though, perhaps, the *pursuit* of pleasure could), hedonism cannot support even the claim that valued projects, of themselves, are welfare benefits, let alone accept *Thesis*. A hedonist might attempt to capture *Thesis* by claiming that people will take greater pleasure in the achievement of long-term goals, or in the maintenance of long-term valued states than they will in the fulfillment of various momentary desires, etc. But this point is far from obvious, and surely depends on the psychological state of any given individual. Hence, it seems to me, there is a limit to the ecumenicalism of *Thesis*, and hence WBM. (Though, like Strong Strong

Subjectivism, I hold that there is greater reason to reject hedonism than *Thesis*.[58])

The basic point of this section has been to show that one needn't commit to, say, "subjective welfarism," or any other particular theory of well-being, to accept WBM. Though WBM rules out some individual theories of well-being, it is broadly ecumenical.

My discussion of the basic minimum has gone down a number of tangents, so I would like to briefly remind the reader of that for which I take to have argued and what I take to have merely left open. First, I argued for *Thesis*, which holds that valued projects are a central element of human well-being. Second, I argued that WBM is defensible as a theory of the basic minimum. In addition, I have responded to three objections. Most importantly, even in light of *Sarah*, WBM is not too low. When it comes to the conceptual nature of a basic minimum, WBM is just right. Furthermore, I have argued that *Thesis* and WBM can be accepted from the standpoint of a wide range of substantive theories of well-being, both objective and subjective.

One important lesson of this chapter is that a non-arbitrary welfarist basic minimum can respect *The Basic Minimum as Proto-autonomy*. However, I have not responded to the second horn of the welfarist's dilemma: it would seem that any view that takes seriously conceptions of the good in defining the basic minimum must succumb to the problem of adaptive preferences. In the next chapter I argue that WBM can avoid this problem – or, at least, can do no worse than Nussbaum's capabilities approach.

58 I shall not spend any additional time rejecting hedonism here. I have tried to show that hedonism is untenable elsewhere. See Dorsey (2011).

CHAPTER 3

Adaptive preferences

The welfarist's dilemma, once again, runs like this: for a welfarist approach to succeed, the basic minimum must be tied closely to the achievement of one's conception of the good. Otherwise, Nussbaum's argument for a capabilities approach sticks: a welfarist approach to the basic minimum *would* insist on a moral reason to force individuals to live lives they do not value. WBM successfully avoids this concern: the basic minimum is not construed as the achievement of particular states or functionings in abstraction from conceptions of the good. The basic minimum is the achievement of a *valued* project.

So far so good. But the second horn of the dilemma looms. To be a valued project, as noted in the last chapter, crucially depends on the attitudes one takes toward this project and its context. But such attitudes are malleable, often in insidious ways. The fact that one values *p* can be shaped by poor circumstances and a lack of opportunity. If so, one should think that the mere fact that A values a particular project is not enough for A to maintain the basic minimum. A's valuing might be the product of adaptive preferences.

The phenomenon of adaptive preferences clearly poses *some* problem for WBM. But the problem it poses is ill-understood and under-theorized. In this chapter, I distinguish two categories of adaptive preferences: *shallow* adaptive preferences, and *deep* adaptive preferences. Shallow adaptive preferences and deep adaptive preferences, I shall argue, pose very different problems for a welfarist approach to the basic minimum. My approach can successfully avoid the problem posed by shallow adaptive preferences. And while it cannot solve the problem of deep adaptation, this should not be held against my view. I argue that deep adaptation is no problem *in itself*.

This chapter is organized as follows. §3.1 discusses the mechanism by which Nussbaum's capabilities approach addresses cases of adaptation. In §3.2, I address the problem of adaptive preferences in more detail. I argue that this problem, far from being a reason to reject welfarism, is actually a problem *internal* to welfare theory. No theory of well-being can possibly be adequate if this theory holds that adaptive preferences improve lives. Indeed, I argue that the problem posed by adaptive preferences (or "shallow" adaptive preferences, at any rate) is that such preferences do not properly characterize a person's genuine conception of the good. In §§3.3–3.4, I offer an account of conceptions of the good that avoids the problem of shallow adaptation. In §3.5 I discuss the problem of deep adaptation; I argue that this problem simply reduces to a problem I call "preference for the worse." As such, it permits of easy solution (if, indeed, a solution is called for at all).

One note before I begin. Generally speaking the phenomenon to which I refer is called "adaptive preferences." I follow the literature on this point. But I treat the term "preference" as a catch-all for pro-attitudes that figure into a person's wider conception of the good (including pro-attitudes that help to determine whether particular projects are valued, e.g., an assessment that *p contributes to a life worth living*, etc.). This makes no difference to the argument of this chapter, however; all such attitudes are subject to adaptation, and my solution applies *mutatis mutandis*.

3.1. NUSSBAUM ON ADAPTATION

Preferences are malleable. But this malleability can cause serious problems for any view that takes the fulfillment of a person's preferences as an important aspect of the basic minimum. The most infamous examples are offered by Amartya Sen: "The hopeless beggar, the precarious landless labourer, the dominated housewife, the hardened unemployed or the over-exhausted coolie may all take pleasures in small mercies, and manage to suppress intense suffering for the necessity of continuing survival, but it would be ethically deeply mistaken to attach a correspondingly small value to the loss of their well-being because of this survival strategy."[1] As Sen notes, the "landless labourer" might adapt to his poor circumstances: because a life of landless labor is the only life to which he has access, he comes to adjust his desires and expectations to his straightened circumstances. Hence, one might think, to index the achievement of the basic minimum to these preferences is "ethically deeply mistaken."

In justifying the rejection of a welfarist approach to the basic minimum, Nussbaum notes the following ways in which preferences can be adaptive: "The normative approach based on human functioning and

[1] Sen (1987), 45–6.

capability . . . rejected utilitarian preference-based approaches as a basis for fundamental political principles precisely because they were unable to conduct a critical scrutiny of preference and desire that would reveal the many ways in which habit, fear, low expectations, and unjust background conditions deform people's choices and even their wishes for their own lives."[2] Elsewhere, Nussbaum writes that the problem of adaptation boils down to the fact that, in cases of adaptation, "an individual's preferences are shaped to accord with the (frequently narrow) set of opportunities she actually has."[3] For Nussbaum, adaptive preferences are shaped by the *particular facts* of an individual's lived life, especially that person's opportunities (or lack thereof). The mechanism by which one's preferences adapt to the "set of opportunities" one actually has can vary. Preferential adaptation can occur as a result of a number of psychological mechanisms: a "survival strategy," as noted by Sen; a lack of "self-worth" as discussed by Jennifer Hawkins;[4] habit, indoctrination, strategic preference engineering, and perhaps many others.

Nussbaum holds that the capabilities approach, unlike "subjective welfarism," can avoid the problem of adaptive preferences. First, for Nussbaum, the basic minimum is not dependent on the fulfillment of preferences. Rather, the basic minimum is identified as the maintenance of the ten central capabilities. An individual must possess these to maintain the basic minimum, and will maintain the basic minimum once these central capabilities are possessed, no matter the content of his or her preferences or pro-attitudes. Hence when it comes to the basic minimum, at least, moral reasons are not sensitive to the content of any individual's preferences, unlike under WBM. Nussbaum writes: "[T]he capabilities account deals well with the problems that plagued the preference-based approach . . . A habituated preference not to have any one of the items on the list (political liberties, literacy, equal political rights, or whatever) will not count in the social choice function."[5] Hence, for Nussbaum, the problem of adaptive preferences is avoided by refusing to index the achievement of the basic minimum to preferences.

However, this response by itself is not satisfying. To see this, consider the central problem for WBM. The only reason WBM might fail in light of the phenomenon of adaptive preferences is that WBM holds that people who live shabby lives as a result of adaptive preferences will, on occasion, obtain the basic minimum. In saying this, WBM is "ethically deeply

[2] Nussbaum (2000), 114.
[3] Nussbaum, "American Women: Preferences, Feminism, Democracy" in Nussbaum (1999), 151.
[4] See Hawkins (2008). [5] Nussbaum (2000), 149.

mistaken." But there is no guarantee that the same will not hold of the capabilities approach. Simply declaring that the ten basic capabilities form the content of the basic minimum still leaves open the possibility that people will maintain, and act on, adaptive preferences, i.e., that people (like the "overexhausted coolie") will live horribly shabby lives despite the fact that they maintain the basic minimum. Without some further mechanism to *overcome* the psychological entrenchment of adaptive preferences, the capabilities approach is impotent to respond to the problem that plagues WBM. Any person who lives a shabby life as a result of adaptive preferences might nevertheless also do so *even if* they secure the ten basic capabilities. If so, people who live shabby lives as a result of adaptive preferences will, at least on occasion, maintain the basic minimum. If this is a problem for welfarism, it is no less a problem for the capabilities approach.

Nussbaum is aware that leaving the matter here is unsatisfactory. Remember that, for Nussbaum, adaptive preferences are a *result* of narrow opportunities or capabilities. If so, there is no reason to fear a refusal to develop valuable functionings once the central capabilities are granted. For Nussbaum, the capabilities *themselves* are mechanism enough to overcome problems of adaptation insofar as adaptation is specifically a result of a lack of capabilities. After all, the overexhausted coolie develops his preferences in light of the fact that "truly human functioning" is not available. *Were* it available, Nussbaum surmises, the overexhausted coolie would not come to prefer the life of overexhausted coolieism.[6] In this way, the capabilities approach not only insists that all persons should be granted the ten basic capabilities, but the capabilities themselves work to combat the existence and development of adaptive preferences. For Nussbaum, the various psychological mechanisms that result in adaptive preferences share a common cause. Adaptive preferences are, at base, the result of facts of unavailability; facts that, if alleviated, would cause us to revert to non-adaptive preferences. In this way, and only in this way, does the capabilities approach alleviate the problem of adaptive preferences.

3.2. ADAPTIVE PREFERENCES AND WELL-BEING

If WBM allows adaptive preferences to determine the content of anyone's basic minimum, it is in serious trouble. Many of the most important cases that motivate a moral commitment to a basic minimum involve people who live shabby lives, cannot get sufficient nourishment, are imprisoned,

[6] Ibid., 155.

or desperately sick. However, given that such people can *adapt* to their straightened circumstances and hence come to value whatever projects they may achieve in such circumstances, it would appear that any welfarist basic minimum is in tension with a major motivation for a basic minimum: to assist those who live shabby lives, cannot get sufficient nourishment, are imprisoned, or desperately sick. Hence because someone might achieve a valued project that is valued only as a result of problematic adaptation (say, for instance, the valued project of being "an overexhausted coolie"), and because WBM only entails a moral reason to promote the achievement of valued projects, there is no mechanism by which WBM might avoid the problem of adaptive preferences. Hence WBM cannot be trusted to properly account for the basic minimum. In this way, the problem of adaptive preferences can be seen as another way of stating a (by now) familiar objection: because many people can adapt to ridiculously poor lives and hence come to adaptively see them as worth living, WBM sets the minimum threshold too low.

But though this may be a problem for WBM, the root of the problem is not simply that WBM is a welfarist approach. We describe the problem of adaptive preferences inaccurately if we say that it is a problem for welfarism generally. Rather, the problem of adaptive preferences is itself *internal* to an inquiry into the nature of human well-being. The fulfillment of adaptive preferences, so I shall argue, does not improve lives. The problem for WBM is its implicit commitment to the claim that the satisfaction of adaptive preferences *is a prudential benefit.*[7] But this is a false claim *about human well-being.*

By way of an example, consider the following case:

Erin: Erin, at t_1, intrinsically preferred a life of excellent achievement in dance to a life of excellent achievement in painting and dedicated years to the achievement of her goal. At t_1, Erin regarded the movement of the human form as a much more meaningful expression of her artistic temperament than mere paint on canvas. However, as a result of years of rejection and failure, she came to a decision. To avoid continued frustration and regret, she would attempt to alter her preferences away from dancing and toward painting. Suppose she is successful: Erin, at t_2, prefers the life of painting to the life of dance.

[7] Indeed, Nussbaum holds something similar. Nussbaum writes: "One might hold that the preference-based view is perfectly all right as a basis for quality of life comparisons, while doubting that it could be an adequate basis for the selection of basic political principles . . . This would, I think, be an implausible position to hold, once one confronts the specific defects of preference-based views: the reasons for thinking them bad bases for political principles are also reasons why they do not do a good job of quality of life measurement" (ibid., 116).

Erin's case is an example of adaptive preferences. Erin, merely because it is available, comes to prefer a life of painting to a life of dance. Hence any theory that draws an important connection between Erin's adaptive preferences and her good must claim that a life of painting is better for Erin at t_2 than a life of dance. But this is counterintuitive. Her preference is an example only of a successful attempt to avoid the predictable and painful frustration that comes along with a preference for that which is simply unavailable. Of course, we are perfectly licensed to say, at t_2, that a life of painting would improve Erin's life over the lack of either activity. Furthermore, it seems right to say, of Erin, that *given* her lack of talent, it is prudentially *rational* to switch her preferences in this way. But insofar as her preferences are merely a result of strategic engineering, of intentional adaptation to her circumstances, it seems wrong to take them at face value. Contrary to her preferences post-engineering, *were* she able to be a dancer at t_2, it seems quite right to say that the life of a dancer would be better for Erin at t_2 than the life of a painter. Thus it seems wrong to say that Erin's t_2 preferences should be authoritative over that which is good for her at t_2.[8] Any theory that admits that the fulfillment of adaptive or distorted preferences improve lives is thus mistaken. Hence WBM has two strikes against it. Not only is it "ethically deeply mistaken" as a theory of the basic minimum, it also seems to rely on a false theory of welfare: that a person's valuing attitudes (some of which will be adaptive) are a guide to the most central elements of a person's life quality.

One might be tempted to claim that this feature of adaptive preferences is good news for a welfarist approach to the basic minimum, if not for WBM: if adaptive preferences are bad guides to an individual's good, then it must be the case that the *proper* account of that which is in an individual's interest might be able to construct an approach to the basic minimum that avoids the problem at hand. But this possibility is complicated by the first horn of the dilemma I posed in Chapter 1: only approaches to a welfarist basic minimum that take an individual's conception of the good (and hence potentially adaptive preferences) seriously in setting the basic minimum can avoid the unacceptable conclusion that people should be forced to live in ways they do not value. Hence if the problem of adaptive preferences

[8] That Erin's preference is not authoritative is not evidence that achievement in painting is not good for her. Indeed, Erin may have some *other* preference, viz., the preference to paint rather than *nothing*, which *is* authoritative. Furthermore, one might also claim that achievement in painting is good for Erin no matter what she prefers. To say that a particular preference is not authoritative is simply to say that this preference is not a guide to an individual's good. It does not entail that the preferred *object* is of no welfare value.

cannot be solved by WBM, it seems unlikely than any welfarist approach to the basic minimum will succeed.

To begin my defense of WBM, I note first that though many agree that adaptive preferences cause problems for particular theories of welfare, the precise nature of the problem appears ill-understood.[9] Hence to address the problem of adaptive preferences, I must first investigate *what*, precisely, this problem is. What *about* adaptive preferences renders them irrelevant to welfare?[10] This question will take up the next three sections.

3.2.1. Preference for the worse

First, one might be tempted to claim that adaptive preferences are welfare-irrelevant because they cause a person to *prefer the worse*; that is, to prefer those things that are worse as a matter of *objective* prudential value. Sen's landless laborer, quite plausibly, prefers the worse insofar as he prefers landless labor to a life of greater achievements, education, relationships, etc. These things are objectively better than landless labor. Hence the landless laborer's preferences are welfare-irrelevant, mistaken.

Preference for the worse is obviously an important challenge to views that posit subjectively defined welfare goods. As such, it will be dealt with in due time. However, the problem of adaptive preferences should be kept distinct from the problem of preference for the worse. A preference can be adaptive without being an instance of preference for the worse. Erin is a prime example. It strikes me as clearly implausible to say that Erin's post-adaptation preferences are for the worse. Erin's preferences are surely adaptive; indeed, they are consciously, explicitly adaptive. If social policy is interested in improving Erin's life, it will not treat her preference for painting as authoritative. But Erin's preferences are not an example of preferring the worse to the better.

Divorcing the problem of adaptive preferences from the problem of preference for the worse sheds some important light on previous attempts to solve the problem of adaptive preferences. One popular solution is to declare that some things are intrinsically bad and some things are intrinsically good for people independently of anyone's preferences for them. One

9 For vastly different approaches to understanding the nature and problem of adaptive preferences, see Elster (1982) and (1983), esp. ch. 3; Nussbaum, "Women and Cultural Universals" in (1999) and (2000), esp. ch. 2; Sumner (1996), esp. ch. 6; Sen (1993), 6–7; Rickard (1995); Qizilbash (2006).

10 I use the term "welfare-relevant" for any preference or element of an individual's conception of the good that can sensibly play a role in determining that which is good for a person; welfare-relevant preferences need not determine the all-things-considered betterness of a preferred object; they are simply one factor among others in determining a person's well-being.

might, for instance, reject subjectivism about well-being on the whole, or adopt a form of Weak Subjectivism, which has the power to declare that some things people prefer are intrinsically worthless. On this view, any preference for, say, overexhausted coolieism is not relevant to welfare; overexhausted coolieism is not a prudential benefit no matter how much it is preferred. However, this solution is insufficient to solve the problem at hand.[11] It conflates the problem of adaptive preferences with the problem of preference for the worse. This conflation leads to a failure to address cases of adaptive preferences that do not *also* involve cases of preference for the worse. Erin's is one such case. It is wildly implausible, it seems to me, to declare that a life of excellent achievement in painting is objectively worse than a life of excellent achievement in dancing. But unless the view in question is willing to take the implausible step of declaring that neither possibility is better for Erin, it cannot simply reject *tout court* the importance of Erin's preferences to her well-being. But any view that takes the plausible step of allowing the occasional authority of preference remains vulnerable to the problem of adaptive preferences whether or not it solves the problem of preference for the worse. Though preference for the worse is an important problem in its own right, solving this problem does not entail solving the problem of adaptive preferences.

3.2.2. *Adaptation and autonomy*

The problem of adaptive preferences goes beyond preference for the worse. But what, then, is the problem? Some have claimed that the distinctive problem illustrated by the phenomenon of adaptive preferences is that some preferences are *non-autonomous*, and hence any theory of well-being that holds that such preferences are welfare-relevant is out of tune with a person's autonomy or autonomous nature. As Sumner writes:

> Why are we reluctant to take at face value the life satisfaction reported by "the hopeless beggar, the precarious landless labourer, the dominated housewife, the hardened unemployed or the over-exhausted coolie"? Presumably because we suspect that the standards which their self-assessments reflect have been artificially lowered or distorted by processes of indoctrination or exploitation. In that case, the obvious remedy is to correct for the conditions under which their expectations

[11] Hawkins proposes a solution that accepts that certain lives can be *bad* for persons regardless of their own preferences, but cannot be *good* for persons without the authority of their preferences. Her proposal accepts a form of Weak Subjectivism. See Hawkins (2008), 167–8. Others have adopted objective theories of well-being to solve the problem of adaptive preferences. See, for instance, Qizilbash (2006) and Rickard (1995). Both strategies fail.

about themselves came to be formed. The problem is not that their values are objectively mistaken but that they have never had the opportunity to form their own values at all. They do not lack enlightenment, or insight into the Platonic form of the good; they lack autonomy.[12]

Sumner speaks of "happiness" or "life satisfaction." But leaving this aside for the moment, a "Sumnerian" approach to adaptive preferences might hold that the problem to be illustrated by adaptive preferences is that adaptive preferences are not properly *autonomous*.[13] For Sumner, problematic forms of adaptation are a result of non-autonomous mechanisms, both social and psychological. On this view, one solves the problem of adaptive preferences by claiming that preferences formed by non-autonomous processes are welfare-irrelevant, preferences that are – or would be – formed by autonomous processes are accepted as welfare-relevant.

Missing from this proposal is a theory of autonomous preference formation. Sumner does not offer such a theory, and does little to clarify what it means for a preference to be formed by a non-autonomous process. However, he does offer a list of preference (or "happiness") formation processes that he regards as non-autonomous:

> Self-assessments of happiness or life satisfaction are suspect (as measures of well-being) when there is good reason to suspect that they have been influenced by autonomy-subverting mechanisms of social conditioning, such as indoctrination, programming, brainwashing, role scripting, and the like. [. . .] [T]he best strategy here is to treat subjects' reports of their level of life satisfaction as defeasible – that is, as authoritative unless there is evidence that they are non-autonomous.[14]

Such socialization processes can surely give rise to adaptive preferences. One might imagine, for instance, that the landless laborer's life of poverty is an importantly non-autonomous preference formation process. But the problem of adaptive preferences cannot be solved by claiming that preferences or reports of satisfaction or happiness are non-autonomous. *Some* psychological mechanisms by which adaptive preferences are formed will be perfectly compatible with a person's autonomy. For instance, it is hard to see Erin's preference revision as non-autonomous.[15] Erin prefers the life of a dancer for its own sake, but finds that she has no talent for it. She then, quite rationally, decides to stop pining away for the life she longed for, and strategically attempts to revise her preferences toward the available: the life of a painter. Indeed, far from being an instance of pernicious socialization, embarking on a strategy of preference revision of this kind

[12] Sumner (1996), 166.
[13] This view is also endorsed in Elster (1982).
[14] Sumner (1996), 171.
[15] Compare Rickard (1995), 289–90.

is straightforwardly rational. Why continue to pine away for something when it is clearly beyond your grasp? Preference switching in this case will lead to far fewer cases of frustration and regret which is surely, all things considered, something to be praised and encouraged.[16]

One might reply that if they are the result of a rational or autonomous process of preference formation, we have no reason to believe that, e.g., Erin's t_2 preferences are not a guide to her good. This suggestion is mistaken. Merely because it is *rational* to at least attempt to switch her preferences, or that in so doing she would be acting autonomously, does not mean that the life of a dancer wouldn't be better for Erin. If she *could* achieve it, we are tempted to say, it would certainly be better for her. Erin's adaptive preferences interrupt the inference from her preference to her good, but not because the process by which the preferences were formed is somehow irrational or non-autonomous.

3.2.3. *Adaptation and proto-autonomy*

Adaptive preferences are welfare-irrelevant not because they are instances of preference for the worse or because they are non-autonomous. But if this is correct, we appear to lack justification for treating Erin's preferences as irrelevant to her good. One might put this point in the following way: once preference for the worse and failures of autonomy have been swept away, why should we believe that, e.g., Erin's welfare at t_2 is determined, not by her preferences at t_2, but rather by her preferences at t_1? On the one hand, it seems right to say that Erin's preferences ought to have some authority over her well-being, especially given that dancing and painting are both worthwhile activities. But on the other hand, we seek to reject the authority of her t_2 preferences given their adaptation. We seem to want Erin's preferences to determine her welfare, and then refuse to grant her preferences such authority. What gives?

To answer this question, we must answer a much more fundamental one. Why should we believe that a person's preferences should have *any* welfare-determining authority at all? Surely at least *part* of the motivation for accepting the prudential authority of preferences is a commitment to the claim that what is good for a person should be – perhaps even only to a very minor degree – determined by his or her *conception of the good*, or

[16] Cf. Rosati (2006), esp. 60–4; Nussbaum (2000), 137–8.

what this person, in the broadest sense, values.[17] And if we are interested in tying Erin's good to her conception of the good, we must say that preferences have at least some authority over her welfare. But this sheds new light. In Erin's case, it seems right to say that her preference at t_2 for painting over dancing does not really capture her conception of the good: her preferences are merely a result of an unusually successful attempt at strategic preference engineering. If so, *Erin's adaptive preferences are not part of her genuine conception of the good*, and hence do not really capture what we care about when we seek to grant welfare-determining authority to preferences.

This verdict appears to generalize: adaptive preferences show that any old preference need not always express its possessor's conception of the good. This holds just as well for Sen's overexhausted coolie as it does for Erin. Though the overexhausted coolie might prefer coolieism as a survival strategy, overexhausted coolieism is not a feature of his true *values*. It is a product, rather, of manipulation by external circumstances, such as a lack of available alternatives. Though it is correct to say that at least some of Erin's preferences shift from t_1 to t_2, such a shift need not entail that her conception of the good *also* shifts. Rather, they are a mere product of circumstance; they reflect, as it were, a strategic "coping mechanism."

My examples here are stylized, but the point holds. It seems right to say that the overexhausted coolie, the landless laborer, etc., do not *really* value the circumstances they are in or the projects they might adopt. Their preferences are a result of a coping mechanism, or simple habit, or a form of indoctrination. Indeed, Nussbaum's own solution to the problem of adaptive preferences relies on this diagnosis. For it to be the case that greater capabilities will yield the reversal of adaptive preferences, Nussbaum must believe that a person's adaptive preferences are not a real part of her conception of the good, but are a mere product of a lack of alternatives. Otherwise there is no reason to believe that additional capabilities will alter the life she leads. To put this another way, in cases of adaptation, *real* preferences are "covered up" by the lack of capabilities, and hence Nussbaum is licensed to expect that *given* further opportunities, people will overcome adaptation, and come to prefer lives that enjoy "truly human functioning."

If my analysis is correct, there need be no tension between the project of avoiding adaptive preferences and the project of accommodating

[17] Again, this claim is perfectly compatible with subjectivist and objectivist theories of the good; objectivist views can claim, plausibly, that the fulfillment of a person's preferences *occasionally* improves their welfare, perhaps when the preference fulfilled is for a valued project.

The Basic Minimum as Proto-autonomy. If adaptive preferences do not reflect an individual's true conception of the good, the project of constructing a basic minimum that does not succumb to the problem of adaptive preferences just *is* the project of accommodating *The Basic Minimum as Proto-autonomy*. Hence, or so it would appear thus far, all that is required to defeat adaptive preferences is to account for a person's "true" conception of the good – a conception of the good not biased toward the status-quo or distorted by facts of unavailability, habit, strategic engineering, etc. If such an account can be found, WBM is under no threat.

3.3. CONCEPTIONS OF THE GOOD: A THEORY

Time to take stock. The problem for WBM seemed to be this: according to WBM, one maintains the basic minimum insofar as one maintains a valued project. But one's "values" can be based on preferences or other pro-attitudes (such as an assessment of a life as worth living, etc.) that are susceptible to adaptation. However, I have so far argued that adaptive preferences do not reflect an individual's "true values" or true conception of the good. Hence to complete the project of accommodating *The Basic Minimum as Proto-autonomy, and* to avoid the problem of adaptive preferences, we simply need a better account of an individual's true preferences that avoids the mechanisms of adaptation. If this can be offered – and this is a big "if" – the welfarist's dilemma is dissolved.

Call my account of a person's genuine preferences "preference coherentism" (PC). I won't be able to defend all the nooks and crannies of PC here; I set out only to show how it might solve the problem of adaptation. There are surely powerful objections to my view; I leave these aside. (For instance, I will not defend my precise conception of coherence. Furthermore, some have argued that my account is circular. I argue elsewhere that it is not, but will leave aside this objection here.[18]) PC declares that a person's genuine conception of the good is constituted by her evaluative beliefs, *rendered coherent and complete*. I present this account in four stages. First, I argue that genuine preferences should be understood as evaluative beliefs rather than desires. Second, I more fully describe the "coherence and completeness" constraints. Third, for the purposes of clarification, I compare my account of valuation to other superficially similar accounts, including a coherentist

[18] I try to specify a working notion of coherence good enough for our purposes here in Dorsey (2006). For a defense against the charge of circularity, see Dorsey (2010b) and (MS).

moral epistemology, and an account of prudential valuing offered by James Griffin. Finally, I argue that PC solves the problem of adaptive preferences.

3.3.1. Beliefs not desires

The first noteworthy feature of preference coherentism is that it understands preferences or other pro-attitudes in terms of evaluative beliefs rather than desires. According to PC, A prefers *p* to *q* to the extent that A believes (under the right conditions) that *p* is better for A than *q*. Understanding preferences in terms of beliefs rather than desires requires defense. Most importantly, the appeal to beliefs rather than desires in defining welfare-relevant preferences can correct the influence of certain adaptation-causing psychological mechanisms. This proposal is intuitive, as noted by Sidgwick: "a prudent man is accustomed to suppress, with more or less success, desires for what he regards as out of his power to attain by voluntary action – as fine weather, perfect health, great wealth or fame, etc.; but any success he may have in diminishing the actual intensity of such desires has no effect in leading him to judge the objects desired less 'good.'"[19] Here Sidgwick notes that one adaptation-causing psychological mechanism is "prudence," or rational suppression of a desire for that which is unavailable. (One might imagine that this mechanism is at work in Erin's case.) But this form of suppression occurs only at the level of desire: according to Sidgwick, this form of adaptation "has no effect in leading him to judge the objects desired less 'good.'"

Other mechanisms by which adaptive preferences may form are limited to desire. To see this, consider Jennifer Hawkins's discussion of a character in Alice Walker's *The Color Purple*:

> Celie's early life is a study in trauma and abuse. From a young age, she is sexually abused by her stepfather (whom she falsely believes to be her biological father) . . . Eventually, Celie escapes this tormentor for a new one – the man her stepfather forces her to marry and who is simply referred to throughout the novel as Mr. —. Mr. — treats Celie like a slave, demanding not only that she care for his unruly children from a previous marriage and maintain a high standard of housekeeping, but that she work in his fields as well. He beats her mercilessly and constantly tells her how stupid and ugly he thinks she is.[20]

[19] Sidgwick (1907), 110. Sidgwick's own account, however, fails to properly address this problem: Sidgwick himself insists that a person's desires are authoritative over his good only among those choices that are "open to him." See ibid., 111–12.

[20] Hawkins (2008), 145–6.

Celie comes to accept this treatment as her lot in life; in describing her condition, Hawkins writes as follows:

> One particularly striking feature of . . . Celie [is her] low sense of self-worth. As I suggested before. . . Celie *feels* worthless. Without a proper sense that she, Celie, matters, her idealized self will be unlikely to give her non-idealized self good advice. Nor will she be able to assess her life fairly in comparison with other lives. Although she may recognize that other lives are happier or more successful, she will not necessarily see them as better for her if she herself feels unworthy of the lives in question.[21]

As Celie seems to clearly illustrate, some people, because of their circumstances, will develop a lack of self-worth and will, as a result, develop preferences that are adaptive or biased toward the status-quo. This might occur not only for people whose lives are objectively bad (such as Celie or the landless laborer), but also in others; one could imagine, for instance, that Erin's preference for painting might arise given a conviction that she is "unworthy" of the life of a dancer. But it is important to note that there are (at least) two ways in which low self-worth could lead to adaptive preferences. First, a person with low self-worth might *believe* that other lives would be substantially better than her current life, but because she has a low sense of self-worth and "feels unworthy of the lives in question" she fails to desire them. Second, a person with low self-worth might simply come to judge that the life in which she is, say, dominated, landless, overexhausted is actually good for her, perhaps because it somehow "fits" her low conception of her own worth.

I will leave discussion of the second possibility until §3.4. But PC's emphasis on beliefs rather than desires helps to address the first permutation of Hawkins's treatment of adaptation: even though Celie might believe herself unworthy of that which she believes is good, she still has a conception of what is good for her – she *believes* that lives other than her own are good for her, or might be better than the one of which she feels herself worthy. Her lack of self-worth causes adaptive preferences only at the level of desire: because she lacks self-esteem, she fails to *want* that which she judges good for her. Though this might not be the only way in which low self-worth can contribute to adaptive preferences, it is certainly *one* way it might do so. Hence understanding genuine preferences in terms of evaluative beliefs rather than desires better explains a person's *true* values. Thus it seems to me there is good reason to understand a person's conception of the good in terms of what this person believes is good for her.

[21] Ibid., 160–1.

3.3.2. Coherence and completeness

Understanding a person's preferences in terms of evaluative belief rather than desire goes some distance toward solving the problem of adaptive preferences. But it does not go far enough. An account of a person's genuine preferences must be abstracted from the person's actual evaluative beliefs, and must be identified with what a person *would* come to believe under certain counterfactual conditions. There are two reasons for this. First, a person's conception of the good might be incoherent, inconsistent, or self-refuting. Second, without such abstraction we leave open the possibility of adaptation. Certainly psychological mechanisms exist (including, e.g., rational preference revision) that could render not just desiderative preferences, but also one's evaluative beliefs, adaptive to one's – potentially quite shabby – circumstances. Taking evaluative beliefs at face value, then, fails to eliminate all mechanisms by which preferences might be adapted, and hence fails to properly accommodate an interest in proto-autonomy.

A person's conception of the good must be abstracted from her actual evaluative beliefs in two ways. First, genuine preferences must be understood not as that which she happens to believe is good, but as that which she *would* believe good *were* her conception of the good rendered *coherent*. Incoherence involves not only contradictory beliefs, but beliefs that are ill-behaved in various ways, including those that display intransitivity.[22] Furthermore, coherent beliefs support each other and provide explanatory and justificatory connections.[23] Though I take this to be a rather weak requirement, we should at least insist that welfare-relevant preferences that purport to reflect a person's genuine conception of the good be supported and warranted by other members of her conception of the good.[24]

Second, conceptions of the good should be construed as arising from a *complete* set of evaluative beliefs. The completeness requirement is really two requirements in one. The first is that welfare-relevant conceptions of the good must yield a *complete ordering* of all possible welfare goods. (If commensurability is limited, A's coherent and complete conception of the good should yield *as complete an ordering as possible*.) By "possible," I mean *metaphysically possible*. Insofar as we believe that a change in A's capacities,

[22] Though transitivity has been denied as a feature of the good, I accept it as bedrock. For conflicting views, see Rachels (1998), Temkin (1996). Arguments, in my view successful, for transitivity are to be found in Broome (2004), ch. 4; Norcross (2002).

[23] One such explanatory connection is exploited in the last chapter: an assessment of a life as worth living must be explained, at least in part, by a further judgment of the value of a global project *p* if *p* is to be a valued project.

[24] I argue for this in more detail in Dorsey (2006).

circumstances, or environment might be good or bad for A, we shouldn't hold these capabilities, circumstances, or environment fixed when issuing a complete account of that which would be better or worse for A. This is a crucial step in avoiding preference adaptation: if one's conception of the good only rank-orders activities or other welfare goods that are possible only in some more restricted sense of "possible" (such as physically possible, economically possible, etc.), this will open the door to adaptation to that which is possible in this more restricted sense. But insofar as any set of preferences are to be a reliable guide to a person's good (at least some of the time), and insofar as we believe that any metaphysically possible life *l* *could* be better or worse for a person, that person's conception of the good should evaluate *l*.

However, to guarantee a complete ordering, a conception of the good must have a sufficient basis to determine a complete ordering without gaps. This consideration naturally leads into the second half of the "completeness" requirement. Evaluative beliefs must be tested against a complete set of *value data*. Complete testing closes potential gaps. Though I now have no beliefs that will yield a proper ordering between the life of an Aztec chieftain or a Mayan chieftain, testing my evaluative beliefs against the relevant value data will close this gap (or, if they are genuinely incommensurable, declare them so). Thus the completeness requirement refers both to the mandated complete ordering, and also to the requirement that any genuine conception of the good survive a counterfactual process of complete testing.

What are value data? On my understanding, a value datum consists of two crucial elements. First, the *information* about *what living a given life would be like*. A value datum will require the full confrontation with the consequences, experiences, achievements, etc., of living some life. There are different ways one might construe this element of value data. One might conceive of it as a "report," i.e., some list of facts about the content of a life, or as an "experience," i.e., the actual *experience* of living a life reported on in the report model.[25] According to David Sobel, the choice is not inconsequential: a mere report, in comparison to the full experience, will fail to accurately convey the bases for a complete evaluation.[26] Sobel's critique seems correct, and hence I will accept it for my purposes here. Thus value data will require full information about what a given life would be like for the person who lives it, conceived of as the experience of actually living it. The second element of value data is a *judgment* about the

[25] Sobel (1994). [26] Ibid., 798.

quality of that life *given* the experience of it. Thus value data is properly conceived of as a belief in the quality of some particular life on the basis of actually experiencing that life, *and on that basis only*. A completely tested conception of the good, then, will be tested against judgments of the quality of all metaphysically possible lives.

One point remains. The coherence and completeness requirements introduce the possibility of recalcitrant data: a belief about the good that conflicts, or renders incoherent, the set of evaluative beliefs it is used to test. If so, revisions to this set with an eye toward renewed coherence will be required. How are we to go about rendering coherent an incoherent set? Here PC is conservative. When revising in light of recalcitrant value data or as a result of incoherence, revisions are made at the "periphery," revising a person's most strongly held preferences only as a last resort. Thus, putting all this together, PC holds that A's genuine conception of the good is constituted by A's set of beliefs about that which is good for A, after having been tested against all possible value data, and revised in light of recalcitrant data and other forms of incoherence by a process of "minimal mutilation."[27]

3.3.3. Some comparisons[28]

PC is a theory of a person's genuine preferences. But before I attempt to show that this account solves problems of adaptation, I should compare my view to some that are similar in certain ways, dissimilar in others. Those uninterested in such comparisons can proceed to the next section.

First, David Brink outlines a coherentist moral *epistemology* identified as follows: "Moral coherentism or a coherence theory of justification in ethics represents the application of coherentism to the justification of moral beliefs. It holds that one's moral belief *p* is justified insofar as *p* is part of a coherent system of beliefs, both moral and nonmoral, and *p*'s coherence at least partially explains why one holds *p*."[29]

Brink's coherentist moral epistemology is similar in many ways to my insistence that a person's genuine conception of the good should be coherent. However, PC makes no claims about the epistemic justification of a person's preferences. Objective theories of welfare might claim that the fact that A values *p* provides some reason for believing that *p* maintains

[27] Quine, "Two Dogmas of Empiricism" in Quine (1981), 42–6.

[28] I'd like to thank an anonymous reader for suggesting these comparisons.

[29] Brink (1989), 103. Brink cites Rawls's reflective equilibrium procedure as embodying an essentially coherentist method of justification.

preference-independent value, but PC itself is agnostic on this point and makes no claims about the evidential strength of a coherent system – evidential, that is, of anything beyond what a person genuinely prefers. It says only that A's coherent and complete beliefs about what is in A's interests constitutes A's genuine preferences and conception of the good. But this is as it should be. When we are interested in a person's genuine preferences, we are interested not in some external order of values to which our beliefs may or may not be reliable guides. Rather, we are interested only in *this person's* pro-attitudes: that which *she* believes is good for *her*. Of course, WBM claims that the fact that a person believes that a particular project *p* is good for her (along with the requisite comparative judgment about the life in which it is led) *renders* this project valuable enough to constitute the basic minimum. But this should be taken, simply, to be the result of an independently plausible claim about welfare (WBM), together with facts about what this person genuinely values.[30]

A second contrast should be drawn here. James Griffin, in *Value Judgment*, offers an account of prudential valuing that is in some ways similar to the approach I offer here.[31] On my view, a welfare-relevant preference is a belief about that which is good for a person, refined by means of coherence and complete testing. Griffin's view is similar. Griffin rejects the idea that "value judgments" are simply desires. According to Griffin, such judgments are a mix of belief and desire, a mix of "recognition and reaction," which includes a crucial cognitive element.[32] Furthermore, Griffin accepts a method of refining one's value judgments that seems to recall certain elements of my account of "value data."[33] For Griffin, the welfare value of something like "accomplishment" is known through a process of "recognition and reaction" of the importance of certain elements in human life; in this way, one might believe that a defect of a person's preferential profile is that this person has not engaged in the sort of reflection that would require confrontation with "value data" concerning a wide array of elements in human life.[34]

However, there is an important difference between Griffin's approach and my own that I should like to spend some brief time on.[35] Griffin

30 This discussion gives rise to a number of questions about my view, including the semantic content of judgments about value ("if they're not about an external realm of value, what are they about?"). I shan't discuss these matters here, except to direct the interested reader to other venues in which I discuss them in much more detail. See Dorsey (2010b). For the purposes of this book, I leave aside such technical matters.

31 Griffin (1996). 32 Ibid., 32–6.

33 See, especially, ibid., 25, 53–9. 34 Ibid., 24–5.

35 A few other differences should be obvious. First, I don't include the "reactional" element in a person's value judgments. Second, Griffin criticizes a model of ethical judgment that is simply coherentist.

writes: "For me to see anything as prudentially valuable, I must see it as enhancing life in a generally intelligible way, in a way that pertains to *human* life, not to any one particular person's life."[36] As noted above, my account of a person's genuine preferences denies this. On my view, A's genuine preferences are taken from A's beliefs about that which is good *for A*, not from A's beliefs about what is genuinely important to human life in any wider sense. Again, Griffin writes:

> For anyone to see anything as valuable, from any point of view, requires being able to see it as worth wanting. This is a perfectly general requirement on values; it is the basis of the distinction between mere wanting and the sort of wanting that connects with values. One way to see something as worth wanting is to see it under the heading of some general human interest . . . So long as one defines "personal values" in terms of what a person wants or cares about, one retains too much of the taste [i.e., desire-based] model.[37]

Griffin's approach seems to have a novel solution to the problem of adaptive preferences: the overexhausted coolie, for instance, will generally not see overexhausted coolieism as "falling under the heading of some general human interest."[38] Why, then, not embrace Griffin's account, rather than my own approach, which focuses on A's judgments about what is good *for A*?

Three considerations tell in favor of my view, at least for the purposes to which I put it here. First, we needn't say that to see something as "worth wanting," we must see it as valuable in terms of *general* human interests. Rather, one way in which I can see something as "worth wanting" is that I can *believe*, in a way that is supported by other such beliefs, that this thing *is good for me*. In this way, some things I want are not worth wanting: they are not things that I believe are good for me. All Griffin's point requires is *some* extra-desiderative account of valuing against which we can test the evaluative quality of desires, not necessarily his particular account.

Second, I think there are very good reasons, in determining what a person's genuine preferences are, to focus on what he believes is good for him, rather than what he believes is valuable for humans generally. For instance, we could imagine a person who believes that something is

Griffin believes that such a model is of only slight benefit if we have no evidence that our ethical beliefs are generally reliable (ibid., 12–18). Of course, Griffin believes that the judgments we form about prudence and human interests are generally reliable (ibid., 66–7), and hence should be taken as good epistemic indicators of value. Again, I remain neutral on this point. I am interested only in the coherence and completeness of an individual's evaluative beliefs, which is necessary and sufficient for such beliefs to be representative of a person's genuine conception of the good.

[36] Ibid., 27. [37] Ibid., 27–8. [38] See, especially, ibid., 27.

valuable for him (in a way that is coherent and complete), but who does not also see this as valuable for humans generally. A person engaged in the project of grass-counting may very well recognize that his pursuit is not for everyone, i.e., that it does not fall "under the heading of some general human interest." However, it seems to me that this latter claim does nothing to diminish our judgment that the grass-counter *values* grass-counting. We may be tempted to say that grass-counting is not in anyone's interest. But this is merely a call to restrict the relevance of this person's genuine preferences in determining that which is in her interests, not to come to a different understanding of what she prefers or values. Furthermore, take a person who judges that a particular *p does* fall under the heading of a general human interest or need. But this person judges also (coherently and completely) that *p* is not good *for him*. Such a belief is not incoherent: this person could believe that he or she is relevantly different than human beings in a certain way, or may believe that it is good for him or her *to* be different in this way. I think we would say quite emphatically that this person does not value *p*.

Third, though we offer different interpretations of prudential judgments, it seems to me that our views are, ultimately, compatible. Griffin takes his account to be answering a very different question than the question my account of preferences addresses. Griffin holds that value judgments must be "reliable beliefs," evidence of *objective* prudential values.[39] Griffin, like Brink, seeks to assess a more general moral epistemological question: what *sort* of beliefs are reliable indicators of an external realm of value? For Griffin, the "recognitional" element of our value judgments is intended to be "a kind of sensitivity to something in the world," which Griffin understands as those things that make human life – rather than any particular person's life – better.[40] If that is correct, Griffin may very well believe that the best way to come to *true* judgments about welfare is to judge things against a background of general human interests, rather than with an eye toward what is good for me, in particular. PC, however, is not advanced as an epistemological guide to this external realm of values. Given this, PC and Griffin's approach to value judgments need not be at loggerheads. As I have so far been at pains to argue, one plausible claim about objective prudential values is that the maintenance of a valued project is a central

[39] See ibid., 29–30, 53–9. Griffin himself objects to the "objective" terminology; however, his view does conform to the idea of "objectivism" as I define it here. Griffin offers us a list of prudential goods, and holds that these goods are valuable "in any life" (ibid., 30). If so, Griffin has an objective view.

[40] Ibid., 57–9.

element of human well-being *in any life*.[41] One might assess this claim given its coherence with our beliefs about what is generally valuable for humans. But if this is correct, a further question arises: what, for A, is a valued project *for A*? The set of beliefs that results from the process embraced by PC helps to answer this latter question, but needn't be construed as answering the wider question concerning whether a valued project is beneficial for persons, generally. Our methodologies respond to different concerns, and are appropriate to the concerns to which they respond.

3.4. COHERENTISM AND ADAPTATION

PC avoids the problem of adaptive preferences by blocking the cognitive conditions that yield adaptive preferences. That which is shared by the cases of adaptive preferences we have so far considered is the extent to which facts about a given person's actual life, including facts concerning what is available to that person, influence the extent to which the person in question maintains a particular preference or pro-attitude. This fact explains any success the capabilities approach may have at avoiding adaptive preferences: we would expect the capabilities approach to correct preferences that arise as a result of a lack of basic capabilities or available styles of life. But when revising a person's set of preferences according to PC, facts of availability are rendered moot. Though it might be the case that Erin cannot live the life of a dancer, and hence develops an adaptive aversion to such a life, the *value data* that are used to revise her evaluative beliefs are not influenced by Erin's actual inability. Any relevant value datum used to revise her set of preferences includes a judgment of the comparative value of a particular life and its various goods given on the basis of a full experience of that life, not whether that life is available or is likely to occur given the facts about the world. Facts of actual availability will not influence the extent to which recalcitrant value data will cause revisions to her preferences. Because all lives are experienced, preferences that depend on facts of availability will be – other things equal – revised. For PC, the life that a person actually leads is simply one among many, and has no special status.

Furthermore, PC can also avoid problems of adaptation that are not simply due to facts of unavailability. Consider, for instance, examples of adaptation through "habit," or perhaps certain forms of social indoctrination. *If* these preferences are not expressive of an individual's true

[41] Griffin seems to accept a claim very much like this in identifying "accomplishment" as a central element of the objective list. See ibid., 29.

conception of the good, we should expect that after having undergone complete testing against all metaphysically possible value data, one's preference for *p* or *q* as a result of social pressure, indoctrination, or habit will be revised as recalcitrant. When experiencing value data, one experiences lives in which one's habits are markedly changed, one's social pressures are very different, and in which one is not indoctrinated. *If* these preferences are genuinely adaptive, we should expect that once these habits, pressures, etc., are removed, the person in question will no longer prefer *p* to *q* – or, at the very least, will prefer *p* to *q* in a way that is reflective of her genuine conception of the good.

Of course, adaptive preferences are an ineradicable feature of value data: the *experience* of living a life will surely present many *examples* of biased or adaptive preferences. But the preferences one has during any particular life are not necessarily representative of one's conception of the good, properly conceived. Though, in life *l*, Erin might strongly prefer painting to dancing, Erin's coherent and complete conception of the good can declare this preference irrelevant to her welfare. And it might do so by comparing the assessment of *l* against an assessment of life *k*, in which a life of dance is available and experienced. The relevant value datum here is likely to declare that dancing is to be preferred, sufficient to override a judgment from within *l* that a life of painting is to be preferred.[42]

It might be objected that PC is still beholden to the (perhaps adaptive) preferences of a person's original set of evaluative beliefs in one sense: conceptions of the good are revised conservatively, i.e., by minimal mutilation, which requires that we override a person's most strongly held judgments only as a last resort. It is not at all guaranteed that preferences that are originally a result of facts of availability will not be among the person's strongest held beliefs from the perspective of her conception of the good. After all, over the course of time and psychological change a person might come to strongly identify with preferences that were originally cases of adaptation, or other forms of psychological distortion. If so, confrontation with value data is insufficient to remove biased preferences because this reflection will surely be done in light of these very preferences. However, PC has resources to alleviate this worry. After all, *for a preference to be adaptive*, there must be some reason for thinking that this preference arises merely given facts about what is or is not available or other various facts about the particular

[42] However, were Erin to judge her life as a dancer worse than her life as painter from the perspective of her coherent and complete conception of the good, being a painter *is* a better life for Erin. Furthermore, if the respective value data judge these lives to be equivalent in value, Erin's conception of the good will also reflect this fact. This is the correct answer.

life a person leads (including habit, social pressures, indoctrination, etc.). Because Erin's biased preferences arise as a result of, and are supported by, these facts, Erin will prefer achievement in dance when these facts are rendered moot. In experiencing value data, there is no longer any feature of the world or of the life one actually lives that would allow biased preferences to develop, or recommend preference revision. All beliefs are subject to revision, and given the nature of adaptive preferences, they are likely to be revised in light of complete testing against value data, insofar as a person's *particular life* is simply one among many metaphysically possible lives.

Thus, returning to WBM, PC solves the problem of adaptation as follows: any judgment that a particular life is worth living, or that a particular project contributes to the worth of a particular life, will not be made on the basis of facts of unavailability habit, indoctrination, etc. Such judgments, if they are to reflect an individual's genuine conception of the good, must survive the process described here. Thus we should not fear anyone's maintenance of the basic minimum on the basis of adaptive preferences. No preferences, pro-attitudes, or other evaluative judgments that are held simply on the basis of the particular facts of a person's actual life will determine whether a given person maintains the basic minimum.

3.5. TOO LOW, PART TWO: DEEP ADAPTATION AND PREFERENCE FOR THE WORSE

PC makes as much headway on the problem of adaptive preferences as Nussbaum's capabilities approach. Recall that Nussbaum's approach treats adaptation as a result of facts of unavailability or narrow sets of capabilities. In correcting these facts, Nussbaum avoids the problematic suggestion that people who possess the basic minimum live shabby lives as a result of adaptive preferences – for Nussbaum, the provision of capabilities is mechanism enough to overcome adaptation. WBM can do just as well. PC, and hence WBM, holds that preferences held simply on the basis of facts about a given person's actual life (such as availability, habit, indoctrination, etc.) will not influence that which constitutes, for them, the basic minimum. Hence, for WBM, people who maintain adaptive preferences will not maintain the basic minimum simply on the basis of fulfilling these adaptive preferences. But there is an important dimension of the problem of adaptive preferences that has so far been left out: adaptation (through whatever mechanism) can give rise to preferences that are *central* elements of a person's conception of the good. So far I have been assuming that adaptive preferences are preferences that do not express an individual's true values. But what if habit, indoctrination, or simple facts of unavailability – perhaps as a result of the sands of time – come to be ingrained as a central part of an individual's conception of the good, which complete testing will not revise?

This question illustrates a difference between two forms of adaptive preferences (to which I briefly alluded in the introduction to this chapter). Call "shallow adaptive preferences" those preferences that are adaptive insofar as they do not reflect an individual's true conception of the good. Call "deep adaptive preferences" preferences that, as a result of various mechanisms of adaptation, are not simply a product of facts of unavailability, but are rather a *central* element in a given person's conception of the good, which the processes central to PC will not alter. Given that PC relies on revision of a person's conception of the good using a rubric of minimal mutilation, there is no guarantee that previously adaptive preferences will not themselves be the most central, important bits of a conception of the good, ruling contrary judgments out on the basis of incoherence. Though PC can solve the problem of shallow adaptive preferences, it does nothing to solve the problem of *deep* adaptation.

In evaluating WBM in light of deep adaptation, however, one must always keep in mind the extent to which its competition can do better. In considering the possibility of deep adaptation, or preferences that are "adaptive through and through," Nussbaum effectively denies their existence. According to Nussbaum:

> the human personality has a structure that is at least to some extent independent of culture, powerfully though culture shapes it at every stage. As the Greek philosophy Sextus Empiricus wrote, "In the person burdened by hunger and thirst, it is impossible to produce by argument the conviction that he is not so burdened." Desires for food, for mobility, for security, for health, for the use of reason – these seem to be relatively permanent features of our makeup as humans, which culture can blunt, but cannot altogether remove.[43]

Of course, we may deny that Nussbaum's psychological claims are correct. If so, deep adaptive preferences are no less a problem for her approach than for mine. But if we accept this psychological claim – which itself seems plausible – this helps to alleviate deep adaptation for welfarism, as well. Few people "burdened by hunger and thirst," or who live lives of subjugation, destitution, etc., etc., will regard any project lived in such a life as valuable: few people would regard these lives as worth living or of positive rather

[43] Nussbaum (2000), 155.

than negative value, after having undergone complete confrontation with all possible value data.

Furthermore, the problem of deep adaptation *in and of itself* is neither a problem for Nussbaum's view, nor for mine. To see this, consider two cases. First, imagine that Erin's preferences shift from t_1 to t_2 as a result of successful preference engineering. Now, at t_n, Erin's adaptive preference for painting has become a central, ingrained aspect of her conception of the good, so ingrained that complete testing against all metaphysically possible value data will not reverse her preference for painting over dancing. In this case, it seems to me difficult to declare that painting would be worse for Erin than dancing. After all, she strongly prefers it, and though this preference did not express her genuine conception of the good at t_2, *it does at* t_n. Hence, it seems to me, there is little reason to believe that Erin's *deep* adaptive preferences are irrelevant to her welfare in the same way that Erin's t_2 *shallow* adaptive preferences are. Once Erin's preferences shift in a way that genuinely reflects her values, there is little call to index her welfare to what her preferences *used to be*. Her current preferences are genuine. However, now compare Erin to Celie. One might imagine that Celie, through a lack of self-worth, comes to value her shabby life. Assume also that this adaptive preference is *deep*: it is a central part of her conception of the good. In this case, deep adaptation is a problem: Celie's preferences, or so it would seem, are not a good guide to that which is in her best interests.

What distinguishes Erin and Celie? It is not deep adaptation: both maintain preferences that are deeply adaptive. Rather, deep adaptation seems problematic only when these preferences are also an example of *preference for the worse*. As I stated before, one prefers the worse insofar as one prefers that which is objectively worse to that which is objectively better. Erin clearly does not prefer the worse; this fact seems to explain our reaction to her deep adaptive preferences. Celie, on the other hand, does.

If this is correct, deep adaptation is not *in itself* a problem for WBM. But Celie's case shows that even though deep adaptation is not a *per se* problem, preference for the worse *is*. There are certain projects we may regard as being "beneath" the basic minimum simply because they are independently of shabby quality: they are objectively bad rather than objectively good. One could imagine that "being a dominated housewife" (like Celie) might very well be a global project that Celie genuinely values. And if that's right, WBM seems to implausibly suggest that Celie maintains the basic minimum. One might be tempted to saddle Nussbaum's approach with exactly the same problematic conclusion. After all, if Celie values her shabby life in a *deeply* adaptive way, wouldn't she continue to live such a life even with greater capabilities? Generally speaking, I think the answer is yes. But WBM has a problem that Nussbaum's view escapes: we might imagine that Celie *prefers* to be non-dominated, and given the capability for non-domination, would avoid it (though being a dominated housewife remains a valued project). If this is correct, the capabilities approach seems to entail that Celie, in maintaining the basic minimum, will avoid being a dominated housewife. WBM, on the other hand, seems to include no such mechanism. In living a life as a dominated housewife, Celie will maintain the basic minimum though she may prefer the non-dominated life. Looked at in this light, the problem of preference for the worse becomes a new way of stating the objection I discussed last chapter: that WBM identifies a basic minimum that is simply *too low*.

However, this objection can be rebutted. Notice that either theories of welfare will, or will not, accept the possibility of "content-based assessment" of valued projects. In other words, some will believe that, in terms of their welfare value, valued projects can be *assessed by the objective value of the projects themselves*. On this sort of view, some projects will maintain preference-independent value, others will not, and preference-independent value is a *pro tanto* determinant of the intrinsic value of such projects for persons. Other theories of welfare will refuse to evaluate valued projects based on content, but will instead rely simply on the preferences of the individual whose projects they are.

The dispute between welfarists who accept content-based assessment of valued projects and those that do not is long, deep, and something I won't settle here. However, it is certainly true that *either* valued projects can be assessed by their content *or* they cannot. But in either case, a welfarist basic minimum survives.

3.5.1. Preference for the worse and content-based assessment

Some will accept that valued projects can be assessed for their welfare value on the basis of content. Some valued projects (like, e.g., being an excellent dancer) will maintain preference-independent value, others (like, e.g., being a dominated housewife) will not. However, if we accept this sort of view, an obvious and immediate response to the problem of preference for the worse arises. Recall that an essential element of any basic minimum is the ability to draw a "dividing line" between lives that maintain some morally or evaluatively essential feature and lives that do not. WBM insists that the dividing line is between lives that do, and lives that do not, maintain a valued project. But if one accepts the possibility of content-based assessment, one might draw the dividing line differently: between lives that maintain valued projects of *preference-independent value*, and those that do not. Consider, then:

Welfarist Basic Minimum 2 (WBM2): A achieves the basic minimum over the course of a life *l* if and only if A successfully achieves or maintains a valued project of sufficient preference-independent welfare value in *l*.[44]

WBM2 insists that valued projects must be of preference-independent value if their fulfillment is to constitute the basic minimum. WBM2 solves the problem of preference for the worse. One might declare that Celie, no matter how deeply she values a life in which she is dominated or treated shabbily, cannot maintain the basic minimum simply given the worthlessness of her project. Of course, WBM2 insists that to achieve the basic minimum Celie must successfully maintain a valued project. But a particular valued project *cannot* be of welfare value sufficient to maintain the basic minimum unless that project is also of sufficient preference-independent welfare value. This solves the problem of preference for the worse.

In interpreting WBM2, two points are worth noting. First, the account of preference-independent value is left open. One might insist that preference-independent value is to be identified as being in accordance with human dignity, nature, or "truly human functioning" (*modulo* my arguments against such possibilities in the previous chapter). Alternatively, one might identify the preference-independent value of valued projects by means of some form of objective list. Second, WBM2 is ecumenical between substantive theories of welfare, just as WBM was. For instance, Weak Strong Subjectivism holds that though the fact that *p* is valued by A is necessary and sufficient for *p* to be of value for A, Weak Strong Subjectivism can declare that the basic minimum requires one not simply to achieve a project one values, but also requires a valued project of preference-independent value. Celie, in other words, is benefited by being a dominated housewife because she values this project. But without maintaining a project that is of sufficient objective value, her life – no matter how many other things she achieves – is not good enough to maintain the basic minimum. Weak Subjectivism, as opposed to Weak Strong Subjectivism, might accept an even stronger claim. Weak Subjectivism needn't declare that Celie's achievement of the projects she actually values is of any benefit to her at all: Weak Subjectivism could say that Celie is benefited *only* when obtaining a

[44] If one prefers the time-relative version of WBM, WBM2 can be translated *mutatis mutandis*.

valued project of preference-independent value. Both Weak Subjectivism and Weak Strong Subjectivism can accept WBM2, and hence can plausibly respond to the problem of preference for the worse. Furthermore – as must be fairly obvious – an objectivist can also accept WBM2. Indeed, an objectivist can either agree with Weak Strong Subjectivism – and claim that being a dominated housewife does benefit Celie, but not enough to obtain the basic minimum – or agree with Weak Subjectivism – and claim that the fulfillment of Celie's preferences for the worse is of no independent welfare value. WBM2 remains widely ecumenical.

WBM2 is thus an option for theories of welfare that accept content-based assessment of valued projects. I leave this possibility fully open, and will indicate in the remainder of the book points at which further discussions will require modification in light of WBM2 rather than WBM. However, I do want to offer a few words in favor of accepting WBM even for theories that allow content-based assessment of valued projects. For starters, whatever else her life is actually like, Celie's life has a self-directed meaning that she regards as being "worth it" rather than not, good rather than bad, etc., in a way that reflects her true conception of the good. As I have so far argued, this is no minor welfare achievement. There may be other very good reasons to assist Celie, even to regard her situation as morally urgent. But she has something important that many other people lack: a life that maintains a self-directed meaning, one that, given her genuine values, contributes to her own assessment of the worthiness of her life. However her values come about, whatever her values really are, they are deeply and essentially *hers*. Thus the difference between deep adaptation and shallow adaptation is of the essence. For a person who lacks shallow adaptive preferences, any life she leads that maintains the basic minimum is genuinely valued. The activities of this life can be said to have a shared meaning, one that this person believes is valuable for her, lived within the context of a life she (coherently and completely) believes is worth living. Viewed in such a light, I have a very hard time accepting the claim that WBM sets the basic minimum too low.

Fair enough, it might be said, when viewed in isolation. But is this really plausible for Celie, even if she regards her project as contributing to an assessment of her life as worth living? I think so. Consider again a simple trade-off of the sort we considered in the previous chapter. Take Glen, who has no valued project at all, but could potentially maintain such a project. Now compare Glen to Celie, to whom we could grant a further valued project of preference-independent value. It seems to me that if we are concerned only with the *promotion of valuable states*, distributional priority ought to go to Glen. Celie, rather than Glen, maintains a life of self-directed meaning that she actually regards as valuable. Glen does not. It seems to me that the dividing line between people who do and do not maintain valued projects is of greater moral significance than the dividing line between people who do and do not maintain projects of preference-independent value. If that is correct, we should accept the claim that Celie maintains the basic minimum. Again, the conceptual structure of any basic minimum looms large: the basic minimum *ought* to be low, low enough to plausibly support upward distribution.

One final problem should be explored. In the face of the problem of preference for the worse, WBM seems to have a frightful moral implication. It would appear that the moral reason to establish the basic minimum could morally justify treating a person like Celie *so shabbily*, or justify subjecting her to such strong brainwashing, that the shabby projects she actually ends up maintaining are a *central* (or "deep") part of her conception of the good, rendering her activities constitutive of the basic minimum. But it seems wrong to say that such actions could be morally justified. In response, WBM can sensibly reject the troubling claim that a person might be morally permitted to engage in such brainwashing for the sake of the achievement of the basic minimum. If we accept the possibility of content-based assessment, we can quite sensibly claim that Celie would be better-off maintaining the basic minimum with a project of preference-independent value than she would be maintaining the basic minimum *as a dominated housewife*. Insofar as one always has a moral reason to provide a person with a better, rather than a worse, life, one always has greater reason (given that we are assuming the possibility of content-based assessment of valued projects) to provide an individual with the achievement of an objectively valuable valued project rather than one that is objectively valueless. If that is right, even if we accept WBM, there is far stronger reason simply in terms of the promotion of valuable states to grant a *more* valuable achievement of the basic minimum than a less valuable achievement of the basic minimum. In addition, we might perfectly well accept reasons not to brainwash or indoctrinate people into living lives they would not otherwise have valued. One might suggest, for instance, that tinkering with someone's conception of the good in this way is a fundamental lack of respect or a violation of that person's autonomy.[45] We can embrace sensible moral restrictions on brainwashing and shabby treatment even if such brainwashing is a means to

[45] See, for instance, Pogge (2001), 37.

the achievement of the basic minimum. Again, the promotion of valuable states need not be all there is to morality.

These considerations seem to me to provide good reason for any substantive theory of welfare, even those that accept content-based assessment, to accept WBM rather than WBM2. But I cannot pretend to have offered anything like a knock-down argument here. Hence I leave WBM2 open for those who are genuinely concerned about preference for the worse. Very little in the remaining chapters will require substantive translation. Whether one accepts WBM or WBM2, however, is less important than the general lesson: a welfarist basic minimum can survive the challenge of preference for the worse, or the claim that the basic minimum is set too low.

3.5.2. Preference for the worse and no content-based assessment

Now assume that we reject content-based assessment. If so, the only relevant facts concerning the merits of valued projects are the extent to which they are genuinely valued. And if *that's* right, Erin's project and Celie's project are of equivalent welfare value (assuming that they are valued to the same extent). Under these conditions, preference for the worse is nonsensical: no valued projects are worse than any others. If such a view is correct, WBM seems the obvious choice.

One might think this is a problem. After all, this would entail that Celie maintains the basic minimum no less than Erin. Surely this is wrong! But if we are genuinely rejecting the claim that Erin's project is any better than Celie's in terms of its content, this is exactly the *right* conclusion. Few would disagree that Erin's great achievement in painting would constitute a life that maintains the basic minimum. But to say that a life that is *just as good as Erin's*, i.e., Celie's, does not maintain the basic minimum one must say that Erin maintains, but Celie does not, some particular non-welfare good *g* that is essential for the basic minimum, but that makes *no difference whatsoever* to the quality of Erin's life. This smacks of the sort of fetishism displayed by the capabilities approach I discussed in Chapter 1: a commitment to the provision of non-welfare goods even when such provision will do nothing to alter the relative quality of lives. But this is surely morally problematic if anything is. If we really agree that there can be no content-based prudential assessment of projects, so long as they genuinely value their projects to an equivalent degree, Erin and Celie live lives that are equally good, and hence it seems correct to say that they equally maintain the basic minimum. WBM survives.

That Erin and Celie live equally good lives, simply on the basis of their own conceptions of the good, may sound absurd, even obscene. This, it seems to me, is less a problem for WBM than it is for the claim that we should reject content-based assessment of welfare goods. However, as I argued in the previous section, there remains good reason to accept WBM even if we accept the possibility of content-based assessment. WBM guarantees not just a life that a person regards as worth living, but a life that includes a valued project that unifies, and provides a self-directed meaning to, one's life and activities. This seems to me a significant welfare achievement, one that we would be unwise to allow the basic minimum to exceed. I leave WBM2 open for those who disagree.

3.6. CONCLUSION

Recall the welfarist's dilemma: either one accepts *The Basic Minimum as Proto-autonomy*, and one succumbs to the problem of adaptive preferences, or one rejects *The Basic Minimum as Proto-autonomy*, and one commits to forcing people to live lives they do not value. But I have shown that this is in fact no dilemma whatsoever. In fact, one can respect individuals' conceptions of the good only if one *also* avoids adaptive preferences. And we respect conceptions of the good and avoid adaptive preferences by better understanding the nature of conceptions of the good. To this end, I have offered a theory of a person's true conception of the good: PC. In addition, I have shown that there is very little reason for a welfarist theory of the basic minimum to fear the problem of preference for the worse. First, preference for the worse is not a genuine problem for WBM, even if we allow for content-based assessment. Second, even *if* we accept that preference for the worse is a problem for WBM, it is not a problem for welfarist theories of the basic minimum on the whole: one can simply accept WBM2. No matter the content of an individual's genuine preferences, maintaining a valued project is a crucial and central welfare achievement; it is the maintenance of a life of unified, self-directed meaning one *genuinely* values.

CHAPTER 4

The intrinsic value of the basic minimum

So far, I have offered a critical analysis of the most important non-welfarist approaches to the basic minimum. I have also argued that at least one welfarist approach (captured by WBM, or the view that the basic minimum is the maintenance of a valued project) can avoid the welfarist's dilemma. But even if we accept WBM (or, in response to the problem of preference for the worse, WBM2), much remains to be done in providing a full welfarist approach to the basic minimum. Though we may know what the minimum threshold is, a well-formed conception of the basic minimum must also account for its comparative moral importance. In other words, we must address a problem I hereby dub "the problem of weight": we must understand the comparative moral weight of the basic minimum against non-minimum states.

To some, an inquiry into the moral importance of the basic minimum might seem quaint. After all, we're talking about a basic *minimum*: surely the most natural way to understand its significance is to insist that the promotion of the basic minimum is, in all cases, of paramount or overriding moral importance. Of course, given BM3, this is not conceptually required: a basic minimum need only take weak moral priority. But surely the most natural view is that the basic minimum (whether welfarist or otherwise) should be the dominant moral concern. This proposal is reflected in the general motivation for a basic minimum offered by Stuart White (among others), and in Nussbaum's *Guarantee*.

Unfortunately, matters are not so simple. One can distinguish two ways in which the basic minimum might have overriding moral importance. The first, the aforementioned *Guarantee*, insists on an overriding moral reason to guarantee the basic minimum for all. The second, which I shall call *Maximize*, posits an overriding moral reason to promote the achievement of the basic minimum (in other words, the basic minimum is the dominant moral concern, but is not a *guarantee*). Both accounts fail: they are simply too strong. Instead, we must allow that the basic minimum can be traded-off against other valuable states of persons. I argue that the best strategy for approaching the problem of the *moral* weight of the basic minimum is to first consider its relative intrinsic value, i.e., how *good* is the basic minimum in comparison to other potentially valuable states? This topic will comprise the bulk of this chapter.

Before I begin, however, I want to say a few words about the overall argument of the chapter, and what I do and do not attempt to accomplish. My main goal in this chapter is to establish two separable theses concerning the relative intrinsic value of the basic minimum (detailed in §4.2). However, the arguments for both theses will rely on general principles of impersonal and personal value I find plausible or natural. And while in most cases I will offer some motivating rationale, I will also rely to a great extent on my own considered judgments. I make no apology for doing so; I hope and believe that the resulting view will be, all things considered, attractive especially in comparison to alternatives, and will – together with the moral principle defended in Chapter 5 – make for a satisfying representation of the traditional overriding view. Nevertheless, as I have so far noted, my approach to the basic minimum is *modular*. Though the argument of this chapter builds on the general account of human well-being I develop in Chapters 2 and 3, nothing in the remaining chapters (nor, for that matter, in the previous ones) depends on the acceptance of the view I advocate here. Hence if readers' considered judgments differ from mine at a crucial point (say, if one chooses to reject the plausibility of the sequence I discuss in §4.5.2), they are licensed to replace either or both of the theses I present here with one that better conforms to their own considered judgments (including, say, one of the options against which I argue in §4.6).

With this caveat in mind, the plan of the chapter runs as follows. The first part, comprising §§4.1–4.2, will discuss two standard accounts of the moral weight of the basic minimum and offer a strategy for progress in light of their failure. §§4.3–4.5 take up the intrinsic value of the basic minimum in comparison to *sub*-minimum welfare states. §§4.6–4.7 take up the intrinsic value of the basic minimum in comparison to *super*-minimum states. §4.8 concludes.

4.1. THE BASIC MINIMUM AS OVERRIDING

As stated above, it seems natural to believe that the moral weight of the basic minimum should be overriding. However, there are at least two interpretations of this natural instinct. The first, *Guarantee*, claims that political institutions, or moral agents more generally, have an overriding moral reason to establish the basic minimum for all. The second, *Maximize*, insists instead that one has a moral requirement to promote the achievement of the basic minimum to the greatest extent possible. Both approaches, I argue, fail.

4.1.1. Guarantee

Guarantee is one of the fundamental elements of Nussbaum's capabilities approach. *Guarantee* states that moral agents (most importantly for Nussbaum, political societies) have a moral reason to establish the basic minimum for all persons and that doing so is a moral requirement in all cases.

> [I]n some form all [ten basic capabilities] are held to be part of a minimum account of social justice: a society that does not guarantee these to all its citizens, at some appropriate threshold level, falls short of being a fully just society, whatever its level of opulence . . . In desperate circumstances, it may not be possible for a nation to secure them all up to the threshold level, but then it becomes a purely practical question what to do next, not a question of justice. The question of justice is already answered: justice has not been fully done here.[1]

Guarantee as stated is an implausible principle – taken literally, no just society could ever exist. *Guarantee* states that a failure in the possession of the basic minimum – any such failure – is a failure to fulfill one's moral obligations. But every society will have persons who, for one reason or another, cannot maintain the basic minimum. If this is the case, and the basic minimum must be guaranteed, no society will fulfill its moral obligations. Any society will have people with adolescent cancers or various genetic defects, say, who have no ability to achieve a valued project. But this is not a failure of justice.

Nussbaum understands the implausibility of these results, and suggests an alternative to the literal reading of *Guarantee*. In essence, Nussbaum allows that a just society will occasionally contain failures of the basic minimum because it is simply impossible to grant the basic minimum to individuals with, say, significant disabilities. Though tragic, such circumstances permit of options consistent with justice.[2] Nussbaum insists that

[1] Nussbaum (2006), 75, 175.

[2] Of a significantly impaired woman, "Sesha," she writes: "Society should strive to give her as many of the capabilities as possible directly; and where direct empowerment is not possible, society ought to give her the capabilities through a suitable arrangement of guardianship. But guardianship, however well designed, is not as good for Sesha as it would be to have the capabilities on her own. We have emphasized the capabilities on the list because they have truly human importance: we have evaluated

states can remain just even in the face of failures of the basic minimum if the state has guaranteed the "social conditions" of the basic minimum to all. Some of these social conditions will include, for instance, appointed guardians or proxies (especially for people with severe mental disabilities).[3]

To put Nussbaum's suggestion in a slightly different way, one might think that there are roughly two types of failure of the basic minimum. The first involves conditions of certain individuals (like, for instance, the severely mentally disabled, or persons who are born with genetic defects, etc.) that political agency could not correct. (This last clause is important: anytime someone could be granted the basic minimum they should be – even if this means correcting certain natural impairments, such as physical or mental illness.[4]) Call these "natural failures." "Social failures" are any failures of the basic minimum that are not natural failures, i.e., that are not the result of particular impairments of individuals. Thus, on Nussbaum's understanding, *Guarantee* yields two paths to injustice. In the first case, if a failure of the basic minimum obtains without an associated natural impairment, this is a failure to conform to overriding moral reasons; a failure of justice. However, in cases of natural failures, we ask: "[h]as the public political arrangement in which she lives extended to her the social basis of all the capabilities on the list,"[5] to the extent that *if she were not suffering from natural failure*, she would obtain the basic minimum? If the answer is no, the society in question is to that extent unjust. If the answer is yes, justice is compatible with failures of the basic minimum.

I am willing to grant that Nussbaum's proposal is successful in dealing with cases such as genetic illnesses or various forms of disability. But the division of failures of the basic minimum into "natural" and "social" is insufficient to salvage *Guarantee*. Consider the following case:

Tsunami: A large and destructive tsunami destroys the homes and farms of six people (A–F). Without access to food, the fast-approaching winter means their deaths. Unfortunately, there is no direct access to deliver food from outside: the society in question does not have the resources to fly them in, and all access roads

these options to function, and we say that they are really important and good. When someone does not attain them, this is an unhappy state of affairs, whether or not this is anyone's fault: the only way that Sesha can ever flourish is as a human being" (ibid., 193).

[3] Ibid., 193. Notice Nussbaum's use of the term "unhappy" rather than "unjust."

[4] Cf. Ibid., 193. Of Sesha, Nussbaum writes: "if we could cure her condition and bring her up to the capabilities threshold, that is what we would do, because it is good, indeed important, for a human being to be able to function in these ways. If such a treatment should become available, society would be obliged to pay for it, and would not be able to offer the excuse that she is impaired 'by nature'. And, further, if we could engineer the genetic aspects of it in the womb, so that she would not be born with impairments so severe, that, again, is what a decent society would do."

[5] Ibid., 193.

have been blocked. Even more unfortunately, the accessible resources are sufficient only to feed five of the six.

If *Guarantee* is true, assuming that these are the only two options, there is no option available consistent with justice. Political society is unjust no matter what it decides to do. In this case, Nussbaum's solution to the problems posed by disabled individuals is of no help: there are no natural impairments involved – no features of particular individuals that entail that they will fail the basic minimum. At least one person will fail the basic minimum because of a sheer lack of food. But why, we may ask, should such a flood turn a just society into an unjust one? It seems that according to *Guarantee*, no matter what it decides, this society is unjust – asking what should be done in this case is a "purely practical" question, rather than a question of justice.

Something has gone wrong here. At first glance, Nussbaum's view displays an internal tension. Nussbaum allows that societies have an escape clause in the case of failure of the basic minimum based on the physical or mental impairments of individuals. Because social systems cannot actually establish the basic minimum for them, social systems are just when they do the most that is in their power, viz., establish the social conditions, or social bases, of the basic minimum *rather than* eliminating all natural failures.[6] It appears that in the case of *natural failures*, Nussbaum wishes to allow that justice should be within reach. But why shouldn't this apply also in *some* cases of social failure, e.g., cases of resource impairment? Why shouldn't we say of *Tsunami* that there are options consistent with justice, just as there are options consistent with justice when it comes to natural impairments? I see very little ground for accepting a less stringent requirement of justice in the case of disabled or impaired persons while placing justice out of reach in other cases in which social or political systems couldn't have done better.

But leaving this point aside, Nussbaum's view here is clearly implausible. Though she claims that cases similar to *Tsunami* present only "practical" questions, it is worth wondering what is to answer them (Nussbaum herself does not offer a response). Surely there are right and wrong answers to these questions. It is not as if, in such a case, moral reasons simply *fall silent*. (To take an extreme case, it would surely be morally wrong to *murder* A–F; this is no mere "practical" question, but a question to which moral reasons respond.) But Nussbaum must claim that even if a society answers these

[6] I hereby ignore the point that establishing the social bases may be absolutely out of reach for some political societies given factors outside their control.

"practical" questions in precisely the morally appropriate way it remains unjust. This position is unduly burdensome and, frankly, unfair to societies that answer these "practical" questions in the right way. We should say, rather, that answering these "practical" questions correctly – however that might be – just *is* what justice requires in tragic cases. Though there are perhaps very good reasons to regard Indonesia as a state that fails the ideal of justice, the mere fact that so many were killed in the 2004 tsunami does not shed *additional* light on this fact.[7]

4.1.2. Maximize

Guarantee is not the only way to understand an overriding approach to the basic minimum. An alternative is a position I call *Maximize.* According to *Maximize*, one is morally required to promote the achievement of the basic minimum *to the greatest extent possible. Maximize* seems better placed than *Guarantee*: because *Maximize* insists only that the basic minimum be established for as many as possible, rather than that the basic minimum should be guaranteed to all, it needn't say that natural disasters, for instance, are failures of justice. Rather, what does entail a failure of justice, or a failure to conform to one's overriding moral reasons, is a failure to promote the basic minimum to the greatest extent one can. In *Tsunami*, there are options consistent with justice, i.e., to promote the basic minimum for the most possible.

But *Maximize*, though it is better placed with regard to our considered moral judgments than *Guarantee*, remains too strong. Consider:

Severe Disability: Elise suffers from a severe disability that makes the achievement of the basic minimum virtually impossible. However, she could maintain the basic minimum were she to be given a radical, and radically expensive, sequence of medical treatments. Doing so – assume – would require the development of a new technology which – though possible – would be so expensive as to require the expenditure of resources sufficient to rule out the promotion of all non-minimum goods for hundreds of millions of people.

[7] One might reply that my criticism of Nussbaum is unfair. After all, I appear to be evaluating her position in abstraction from her own theory of the basic minimum, viz., the capabilities approach. Two points. First, even if *Guarantee* is plausible when conjoined to Nussbaum's preferred theory of the basic minimum, there are other reasons to reject her preferred theory of the basic minimum, and hence (given what I have said so far) reasons to reject *Guarantee.* Second, it seems to me that *Guarantee* is no less implausible when conjoined to Nussbaum's preferred theory of the basic minimum. *Tsunami* is a problem for the capabilities approach no less than for WBM. Even on her view, a number of problems that could not have been prevented will affect any given society's ability to provide the ten basic capabilities, yielding the same problems that confront *Guarantee* when conjoined to WBM.

For *Maximize*, the reason to establish the basic minimum for Elise overrides all other moral reasons to promote any other non-minimum goods for others. But stated this way, *Maximize* is not plausible. In *Severe Disability*, the particular society in question could establish the basic minimum for Elise, but her basic minimum cannot be had at reasonable cost in terms of other, non-minimum goods. It seems quite wrong to say that the achievement of the basic minimum for a single individual would outweigh the achievement of all sub-minimum goods for any finite number of individuals, *and* all super-minimum goods for any finite number of individuals. The basic minimum is surely important, but it is not *that* important.

One might respond on behalf of *Maximize*. I have so far assumed that *Maximize* insists that the promotion of the basic minimum is overriding, i.e., is itself decisive with respect to the promotion of all other valuable states (even when taken together). But one might reject the claim that the promotion of the basic minimum is overriding and instead believe that it must be balanced, though perhaps heavily weighted, against the promotion of non-minimum states. I believe this is a plausible route to follow, but along this route lies the death of *Maximize*. In balancing the importance of the minimum against non-minimum states, one no longer has a moral obligation to maximize the achievement of the basic minimum. The basic minimum becomes simply one important, promotion-worthy state among others that must be weighted appropriately. On this proposal, the relative moral significance of the basic minimum is left indeterminate.

We should reject the natural, though mistaken, interpretation of the basic minimum as morally overriding. But in rejecting *Guarantee* and *Maximize* we must look for an alternative solution to the *problem of weight*, one that, ideally, can accommodate at least *much* of what is plausible about the traditional overriding approach (without, one hopes, its excesses). Indeed, this question cannot be simply put off or ignored. Without a solution to the problem of weight, we cannot adequately characterize the moral structure of the basic minimum.

4.2. STRATEGY

How are we to make progress on the problem of weight? How are we to determine, in more or less precise fashion, how important the basic minimum is in comparison to other social goals? I propose the following strategy. Though such an inquiry may not settle all moral questions that surround the basic minimum, we certainly make progress on the problem of weight by determining the relative goodness or intrinsic value of the basic minimum in comparison to non-minimum goods. After all, there appears to be at least a *pro tanto* moral reason to favor *p* over *q* if it can be established that *p* is *more valuable* than *q*. It seems a reasonable default presumption, then, that if the axiological weight of the basic minimum in relation to some non-minimum good *q* is *n*, the basic minimum should have the same relative moral weight (though, of course, this default presumption could be overridden by a number of potentially important moral reasons). Therefore a sensible place to begin an examination of the basic minimum's relative moral importance is to consider the basic minimum's relative *worth*.

In this chapter, I defend two general claims. These claims run as follows. First:

Lexical: the intrinsic value of the basic minimum lexically dominates the intrinsic value of sub-minimum welfare goods.

Lexical is strong; indeed, *Lexical* grants the strongest possible axiological priority to the basic minimum in comparison to sub-minimum goods: a single achievement of the basic minimum is better than any finite amount of sub-minimum welfare goods. Second, I defend:

Prioritarianesque: Super-minimum project-improvements for the better-off are less intrinsically valuable in comparison to the basic minimum than super-minimum project-improvements for the worse-off.

Prioritarianesque – as the name suggests – holds that the basic minimum takes a roughly prioritarian weighting against valued projects above the minimum: the better-off your are, the less intrinsically valuable your valued project is in comparison to the basic minimum. Putting *Lexical* and *Prioritarianesque* together, I defend a view that, at least in axiological terms, retains much of the traditional overriding approach to the basic minimum, including the lexical dominance of the basic minimum in comparison to *sub*-minimum states.

My argumentative strategy runs as follows. Both *Prioritarianesque* and *Lexical* are statements of impersonal value: the extent to which the basic minimum improves a state of affairs *tout court*. However, surely an important aspect of impersonal value is *personal* value: the extent to which the basic minimum is better *for people*. One default position is that *p* is impersonally better than *q* to the extent that *p* is better *for people* than *q*. This follows from a plausible "person-affecting" claim about value, i.e., that the improvement of states of affairs is a function of the improvement of the welfare of persons in those states of affairs.[8] But even if this is incorrect, relative welfare value (or "personal" value) is surely one important aspect of impersonal value. And this is where my argument for *Lexical* will begin. I argue that *Lexical* is a natural conclusion in light of a plausible thesis concerning the relative welfare value of the basic minimum in comparison to satisfactions. After considering an important objection to *Lexical*, I argue that *Prioritarianesque* is also a natural result of an inquiry into the comparative welfare value of valued projects for persons at higher and lower levels of welfare.

Before I begin, a terminological note. In discussing the prudential weight of the basic minimum, one important topic is the relative weight of the basic minimum against other marginal project-improvements of – in terms I shall adopt here – greater and lesser "magnitude." Hence, it is important to understand what this means and, relatedly, what it means for one person to be better-off in terms of the achievement of valued projects. This question turns out to be surprisingly difficult to answer in a way that is fully ecumenical between subjective and objective theories of the good and so I won't offer a general theory of magnitude here. But it seems to me sensible to say that any theory of the good will choose from among the following two methods of judging the magnitude of a given project-improvement. First, any individual's conception of the good (complete, coherent) will display preferences among projects and among groups of projects given experience with the attendant value data. Hence one might judge the magnitude of a project-improvement by the extent to which this project-improvement satisfies the preferences of the person whose project-improvement it is. Second, for those who accept content-based assessment of valued projects, a project-improvement might be of greater magnitude than another when it maintains greater preference-independent value. In principle, a substantive theory of well-being could mix and match, and adopt different weightings of, these dimensions. I will remain ecumenical here, and refer generically to "project-improvements," and their greater or lesser magnitude; the reader is free to fill in the details as appropriate. (When I refer to "project-improvements," I mean marginal improvements among *valued* projects, unless otherwise noted.) Furthermore, I will speak generically of a person's being "better-off" or "worse-off" in terms of valued projects. A's being better-off in terms of project-achievement than B will be assessed along the same dimensions as the question of magnitude: the satisfaction of preferences among projects, and the preference-independent

[8] See, for instance, Holtug (2007a), 129.

value one's projects maintain. Again, different theories of welfare will fill in the details in different ways; I remain neutral here.

4.3. THE BASIC MINIMUM AND SUB-MINIMUM GOODS

There are two potential marginal welfare benefits one could obtain while failing the basic minimum, both of which must be explored before any broad conclusion about the relative intrinsic value of the basic minimum can be drawn.[9] Because WBM claims that the basic minimum is the achievement of a valued project, one can improve in terms of satisfactions without maintaining the basic minimum. Hence to properly determine the intrinsic value of the basic minimum in comparison to sub-minimum states, we must first better understand the value of the basic minimum in comparison to *satisfactions*. In addition, because WBM declares that the basic minimum is the achievement of a *valued* project, marginal improvements among *un*valued projects are also available to those who do not obtain the minimum. For instance, someone might fail to value global project *p* and global project *q*, but might prefer *p* to *q*. If so, the move from *q* to *p* is a marginal sub-minimum welfare benefit, i.e., an unvalued project-improvement. Alternatively, for those who accept content-based assessment of valued projects, one might fail to value *p* and *q*, but it might be that *q* is more objectively valuable than *p*; hence a move from *p* to *q* might be a marginal welfare benefit. Hence to determine the relative goodness of the basic minimum, we must also determine the relative goodness of the basic minimum in comparison to improvements among *unvalued* projects.

4.3.1. Sub-minimum goods: satisfactions

The first category of sub-minimum goods to be weighed against the basic minimum is sub-minimum satisfactions. Given *Thesis*, we should say that

[9] If one accepts WBM2, the number of marginal welfare benefits one can obtain without obtaining the basic minimum rises to three: satisfactions, unvalued project improvements, and valued project improvements that do not meet a "preference-independent" value threshold. I shall not discuss the third marginal benefit in much detail except to say that it does not seem to me to change the axiology I accept to any great degree. WBM2 is still compatible with *Lexical*: one would expect that if the true "dividing line" is between lives that maintain objectively valuable projects and those that do not, sub-minimum valued project improvements should be fungible against satisfactions. If so, the argument offered in §4.3.2 applies *mutatis mutandis*. I offer this suggestion tentatively, however, and leave it to those who favor WBM2 to provide a more substantive account of the relative value of the basic minimum in comparison to valued project improvements of insufficient preference-independent value.

valued projects (and hence the basic minimum) are prudentially more important than satisfactions, including sub-minimum satisfactions. One possibility, when considering the relative welfare value of the basic minimum in comparison to satisfactions, is to adopt a very strong relative weighting. Consider, then:

Thesis:* the welfare value of the basic minimum lexically dominates the welfare value of satisfactions.

I think we should accept *Thesis**. Take the following case:

Greta: Greta maintains no valued projects, but would value, and could become, a very successful "outsider artist." Becoming such an artist would unify and provide a shared explanation and meaning to Greta's activities over the long term; in short, it would qualify as a global project. Alternatively, Greta could eschew becoming a successful artist in favor of n satisfactions (say, n moments of mild pleasure).

Greta has two options. She could either obtain a valued project, i.e., being an outsider artist, or grab some minor satisfactions. In considering Greta's case, the obvious question becomes not the point at which n satisfactions are sufficient to outweigh her potential valued project, but whether there is *any* n, such that n satisfactions is sufficient to outweigh this project. The answer to this question seems clear: there is no such n. For Greta, though minor satisfactions would improve her life over neither being an artist nor achieving any satisfactions, it seems decidedly implausible to say that, faced with the possibility of maintaining a valued project over the course of her life, it would be better simply to opt for the life lacking in valued, self-directed meaning, whatever the value of n.

One can see this conclusion by considering a further case. Take again Velleman's politician. Assume that, for A, being a successful politician is a valued project, the pursuit of which resulted in failure. We might be tempted to ask ourselves what might *compensate*, in terms of A's life quality, for his failure to be a successful politician. In other words, and more pointedly, could it be the case that A's failure to be a successful politician could be compensated by *some* amount of satisfactions, rather than valued projects? I submit that the answer to this question is no. Imagine that A fails to become a successful politician, but has the opportunity to become a successful writer, a project he values. Imagine also that A could, instead, refrain from developing any valued projects, but instead simply pursues momentary cheap thrills that are in no way narratively unified. Of course, any halfway plausible theory of welfare will hold that the achievement of pleasure (even if it's a simple cheap thrill) is a welfare benefit. But, plausibly, there is *no amount* of cheap thrills that would compensate A for his failure to be a successful politician to the same degree as becoming a successful writer, especially when we consider that otherwise A would achieve no valued projects whatever. Recall that the maintenance of valued projects seems to be the primary data by which we understand our lives and their quality: to maintain a valued project means that one's activities participate in a shared, self-directed meaning over the course of a life. I doubt very much that a life without such meaning could be better than a life *with* the sort of unity provided by a valued project. If so, it would seem, the value of the basic minimum lexically dominates the value of satisfactions. The alternative suggestion seems crass, at best.

Of course, there is a limit to the plausibility of such a claim. For instance, someone might maintain a project which, for this person, would constitute the achievement of the basic minimum. One could imagine, however, that this project reaches a point at which success is so costly in terms of satisfactions (say, massive and constant headaches) that under these conditions it seems reasonable for such a person to give up this project in favor of restoring satisfactions. But my view is compatible with this sensible suggestion. As I noted in Chapter 2, projects are valued or unvalued *in context*. Some might value some project p in circumstances C but not in circumstances D. Given sensible assumptions about the psychology of valuing, we should expect that any successful project with a correspondingly extreme cost in momentary satisfactions would *not* be valued. This does not show that satisfactions are fungible against the basic minimum; it merely shows that sometimes satisfactions, or the lack thereof, can affect the extent to which any particular global project is a *valued* project.[10]

However, if a person, even with these accompanying headaches, views a particular project favorably, and sees the life in which it is led as being worth living, we should hesitate to say that this project could be traded-off for mere momentary goods. Insofar as valued projects constitute the major, long-term elements of our lives, elements that explain and provide our activities and decisions with a shared, self-directed meaning, we should refuse to trade-off such projects for a life barren of such meaning (though perhaps filthy with satisfactions). This conclusion seems to me to be a

[10] Consider, for instance, a project someone might value, a project of "total headache avoidance." (This project is assuredly an odd one, and is likely to be ruled out for those who prefer WBM2 to WBM, but leave this aside.) In this case, even a single headache would eliminate the fulfillment of such a project. However, this again does not show that the satisfaction of headache relief is intrinsically fungible against the achievement of the basic minimum. Rather, it shows only that in some cases the suffering of a headache can be instrumentally damaging to the fulfillment of a valued project.

natural, if not strictly *forced*, result of our reflections in Chapter 2: that the quality of our lives is determined, first and foremost, by the extent to which we maintain valued projects.

4.3.2. Sub-minimum goods: marginal, unvalued project-improvements

I claim that, at least in terms of welfare value, the basic minimum lexically dominates satisfactions, and hence sub-minimum satisfactions. However, to determine the proper comparative welfare value of the basic minimum against *all* sub-minimum benefits, one must consider the welfare value of the basic minimum in comparison to a marginal improvement among *unvalued* global projects. For instance, one might be better-off living according to some unvalued projects rather than others; because I prefer to be a Grand Central Station janitor rather than to be the king's food taster, the former is better for me than the latter, though I fail to value both. Hence becoming a Grand Central Station janitor, which replaces the project of being the king's food taster, is a marginal welfare benefit.

The relative welfare value of the basic minimum against unvalued project-improvements is not as complex an inquiry as might first be thought. Indeed, *Thesis** helps answer it. Specifically, it seems right that there is *some* amount of satisfactions – whatever it is – that could make up for the loss of an unvalued project improvement. Imagine, for instance, that I am the king's food taster. However, I could either be made better-off by becoming a Grand Central Station janitor or by living a life that is otherwise extremely rich in mere momentary enjoyments. Could it be that there is *some* amount of momentary enjoyments that is better for me than an unvalued project-improvement? Though this question is to some degree esoteric, I maintain that the answer is yes: surely it's the case that *some* amount of satisfactions could compensate for the loss of an *unvalued* project improvement. After all, though I prefer being a Grand Central Station janitor under the properly specified conditions to being the king's food taster, I either don't regard my life as a Grand Central Station janitor as worth living, or I don't see that project as *contributing* to the worthiness of my life as a whole. Given my attitude toward my project, given that it is not *valued* by me, there is surely *some* amount of, say, momentary hedonic satisfactions or other, more momentary preferences satisfied that could make up for the loss of unvalued project improvements, whatever their magnitude. (In other words, for any m, there is some n such that n satisfactions are better than a magnitude m unvalued project-improvement.)

But if unvalued project-improvements are fungible against satisfactions, and satisfactions are *non*-fungible against the basic minimum, it must also be the case that unvalued project-improvements are *non*-fungible against the basic minimum. This claim is reflective of the transitivity of the "is better than" relation. Assume "is better than" is transitive. Now assume that for some *m*, an unvalued project-improvement of magnitude *m* for B is better than B's achievement of the basic minimum. If this holds, and if there is some *n* satisfactions that is better than an unvalued project-improvement of magnitude *m* (by the fungibility of satisfactions and unvalued project-improvements), *n* satisfactions for B must be better than B's achievement of the basic minimum. But this violates *Thesis**, and hence we must reject the claim that there is some magnitude unvalued project-improvement that can outweigh the achievement of the basic minimum.

This claim is susceptible to the following objection. There may be very little difference between a project that is *barely* valued by a given individual and one that is *barely* unvalued. Assume that I barely value a given project *p*, and barely do not value a given project *q*. But it could be that *p* and *q* are nearly identical projects, differing in only a few minor points (say, one or two minor annoyances). If this is correct, why should *p* be better than any magnitude *m* of *q*-like projects? This objection, however, does not fully make clear the crucial evaluative difference between *p* and *q*. At some point, small differences in projects will change my attitude toward them enough to render them unvalued. But though these differences may be small in descriptive terms, they are very large in evaluative terms. Maintaining a valued project means being able to look at the projects one adopts as being contributors to a life's worthiness to be led. In the current example, *p* provides my life with a narrative unity that resonates with me. *q*, though it may be very nearly identical, does not. But if this is correct, the evaluative difference between *p* and *q* is no minor matter. To believe that the central element of my life's story, and the central explanation of my life's activities, is *good for me*, in a coherent and complete way, makes a tremendous evaluative difference to the quality of my life. Small differences may determine my relative attitude toward *p* and *q*. But it is the attitude taken toward them, not their descriptive similarity or dissimilarity, that is essential.

Thus *Thesis** indirectly, but nevertheless significantly, draws a very sharp distinction between the welfare value of fulfilling a *valued* project and an *unvalued* project. But this distinction is independently motivated. There is something *special* about welfare goods that find – in the words of Peter Railton – an "internal resonance" in, or that are "compelling or attractive" to, the person for whom they are good.[11] It does seem to me correct to say that my valuing of individual projects – the internal resonance of *that particular project*, and the sense in which maintaining that project contributes to a life worth living – really is a crucial part of what makes projects evaluatively *special*, insofar as they are.

This "specialness" comes with a limit that I explore below. While I think it is plausible to believe that the achievment of *a* valued project (i.e., the achievement of the basic minimum) dominates unvalued, marginal project improvements, we should resist the claim that super-minimum project-improvements are lexically dominant in a similar way. To do so takes some doing, however; I address this in §4.5.2.

4.4. *LEXICAL*

*Thesis** states that, in terms of personal or prudential value, the basic minimum lexically dominates satisfactions. This claim indirectly implies that, again in terms of prudential value, the basic minimum also lexically dominates sub-minimum unvalued project-improvements. Furthermore, or so I shall argue here, *Thesis** implies *Lexical*, i.e., that the basic minimum lexically dominates sub-minimum goods when it comes to the *im*personal evaluation of states of affairs.

The argument runs as follows. Though it seems right to say that, in terms of prudential value, valued projects are non-fungible against momentary satisfactions, it would seem odd to say that these momentary satisfactions are impersonally non-fungible against *each other*. If so, the following principle seems plausible:

Impersonal Satisfaction Fungibility: for any two people A and B, and for any *n*, there is some *m* such that *m* satisfactions for A is better than *n* satisfactions for B.[12]

Now take two people, Jones and Brown. Assume that some amount of Jones's satisfactions, *s* ("*s*Jones") is impersonally better than Brown's basic minimum ("*bm*Brown"). Given *Impersonal Satisfaction Fungibility*, it must be the case that there is some *r* such that *r* Brown's satisfactions ("*r*Brown") is better than *s*Jones. But if this is correct, Brown's basic minimum is fungible against Brown's satisfactions. Assuming that "better than" is transitive, if *s*Jones is better than *bm*Brown, and *r*Brown is better than *s*Jones, it must be that *r*Brown is better than *bm*Brown. But, given *Thesis**, no amount

[11] Railton (2003), 47.

[12] This principle is plausible on its face, but is also supported by a sequence argument of the form considered in §4.5.1.

r of Brown's satisfactions is better than Brown's basic minimum.[13] Hence Brown's basic minimum must lexically dominate Jones's satisfactions. A parallel argument establishes the lexical dominance of Brown's basic minimum in comparison to Jones's unvalued project-improvements. Hence, *Lexical.*

Lexical implies a number of claims that may seem implausible at first glance. After all, how could it possibly be true that no amount of satisfactions for people who fail the basic minimum – people who are, incidentally, very poorly-off – could outweigh the basic minimum for only one person? Doesn't this entail that it would be better to sacrifice millions (billions!) to total misery than to sacrifice a basic minimum for a single person? *Lexical* seems to offer an affirmative answer to such questions, and hence might be thought too strong.

However, though I shan't gainsay the contrary considered judgments, it seems to me that the balance of reasons supports *Lexical.* First, *Lexical* represents at least one element of the traditional, overriding approach to the morality of the basic minimum. At least in terms of its relative intrinsic value, the basic minimum *overrides* sub-minimum states. Hence, if we have a reason to morally favor better states of affairs we have at least *a* reason to treat the promotion of the basic minimum as of absolute moral priority. (More on this in the next chapter.)

Second, and more importantly, any potential axiological weight of the basic minimum against competitor states is bound to have problematic consequences. To successfully solve the problem of weight, therefore, any particular view must do the best job of managing counterintuitive verdicts. But to reject *Lexical* simply on the basis of its own counterintuitive verdicts is to ignore problems that accompany its denial.

Compare two states: one state (S1) in which many of the very well-off, the best of the best, obtain a minor satisfaction. In the second (S2), the best-off

[13] Of course, *Thesis** does not strictly imply this conclusion. As I've so far indicated, "is better than" is really two different predicates, viz., "is personally better than" (or "is better than in terms of welfare value") and "is impersonally better than" (or "better *tout court*"). *Thesis** implies only that the basic minimum and satisfactions are not *intrapersonally* fungible. But if so, one might say that the *impersonal* fungibility of Jones's satisfactions against Brown's satisfactions, and the *impersonal* fungibility of Jones's satisfactions against Brown's basic minimum, imply only the *impersonal* fungibility of Brown's basic minimum against Brown's satisfactions, and does not violate *Thesis**. This is correct, but in light of *Thesis**, this proposal is wildly implausible. This view would have it that we can improve a state of affairs by doing nothing but making Brown worse-off, i.e., by treating his satisfactions as fungible against his achievement of the basic minimum. Hence we should accept that the fungibility of Brown's against Jones's satisfactions, and the fungiblity of Jones's satisfactions and Brown's basic minimum, entail that Brown's basic minimum is fungible against Brown's satisfactions.

don't get this benefit, but one additional person obtains the basic minimum. S2 seems better. Indeed, this judgment is robust: there can be *no* number of extremely minor satisfactions (such as the relief of an extremely minor headache) for the best-off that could outweigh the achievement of the basic minimum for one. After all, not only are these individuals very well-off, but it is also the case that the welfare benefits they receive are absolutely insignificant in comparison to the maintenance of a life of valued and self-directed meaning. However, given *Impersonal Satisfaction Fungibility*, there is some amount of satisfactions for very well-off individuals that will outweigh any amount of satisfactions for very poorly-off individuals. But if that's correct, and "better than" is transitive, to deny that minor goods for the best-off could outweigh the basic minimum for a single person, we must also say that the basic minimum for a single person outweighs satisfactions for individuals who are below the minimum.[14]

To deny *Lexical*, one must either deny that "better than" is transitive, deny *Impersonal Satisfaction Fungibility*, or accept the conclusion that some number of very minor satisfactions for extremely well-off individuals are better than the achievement of the basic minimum for one person. Of course, some have denied that "better than" is transitive.[15] But this view comes with a remarkable number of puzzling and problematic implications.[16] One might try instead to deny *Impersonal Satisfaction Fungibility*. But this also seems hard to do, especially in light of the possibility of so-called "sequence arguments," which I consider in the following section. Furthermore, one could accept that some number of very minor satisfactions for extremely well-off individuals might outweigh the basic minimum for a single individual. But, again, this conclusion seems quite implausible. Indeed, it smacks of a traditionally loathed trade-off in moral theory: the possibility that we might kill one person to save billions from a minor headache.[17] And though the acceptance of this possibility says nothing about killing, it does say that it is better to trade-off what is the most central element of human well-being for a person, even in its most basic form, for the furtherance of minor satisfactions (like the relief of very minor headaches) for the best-off. This verdict is no less loathsome.

[14] Of course, there are other ways out of this proposal. For my purposes, however, I am assuming that satisfactions for individuals of a fixed welfare level are interpersonally aggregative, and that these satisfactions do not permit of a value limit. Both these assumptions are plausible. See, for instance, Dorsey (2009), 37–9.

[15] See Rachels (1998), Temkin (1996).

[16] For the most puzzling, see Norcross (2002), 308–9. See also Dorsey (2009), 38n6.

[17] See, for instance, Thomson (1990), 169. See also Kamm (1993), 101.

I recognize that *Lexical* is very strong, perhaps stronger than many will care for. However, the alternatives are no less implausible, and *Lexical* seems to me supported by a robust conception of the nature of human well-being. If so, *modulo* two objections to be considered directly, the balance of reasons requires that we accept *Lexical*, warts and all.

4.5. TWO OBJECTIONS TO *LEXICAL*

This section responds to two objections to *Lexical*. Of course, there are many more than two; I limit myself simply for the sake of space. However, I should note that I consider a number of arguments against a similar principle elsewhere.[18]

4.5.1. The sequence

To defend *Lexical*, one must defend the existence of lexical priority relations. And the most important objection to lexical priority relations is the classic *sequence* argument, given voice here by Alastair Norcross:

> For each misfortune short of the worst possible one, there is a worse misfortune that can be individually outweighed by a sufficient number of the lesser one. In particular, it seems plausible that there is some misfortune short of death, perhaps some kind of mutilation, that can, if suffered by enough people, outweigh one death. Consider now a sequence of judgments, *S*, that begins as follows: one death is better than n^1 mutilations; n^1 mutilations are better than n^2 *x*s (where *x* is some misfortune less bad than mutilation). *S* continues with the first term of each comparison being identical to the second term of the previous comparison, until we reach the last two comparisons: n^{m-2} broken ankles are better than n^{m-1} mild ankle sprains; n^{m-1} mild ankle sprains are better than n^m mild headaches. If we have *S*, we can conclude, by the transitivity of "better than" that one death is better than n^m mild headaches. In which case, we must reject [lexical priorities].[19]

For any lexical dominance thesis, it must be the case that the value given lexically prior status can stop the sequence. But, as Norcross so graphically suggests, it would appear that finding a stopping point between the most-bad bad and the least-bad bad is extremely difficult and likely to be arbitrary. But I think the centrality of valued projects *qua* welfare goods helps to stop the sequence without sounding arbitrary. Indeed, in outlining his sequence, Norcross considers only the badness of these various states of bodily injury in and of themselves. He does not consider the effects of these various states

[18] See Dorsey (2009). [19] Norcross (1997), 138–9.

on *other* indices of value. But states of bodily injury can also affect the extent to which we achieve valued projects, in particular *the basic minimum*. But if we focus on *this* dimension of intrinsic value, that there should be such a sequence begins to look less plausible.

Assume that a broken ankle carries with it a certain degree of pain, while the next point in the sequence carries with it *slightly more* pain, but that a broken ankle *and not the very next point in the sequence* is compatible with the achievement of the basic minimum. I claim it is much less plausible to insist that the badness of broken ankles can outweigh the badness of the next point in the sequence, assuming that the next point in the sequence is not compatible with the achievement of the basic minimum. If the sequence is carried out only along the index of satisfactions, and leaving aside valued projects, it would appear that the sequence works: any disadvantage could be outweighed by enough of any other, insofar as satisfactions are clearly intrafungible. In other words, the sequence argument seems to establish, with very little doubt, a principle like *Impersonal Satisfaction Fungibility*. But intrinsic value, at least on my view, is more complicated: value breaks down (at least) into satisfactions, unvalued project-improvements, and valued project-improvements (including the achievement of the basic minimum). (Those who accept content-based assessment of valued projects, including those who accept WBM2, will suggest that value breaks down further: satisfactions, unvalued project-improvements, valued project-improvements, and valued (and unvalued) project-improvements of preference-independent value.) And when we import a further dimension of value to which these various bodily injuries may be instrumental, we find a stopping point: the basic minimum.

Of course, we might attempt to construct a Norcross-like sequence while taking seriously the distinction between indices of value. In other words, we may try to run a sequence while noting that certain points in the sequence are compatible with the achievement of the basic minimum, others are not. But this is difficult. The loss of the basic minimum entails the lack of the central element of human well-being, that which provides a unifying, narrative structure to a person's life and activities. If one wishes to construct a sequence running from the basic minimum to various minor satisfactions (including headache relief), the sequence goes wrong in its very first step: trading the basic minimum for satisfactions is worse. Stopping the sequence at the loss of the basic minimum is neither arbitrary nor unmotivated: valued projects are simply a different *sort* of good: they have an impact on a person's life quality that satisfactions could not outweigh.

4.5.2. A distributive objection and varieties of lexical dominance

Another objection to *Lexical* begins by noting that there is a difference between saying that the basic minimum should dominate sub-minimum goods and saying that *all* valued projects lexically dominate sub-minimum goods. Of course, *Lexical* itself says nothing about the weight of super-minimum projects against sub-minimum benefits, only about the weight of the basic minimum in comparison to sub-minimum benefits. However, there is a straightforward argument that *Lexical* implies not just the lexical dominance of the basic minimum against sub-minimum benefits, but the lexical dominance of *all* valued projects, including those for the very well-off.

This argument begins by noting a plausible claim about the evaluative relationship between project-improvements. Recall *Severe Disability*. Leaving aside the moral question, it seems wrong to say that the basic minimum for Elise is worth whatever the cost in super-minimum goods for any number of persons. Hence, it would seem sensible to accept the claim that the basic minimum is fungible, if not against satisfactions (as per *Thesis**), against project-improvements for the better-off. But if the basic minimum is fungible against project-improvements for the better-off, it would seem odd to say that some less significant good (i.e., some super-minimum project-improvement) should be non-fungible against higher level project-improvements. If this is correct, the following proposition seems natural:

Impersonal Project Fungibility: For any two people A and B, and for any n there is some m such that a magnitude m project-improvement for A is better than a magnitude n project-improvement for B.

Impersonal Project Fungibility is also supported by sequence arguments of the form we encountered in the last section. Here's an example: from the worst-off person A to the best-off person Z there is a finite sequence of individuals, each better-off than the last by a marginal amount. For any arbitrary person Q in that sequence it seems right to say that a project-improvement of a sufficient magnitude for Q will outweigh a project-improvement of any magnitude for the next-worse-off person. If there is such a sequence, *Impersonal Project Fungibility* follows.

However, if we accept *Impersonal Project Fungibility* and *Lexical*, trouble brews. Take the following case:

Roy, Gus, and Lee: Roy is extremely well-off, and obtains a number of extremely worthwhile valued projects and satisfactions. Gus does not maintain the basic minimum, but could obtain it. Lee, on the other hand, is extremely poorly-off and has no hope of obtaining the basic minimum, although he can get further satisfactions.

If we accept *Impersonal Project Fungibility*, there is some magnitude project-improvement for Roy (and perhaps others of Roy's welfare level) that would trade-off against Gus's basic minimum.[20] But if this is correct, it must be the case that Roy's valued projects *also* lexically dominate sub-minimum satisfactions. Assume that a project-improvement of magnitude *m* for Roy ("*m*Roy") is better than the basic minimum for Gus ("*bm*Gus") (*m*Roy>*bm*Gus). If we assume that Lee's satisfactions are fungible against Roy's project-improvements, there must be some amount *s* of Lee's satisfactions ("*s*Lee") that is better than *m*Roy (*s*Lee>*m*Roy). If so, by the transitivity of "better than," *s*Lee must be better than *bm*Gus. But given *Lexical*, *bm*Gus is better than *s*Lee. Hence we must reject the claim that there is some *s* such that *s*Lee>*m*Roy. But this seems to imply that Roy's project-improvements lexically dominate Lee's satisfactions. And hence we arrive at the result this objection seeks to pin on *Lexical*. (A parallel argument can be run when it comes to Lee's unvalued project-improvements.)

This result is problematic and should be avoided. Two reasons. First, it is *im*personally problematic. It seems right to say that, at some point, a single valued project for a very well-off person could be outweighed by, for instance, the relief of suffering for a large number of persons who are below the basic minimum. Second, it is *intra*personally problematic. The greater one's accumulation of valued projects, the greater the possibility that one could improve one's life *more* by pursuing satisfactions (in sufficient amount) rather than improvements among valued projects. The lexical dominance of the basic minimum seems plausibly motivated by the fact that without the basic minimum, one does not maintain a life of valued, self-directed meaning. This, it seems to me, drives much of our intuitive reactions in Greta's case, and the case of Velleman's failed politician. But once the basic minimum is maintained, any additional valued projects, though surely very significant welfare goods, will not spell the difference between a life that maintains a valued, self-directed meaning and a life that does not. Hence it is implausible to say that super-minimum project-improvements lexically dominate satisfactions. Or, at least, so say my considered judgments.

[20] *Impersonal Project Fungibility* is supported by the same sort of sequence arguments that supported *Impersonal Satisfaction Fungibility*. One potential argument against this view is offered by Roger Crisp, which I discuss in §4.7.4.

However, I think *Lexical* can escape. In particular, the argument for the claim that *Lexical* implies that Roy's valued project lexically dominates Lee's satisfactions contains a fatal error. The error is in taking the conclusion that *m*Roy must be better than *s*Lee (which is implied by *Lexical* and *Impersonal Project Fungibility*, for any *s*) to imply that *any* magnitude project-improvement for Roy is better than *any* amount of Lee's satisfactions. Consider two ways goods might be lexically dominant. One might call the first way:

Total Lexical Dominance: p totally lexically dominates *q* if and only if any amount of *p*, no matter how small, is better than any amount of *q*, no matter how large.

Now consider a somewhat weaker relation:

Mitigated Lexical Dominance: p mitigatedly lexically dominates *q* if and only if there is some amount *n* such that *np* is better than any amount of *q*, no matter how large.[21]

Mitigated lexical dominance can allow that there is some number *n*' ($n' < n$) such that a sufficient amount of *q* is better than *n'p*.

When it comes to individuals of high well-being levels, it seems to me right to say that, at least under certain conditions, project-improvements *should* trade-off against satisfactions. I think there is a limit to this fungibility; there is surely *some* magnitude *n* project-improvement for Roy against which Lee's satisfactions would not be fungible. At a certain magnitude, given their status as a central element of well-being, projects for individuals at any welfare level should not trade-off against satisfactions. But this claim would allow that some (magnitude $<n$) project-improvements for Roy could trade-off against Lee's satisfactions; this would allow the both personally and impersonally plausible value claim that satisfactions for the better-off, in certain cases, can outweigh project-improvements. Hence we should say that valued projects, including the basic minimum, *mitigatedly* lexically dominate sub-minimum satisfactions. For some *n*, a project-improvement for Roy of sub-*n* magnitude is fungible against some amount of satisfactions. If so, just because there is no amount of Lee's satisfactions that would be better than *m*Roy, it could be that *s*Lee is better than some lesser magnitude (*n*') project-improvement for Roy.

[21] Mitigated lexical dominance is reminiscent of the "discontinuity" principle discussed by Griffin (1989), 85–9, whereas total lexical dominance is reminiscent of Griffin's "trumping" relation.

But hang on. If we accept the mitigated lexical dominance of valued projects against satisfactions, how can we accept *Lexical*? *Lexical* implies the total, rather than mitigated, lexical dominance of the *basic minimum* against satisfactions. But how can we make this claim if valued projects (of which the basic minimum is one) do not totally lexically dominate satisfactions, but rather only mitigatedly lexically dominate satisfactions? Here's how: we should expect that, as a person gets better-off in terms of project-achievement, the fungibility of marginal project-improvements against satisfactions increases. Plausibly, as Roy gets better-off, additional valued projects become less central to his welfare and hence *more* fungible against satisfactions. I think the right way to express this idea is to say that as Roy gets better-off, *n* – the magnitude of his valued project-improvements that is no longer fungible against satisfactions – increases. As Roy gets worse-off, *n* decreases.

However, if we accept this, we can accept *Lexical*, *Impersonal Project Fungibility*, and also hold that Roy's valued projects of a lesser-than-*n* magnitude (*n*'Roy) are fungible against sub-minimum satisfactions. For Gus, we should expect that even a minute project-improvement will be better than any amount of satisfactions, i.e., for Gus, and for anyone else who fails the minimum, $n<1$. Hence the basic minimum, as per *Lexical*, totally lexically dominates satisfactions (and other sub-minimum goods). But as one gets better-off, the magnitude (*n*) of one's project-improvements required to render project-improvements non-fungible against satisfactions increases. If so, we can accept that *n*'Roy is fungible against *s*Lee (given that $n'<n$).

However, one further principle is required. To maintain the transitivity of "better than," we must also say that *bm*Gus is better than *n*'Roy, and any other sub-*n* magnitude project-improvement for Roy (otherwise, we must accept that *s*Lee>*n*'Roy, *n*'Roy>*bm*Gus, but *bm*Gus>*s*Lee, violating transitivity). With these pieces in place, we solve the problem at hand: *s*Lee>*n*'Roy (which accommodates the sensible point that Roy's project-improvements do not totally lexically dominate Lee's satisfactions), *bm*Gus>*s*Lee (for any *s*, accommodating *Lexical*), but *m*Roy>*bm*Gus (accommodating *Impersonal Project Fungibility* given, once again, that $m>n$). Thus *Lexical* need not imply either the lexical dominance of the basic minimum in comparison to super-minimum projects *or* the (total) lexical dominance of super-minimum projects in comparison to sub-minimum benefits. The view here is not only independently plausible, but also avoids a potentially serious worry for *Lexical*. This is reason enough to accept it.

4.6. SUPER-MINIMUM GOODS: A SIMPLE SOLUTION

I have already offered an account (*Lexical*) of the axiological weight of the basic minimum in comparison to sub-minimum goods. What remains is to consider the value of the basic minimum in comparison to super-minimum goods. But this task is comparatively simple. The groundwork for a solution to this problem has already been laid in the acceptance of *Thesis**. First, because some super-minimum goods will be satisfactions, and because *Thesis** holds that the basic minimum lexically dominates satisfactions, the basic minimum will take lexical priority to all super-minimum satisfactions. The same holds for super-minimum *un*valued project-improvements.

Second, the previous section's examination of the relative value of valued projects and satisfactions has already laid the groundwork for the relative evaluative weight of the basic minimum versus super-minimum project-improvements. Speaking strictly in terms of welfare value, valued projects for individuals at very high levels of well-being should only mitigatedly lexically dominate satisfactions. Someone who is very well-off might be better-off in pursuing additional satisfactions rather than additional valued projects up to a magnitude *n*. But *Thesis** holds that the basic minimum is *not* fungible against satisfactions. If so, assuming the transitivity of "better-than," it would appear that the basic minimum must be worth more than magnitude *n* project-improvements at higher levels of well-being.

But recall that a further claim is also plausible. The better-off a person gets, the *more* fungible additional valued projects become against satisfactions. In other words, at increasing levels of welfare it takes a greater magnitude project-improvement to render those project-improvements non-fungible against satisfactions (*n* increases as one gets better-off). If so, it would appear, the prudential weight of the basic minimum must increase in comparison to project-improvements of a fixed magnitude at increasing levels of welfare. As a matter of strictly prudential value, the basic minimum outweighs greater magnitudes of valued project-improvement as one's welfare increases.

Thus the basic minimum is worth more in terms of *welfare* value in comparison to project-improvements of a fixed magnitude for people of increasing levels of well-being. But if this is correct, a parallel principle is naturally suggested for the *im*personal domain. And this just *is Prioritarianesque* which, as you'll recall, runs as follows:

Prioritarianesque: Super-minimum project-improvements for the better-off are less intrinsically valuable in comparison to the basic minimum than super-minimum project-improvements for the worse-off.

It is worth comparing *Prioritarianesque* to the more traditional understanding of its namesake, *prioritarianism*. According to prioritarianism, the impersonal value of equivalent welfare benefits increases as that benefit is obtained by a worse-off person. Paul Weirich, in introducing prioritarianism, describes it this way:

The principle first weights utility gains according to the situations of the individuals to whom they go. The weight of a utility gain decreases as the utility of the recipient's situation increases. More precisely, the weight is inversely proportional to the utility of the recipient's situation. Then the principle says to maximize weighted utility gains. This principle can claim to mediate between utility and equality because, although it gives some weight to every utility gain, it gives more weight to utility gains for those less well-off and so helps them to catch up.[22]

Prioritarianesque implies that the relative weight of the basic minimum against super-minimum project-improvements is, literally, "prioritarianesque": the value of project-improvements of a fixed magnitude decreases in comparison to the basic minimum as the welfare of those who stand to achieve such projects increases. *Prioritarianesque* is not a version of prioritarianism, at least as Weirich understands it. *Prioritarianesque* says nothing about the comparative impersonal weight of *equivalent welfare benefits* for the worse-off and better-off. Because valued projects of a fixed magnitude are of diminishing *welfare* value as one's welfare increases, *Prioritarianesque* is compatible with a view that holds that equivalent welfare benefits are of equivalent impersonal value.

Before I address alternatives to *Prioritarianesque*, I should note that I will not address the traditional prioritarian view, as expressed by Weirich. Indeed, I believe that the traditional version of prioritarianism has much to say for itself; I will offer a truncated argument for prioritarianism in §5.3.3. Accepting the traditional version of prioritarianism (if one chooses to do so) does not threaten *Prioritarianesque*: doing so will have only the affect of increasing the concavity of the impersonal prioritarianesque value curve.

[22] Weirich (1983), 424.

4.7. ALTERNATIVES TO *PRIORITARIANESQUE*

Prioritarianesque, it seems to me, is strongly suggested by my method of treating valued project-improvements as mitigatedly lexically prior to subminimum welfare goods. Of course, it does not strictly follow. One could accept the claim that the welfare value of project-improvements permits of a prioritarianesque treatment, but reject the claim that *Prioritarianesque* is a reasonable principle of impersonal value. I consider four alternatives to *Prioritarianesque* here: neutrality, egalitarianism, leximin, and sufficientarianism. Far from being a reason to reject my view, I claim that consideration of these alternatives serves my argument for *Prioritarianesque*; each has important problems *Prioritarianesque* helps to address.

Three notes. First, my discussion of these views is compact, and does not attempt to address all points in favor or against. But the objections I discuss here, though generally well-known, nonetheless appear to me to get to the heart of the matter. Second, many of the views I discuss here receive their initial statements as *deontic* or moral principles, rather than evaluative or axiological principles. I take the liberty of translation. Finally, some views on offer here are not strictly compatible with *Lexical* (such as leximin and strong versions of egalitarianism). However, for the sake of charity, one can easily hold that the views on offer apply to the axiological weight of project-improvements *only*, and hence that any proposal is *Lexical*-compatible. I will adopt this interpretive rubric here.

4.7.1. Neutrality

A natural competitor to *Prioritarianesque* claims that, speaking impersonally, project-improvements are of equivalent value: leaving aside non-project goods, when seeking to promote the best state of affairs, we simply promote the state of affairs that maximizes total project-improvement. Under this assumption, the one should be indifferent between a project-improvement for Roy and a project-improvement for Gus.

Neutrality fails if for no other reason than it delivers verdicts that are straightforwardly implausible. First, it seems right to say that, other things being equal, a project-improvement for a better-off person is not as valuable as a project-improvement for a worse-off person. At best, a neutralist view can only offer justification for granting priority to the worse-off in terms of the *means* to project-improvements. But there seems to be broad agreement that, other things being equal, a valued project granted to a worse-off person is better than a valued project granted to a better-off person. The proposal that a project-improvement for a person who obtains no such projects is of equivalent axiological weight to a project-improvement for an individual who already lives a life with a valued long-term structure stretches believability.

Furthermore, when combined with *Lexical*, this view would appear to claim that a single project-improvement for an exceedingly well-off individual also lexically dominates sub-minimum satisfactions. If this project-improvement for a well-off individual is equivalent in value to the basic minimum, and the basic minimum is better than any finite number of sub-minimum satisfactions, a valued project for a better-off person must also be better than any finite number of sub-minimum satisfactions. This leads us back to a claim we worked hard to avoid in §4.5.2.

The foregoing reasons are sufficient to reject a neutralist stance. But the following objection is also decisive. If my account of intrapersonal welfare is correct, a neutralist view would reject priority of project-improvements for the worse-off in a way that would actually *decrease* aggregate achievement of well-being. I can understand the claim – made by many traditional utilitarians – that we should not grant priority to welfare benefits for the worse-off because doing so reduces aggregate welfare. But I don't understand a refusal to grant priority to project-improvements for the worse-off when doing so actually *increases* aggregate welfare. Hence, it seems to me, a neutralist view is without motivation.

4.7.2. *Egalitarianism*

Egalitarianism comes in many shapes and sizes. Call "strong egalitarianism" the view that rank-orders states of affairs based only on the extent to which these states of affairs display an egalitarian distribution of welfare (perhaps admitting total welfare as a tie-breaker). On a strong egalitarian interpretation of the comparative value of the basic minimum and super-minimum goods, one might hold that a state of affairs gets better as the distribution of project-improvements gets closer to equality. On this view, the value of the basic minimum against super-minimum achievements is up for grabs: it solely depends on whether granting the basic minimum increases equality (the determination of which is itself a complex matter).[23]

Of course, in all but unusual cases, granting priority to project-improvements for those below the line of equality will improve overall equality, and hence strong egalitarianism is very likely to grant priority

[23] See, for instance, Temkin (1993), ch. 2.

to the achievement of the basic minimum in comparison to benefits for the well-off. If so, an egalitarian distribution of project-improvements may seem attractive to those who are concerned about the problematic features of a neutralist stance. Even if this is true, however, a number of problems with strong egalitarianism are obvious. One such worry is the classic

Leveling-Down Objection: According to strong egalitarianism, simply reducing the welfare of the better-off, with no attendant benefit for the worse-off, makes a state of affairs better rather than worse.[24]

Strong egalitarianism clearly embraces the value of leveling-down. Whether this is a problem in all cases is controversial. Even so, however, strong egalitarianism appears to be committed to leveling-down in circumstances in which leveling-down is uncontroversially repugnant. Strong egalitarianism will claim that leveling-down is acceptable even when the welfare level to which people are leveled-down is extremely low.

Furthermore, on straightforward assumptions about the nature of inequality, improvements to the worst-off can sometimes increase inequality, if a means to or necessary side-effect of such improvements are larger improvements for the better-off. So, for instance, if one person fails the basic minimum, and a necessary side-effect of granting the basic minimum to that person is to grant *many* valued projects to persons better-off, strong egalitarianism would rank this transfer as a value loss, even though *both* the worse-off person and the better-off person improve. Strong egalitarianism is thus unacceptable.[25]

Most egalitarians attempt to avoid the leveling-down objection by adopting a form of pluralism. On this view, overall welfare has impersonal value, but value that competes with the value of equality.[26] But, in refusing to level-down, this view appears to have given up on a distinctive egalitarian axiology. As Brighouse and Swift note: "Egalitarians can be pluralists about value. They think that there is a reason to level-down – where doing so will make a distribution fairer – but to recognize that there are also reasons not to. We are sympathetic to this response, but the result is to leave egalitarianism without much bite. The (non-person-affecting) reason to level down is unlikely to outweigh the reasons there are to prefer people to be better rather than worse-off."[27] In refusing to level-down, the egalitarian

[24] For a detailed discussion of the leveling-down objection, see Holtug (1998). Notice that my view states a slightly weaker leveling-down objection than the one discussed by Holtug, which applies not only to strong egalitarianism, but to other, pluralist forms of egalitarianism as well.

[25] See also Rawls (1971), §§13, 26.

[26] See Temkin (1993), 161.

[27] Brighouse and Swift (2006), 472.

holds that the value of equality can never outweigh the value of marginal welfare benefits. This view lacks "bite": equality adds only marginal value to project-improvements for the worse-off (given the assumption that a benefit to the worse-off improves equality[28]). However, specified in this way, it would appear that this form of egalitarianism is more-or-less equivalent to the value curve defended by *Prioritarianesque*. If so, it seems hard to justify insisting on the *per se* value of equality for a view that differs from a far more parsimonious view only at the margins.

Even if one abstracts from the above worry, some have objected to this form of pluralist egalitarianism. The leveling-down objection arises again in a slightly different form. Note that any view that tolerates even the slightest non-zero intrinsic value of equality is forced to admit that leveling-down a state of affairs makes that state of affairs better *in at least one respect* (i.e., in respect of equality), even though this state of affairs might, given the loss of overall welfare, be all-things-considered worse.[29] In rejecting any commitment to the value of equality, *Prioritarianesque* avoids this problem; hence for those who believe that leveling-down never improves a state of affairs in any respect, there is reason to prefer *Prioritarianesque* even to this comparatively weak egalitarianism.

Two further egalitarian views are worth brief consideration. "Conditional egalitarianism" declares that equality is intrinsically valuable, but only conditionally; an egalitarian state of affairs is more valuable than an inegalitarian state of affairs if and only if at least one person is better-off in the more egalitarian state of affairs. In advocating just such a position, Andrew Mason writes: "When some benefit from equality, we should value it for its own sake even though its value is partly grounded in its benefiting some. If no one benefits from equality, then it lacks non-instrumental value."[30] This view is similar to a view described by Bertil Tungodden and Peter Vallentyne under the heading "Paretian egalitarianism." As stated by Tungodden and Vallentyne, Paretian egalitarianism is the conjunction of a concern for a weak efficiency requirement with a concern for equality. On this view, whenever two states of affairs are Pareto-incomparable (i.e., one state of affairs is better for some and worse for others than another), "equality is determinative of justice."[31] (These views are similar given that both

[28] Of course, this doesn't hold in all cases. See Temkin (1993), 71–6.

[29] See Holtug (2003). [30] Mason (2001), 248.

[31] Tungodden and Vallentyne (2005), 131. It is no accident that Tungodden and Vallentyne use the term "justice" when describing Paretian egalitarianism. According to them, a *deontic* form of Paretian egalitarianism is a distinct position, but an *axiological* form is not: axiological Paretian egalitarianism is simply equivalent to a form of leximin.

views will declare an egalitarian improvement worse only if it is worse for at least one and better for none. In all other cases, egalitarian improvements are better.)

Though these views can retain at least some of the bite of a more traditional egalitarianism, they should be rejected. Nils Holtug argues (successfully, in my view) that conditional egalitarianism (and given their similarity, Paretian egalitarianism) appears committed to the denial of the transitivity of "better than."[32] Holtug compares three states: S1: {A: 5, B: 5; C: 5; D: 5}, S2: {A: 10, B: 10; C: 4; D: 6}, S3: {A: 30, B: 20; C: 10; D: 5}. For conditional and Paretian egalitarianism, S1 must be better than S2 (given that S1 is more egalitarian, and is better for at least one person, than S2), S2 must be better than S3 (given, plausibly, S2 is more egalitarian, and is better for at least one person, than S3), and S3 must be better than S1 (given at least one person is worse-off in S1, and none are better-off). Hence these views are intransitive. The culprit here is the refusal to level down, i.e., the refusal to describe S1 as better than S3.

Furthermore, conditional and Paretian egalitarianism have results that are only slightly less unpalatable than those of strong egalitarianism. The following states of affairs are Pareto-incomparable (assume that level 10 roughly corresponds to the achievement of the basic minimum, 1000 corresponds to a high level of project achievement): S1: {A: 50, B: 50, C: 1000}, S2: {A: 1, B: 51, C: 51}. Assuming that S2 is more egalitarian than S1, Paretian and conditional egalitarianism would appear to declare that S2 is better than S1 given that (a) they are Pareto-incomparable and (b) S2 is more egalitarian. These views are incorrect.

I here conclude my examination of egalitarianism. This view has a rich tradition, and my treatment of it here is admittedly cursory. Nonetheless, I think egalitarianism has serious problems, problems that are perhaps not decisive, but weighty. Much more should be said to defend any *all-things-considered* rejection of egalitarianism (though many have relied, simply, on some version or other of the leveling-down objection). In any event, I will leave aside egalitarianism here.

4.7.3. *Leximin*

Leximin (or, at least, the version I intend to discuss here) holds that project-improvements for any worse-off person lexically dominate such improvements for any better-off person. Hence, in a comparison between

[32] Holtug (2006).

super-minimum project-improvements and the basic minimum, the basic minimum maintains *absolute* priority: the worse-off – those who fail the basic minimum – will always take priority to project-improvements for those who are better-off (those who maintain the minimum).

Though many have accepted leximin in some form or other,[33] this view is difficult to sustain plausibly. When it comes to the distribution of project-improvements, leximin is too extreme. Arneson (referring to "maximin") notes that a leximin-style view

> would prefer the outcome in which a single worst-off person gains a penny's worth of benefit at the cost of the loss of thousands of dollars for each of thousands of the better-off. A maximin rule introduces a strict lexical priority for the interests of the worst-off, however slight, when they conflict with the interests, however great, of the next worst-off... In the context of the distribution of social benefits as assessed by social justice principles, leximin is implausibly extreme.[34]

Arneson's point is a perfectly cogent criticism of the claim that projects for the worst-off have lexical priority to projects for the better-off. This view is too strong.[35] One way to see the strength of leximin is to consider the following possibility. Imagine that, in a particular society, there are millions of people who are doing just better than the minimum; in other words, they achieve the minimum but just barely. Leximin would hold that the basic minimum for only one person takes priority to project-improvements of *any* magnitude for *all* the rest. This is far too strong, as we have seen in *Severe Disability*; *Leximin* would hold that it is better to grant Elise the basic minimum than to grant any number of others project-improvements of any finite magnitude. This is beyond belief.

4.7.4. *Crispian sufficientarianism*

In recent years, *sufficientarianism* has emerged as a powerful competitor to egalitarian accounts of distributive justice, morality, and axiology. Sufficientarianism might thus be profitably canvassed for an account of the axiological relationship between the basic minimum and super-minimum project-improvements. The basic idea behind sufficientarianism is to identify a line of "enough," i.e., a particular welfare achievement, and declare that it is the achievement of *enough*, rather than the relative welfare levels of the better-off and worse-off, that takes evaluative priority.

33 See, for instance, John Rawls's "difference principle" in Rawls (1971).

34 Arneson (2000c), 237–8.

35 Larry Temkin also argues convincingly against leximin in (1993), 103–5. For a response to Temkin, see Mendola (2005).

I limit my discussion here to a view I call "Crispian Sufficientarianism," after its innovator, Roger Crisp. Though there are other accounts of sufficientarianism,[36] Crisp's is by far the most thoroughly articulated. His view begins with a form of prioritarianism: granting axiological priority to equivalent benefits for the worse-off. But it deviates from prioritarianism in two important ways. First, Crispian Sufficientarianism would set some particularly important line of welfare achievement, and declare that benefits below the line are to take absolute priority to benefits above the line.[37] Second, above the threshold benefits for the worse-off are to be given no priority.[38]

What might this say about the intrinsic value of the basic minimum in comparison to super-minimum projects? Crispian Sufficientarianism would accept a prioritarianesque value curve below the threshold, though sharper than the curve required by *Prioritarianesque* (given the prioritarian treatment of marginal benefits for the worse-off). The comparative weight of valued project-improvements above the threshold would take a *Prioritarianesque* structure, but without additional priority for the worse-off. And the axiological weight of project-improvements above the line in comparison to those below the line is the strongest possible: project-improvements below the line, including the basic minimum, trump those above the line.

This is an interesting view and is worthy of serious consideration.[39] However, I argue that Crisp's view is unstable. It seems to me implausible to say that valued project-improvements for individuals below a sufficient threshold take lexical priority to identical benefits above that threshold. But if we reject this form of lexical dominance, I shall argue, we cannot accept the claim that below this threshold, benefits are ranked in a prioritarian way and above the threshold no prioritarian weight is given. To put this another way, the stability of Crisp's view depends on the lexical dominance of benefits below the line to benefits above. But this should be rejected.

Crispian Sufficientarianism requires the specification of a morally or evaluatively significant threshold. On Crisp's view, the smallest project-improvement for a person *just below* the threshold would be enough to outweigh project-improvements of *any magnitude* for *any amount* of people

36 See, for instance, Frankfurt, "Equality as a Moral Ideal" in Frankfurt (1988).

37 Crisp (2003), 758.

38 Ibid. I have left out a further element: Crisp claims that the priority for the worse-off is void in cases of merely trivial benefits for the worse-off. This shan't play any role in my discussion here, as the main problem concerns distribution of project-improvements, which I take to be non-trivial benefits.

39 There is a large literature on Crisp's position. See Temkin (2003b). See also Brown (2005), Benbaji (2006).

just above the line. This, then, must be a threshold of *extreme* significance.[40] But maybe there is such a line. Crisp suggests that the proper threshold should be set at "the point at which [a person] has a level such that [she] can live a life which is sufficiently good."[41] Indeed, thought about in this way, Crisp's view is tremendously plausible. Why believe that, insofar as one's life is sufficiently good, benefits should be fungible in comparison to benefits for those whose lives are not sufficiently good? Call the line of "sufficient goodness" *l*.[42]

I argue that no *l* can support the lexical dominance of sub-*l* benefits to super-*l* benefits. To see this, consider first that *l* cannot be identified as the basic minimum (Crisp agrees[43]). To set *l* at the line of the basic minimum is to render the lexical dominance of benefits below the line moot: there are no valued project-improvements below the basic minimum; Crisp's view would then simply become extensionally equivalent to *Prioritarianesque*.[44] But if *l* is set above the minimum, Crisp is in the position of claiming that a valued project of minimal magnitude for a worse-off person lexically dominates a valued project of any magnitude whatever for a better-off person. But this violates *Impersonal Project Fungibility* and is implausible to boot. Recall that I was able to avoid Norcross's sequence argument by claiming that the sequence could be stopped by concentrating on different indices of value, i.e., the distinction between valued projects and, e.g., satisfactions. But Crisp's view is required to draw a lexical superiority along a single scale: the scale of project-improvements themselves. But it is hard to see how one could accept a lexical dominance thesis along the scale of valued projects *only*. Recall that it seemed right to say that if we draw a finite sequence of individuals from the worst-off person A to the best-off person Z, any magnitude project-improvement for an arbitrary person in that sequence could be outweighed by *some* magnitude project-improvement for the next best-off person.

Crisp might respond by claiming that there *is* a natural division in the sequence: the point at which Q maintains, and a person slightly worse-off than Q does not maintain, a life of *sufficient goodness*. This response begs

40 For a brilliant critical examination of sufficientarianism along these lines, see Casal (2007), 312–14.

41 Crisp (2003), 761.

42 Crisp also identifies the threshold as the point at which "compassion gives out." But insofar as he identifies the point at which compassion gives out with the point at which a person's life is sufficiently good, it seems better to concentrate on the latter formulation. See ibid., 761–2.

43 Ibid., 759.

44 Furthermore, even if we accept an interpretation of Crispian Sufficientarianism that evaluates non-project goods, it would hardly be plausible to say that all benefits above the basic minimum are lexically dominated by even the slightest benefit below the minimum.

the question. The objection I seek to press is that there is no threshold of sufficient goodness *l* such that it is plausible to declare that benefits for individuals above the threshold are lexically dominated by benefits for individuals below the threshold. To be told that the sequence argument can be avoided by positing a threshold of sufficient goodness thus is unsatisfying: we must know what this threshold is, sufficient to provide plausible support for Crisp's axiological claims. But a Norcross-like sequence seems to show that there is no such threshold.

Alternatively, Crisp might insist that there is a natural division between valued projects. If Crisp accepts that one's valued projects are susceptible to content-based assessment, one might say that *l* is set at the point at which a person maintains a valued project of preference-independent value. Projects of preference-independent value might be significant enough to blunt the force of any sequence argument: no project-improvement of any finite magnitude for a person who already maintains a valued project of preference-independent value will outweigh any goods of any magnitude for a person who does not. But this suggestion is independently implausible. Take an example. Imagine that A lives a life that is, from A's perspective, *nearly ideal.* A maintains many valued projects, but none that are of preference-independent value. B, on the other hand, does maintain a valued project of preference-independent value. But just barely, and only one. On this view, project-improvements for A would take absolute priority to project improvements for B. This is implausible. Crisp might respond by claiming that A *could* be above the threshold; i.e., there are two (or perhaps more) ways to maintain the threshold: live a life that conforms to one's preferences among valued projects, or maintain a project of preference-independent value. But this suggestion, which seems a sensible amendment, leads us back to the sequence argument. If A lives a life of sufficient goodness, Crisp must draw a threshold between A and another person C, whose projects are also objectively valueless, but who does not maintain the threshold of sufficient goodness. But I see no plausible way to identify a threshold *in terms of objectively valueless projects* that would sustain the strong axiological priority that Crisp requires; this suggestion obviously permits of the same sort of sequence at which I gestured in previous paragraphs.[45]

[45] One might complain that I have been unfair to Crisp. After all, he explicitly accepts a theory of welfare that would permit of no distinction between satisfactions and valued projects: hedonism (see Crisp (2007), ch. 4). For my purposes, however, this point is irrelevant. Even if we reject a substantive theory of welfare that allows for the distinction between valued and unvalued projects, this does not eliminate the trouble for Crisp's view. For *any* theory of welfare, Crisp's view implies

Crisp might respond in the following way: "You're one to talk! After all, not only do you posit an evaluatively significant threshold (i.e., the basic minimum) you claim that the achievement of the threshold lexically dominates benefits below the threshold. So why reject my view, which also posits such a threshold, and also posits a lexical ordering of benefits above and below the threshold?" The answer is this. *Lexical* is justified in part by the fact that welfare goods below the basic minimum are of a fundamentally different order than the basic minimum itself. The maintenance or failure of the basic minimum means either that someone will, or that they will not, maintain the central element of welfare; will, or will not, maintain a life of valued, self-directed meaning. This, as I have argued at length, is no arbitrary division. But in setting the threshold above the line of the basic minimum, Crispian Sufficientarianism must draw a threshold *between* people who *already* maintain a life of valued, self-directed meaning, but who differ only along the dimension of super-minimum project achievement. Thus any threshold set above the line of the minimum seems arbitrary: it is a division between people who are slightly worse-off, and slightly better-off, in terms of valued projects alone.

So let's leave aside the first element of Crisp's view. What about the second? What about the suggestion that above a certain threshold, priority is not to be granted to the worse-off? Surely *this* element of Crisp's view is plausible. Whereas below the line, the traditional form of prioritarianism is plausible, above a certain threshold, who cares if someone is better-off or worse-off? We might be tempted, then, to accept this feature of Crisp's view, even if we jettison the first element.

But if we do not treat benefits below the line as lexically prior to benefits above the line, a problem arises. Assume that A is below *l*. Assume that B is just above *l*. Assume that C is *wildly* above *l*. And, finally, assume that a valued project-improvement of magnitude *n* is *just barely* larger than a valued project-improvement of magnitude *m*. On these assumptions, a valued project improvement of magnitude *n* for C (*n*C) is better than a valued project-improvement of magnitude *m* for B (*m*B). But we could surely imagine the following possibility. Assume that *m*B is barely better than a valued project-improvement of very insignificant magnitude *i* for A (*i*A) (recall that we are assuming that benefits for A are not lexically dominant). But given that C is *wildly* better-off than B, and given that *n*

that a *p*-good for a person below the threshold takes lexical priority to an identical good for a person above the threshold. In terms I have already had occasion to use, this view requires a lexical priority along a single evaluative scale. But insofar as such views permit of refutation *via* sequence arguments, altering the theory of welfare at hand cannot save Crisp's view.

is *barely* more significant than *m*, it would appear that *i*A is better than an *n*C, though not better than *m*B. But if this is correct, "better than" is intransitive. *n*C is better than *m*B which is better than *i*A. But *i*A is better than *n*C. One could avoid this conclusion by claiming that benefits to A take no *greater* priority to benefits for C than for B and hence *n*C>*i*A. But this seems implausible. After all C is *wildly* above the threshold, B just *barely* above the threshold. Though it might seem plausible to say that *m*B is better than *i*A, it seems decidedly implausible to say that an equivalent improvement for C takes the same priority. If one insists that "better than" is transitive, however, and insists that A's benefits take greater priority to C's benefits than to B's, one must say that B's benefits also take priority to C's benefits, and hence that *m*B is better than *n*C. The lesson here is that once we eliminate the lexical dominance of benefits below the line to benefits above the line, Crisp's view destabilizes: we can no longer claim that there is no priority to be given to the worse-off above the threshold.

Crisp's view is an important innovation. Indeed, his account captures a number of plausible considered judgments. However, we should not accept the claim that benefits below the threshold lexically dominate benefits above the threshold. And if we reject this, the remainder of Crisp's view cannot be plausibly sustained.

4.7.5. Prioritarianesque *as Solution*

Return now to *Prioritarianesque*. Though other views may have some hold on important considered judgments, they are either too strong, or violate axiological considerations there are good reasons to believe. (This argument from elimination is certainly not decisive: there are a number of views I have not considered.[46]) Hence it seems to me that *Prioritarianesque* is the best option. (So far, anyway.)

Prioritarianesque, unlike egalitarianism, needn't be committed to the value of leveling-down: for *Prioritarianesque*, leveling-down never improves a state of affairs in any respect. (In addition, if we also accept a version of prioritarianism, *Prioritarianesque* can accept one of the fundamental motivating principles of egalitarianism: that benefits to the worse-off should be given axiological priority to equivalent benefits for the better-off.) Furthermore, *Prioritarianesque* corrects the defects of a leximin approach. *Prioritarianesque* declares that significant enough project-improvements for people who are *barely* above the minimum can outweigh the minimum,

[46] See, for instance, Roemer (2004).

although the minimum is more intrinsically valuable than a single instance of a project-improvement of equivalent magnitude. Furthermore, *Prioritarianesque* does not commit to a particular, super-minimum threshold of extreme evaluative importance, unlike Crisp's view.

But not only does *Prioritarianesque* correct severe defects in alternative approaches, it is plausible in its own right. *Prioritarianesque* holds that the achievement of the basic minimum is of crucial importance in the improvement of states of affairs. But it also accommodates the plausible view that it is worse for those people who live lives that are *just* above the minimum to sacrifice project-improvements for the sake of the achievement of the basic minimum than it is for those who are well above the minimum to undertake a similar sacrifice. Hence, I conclude, *Prioritarianesque* is independently plausible, as well as a proper fix for the defects of alternative accounts of the relative weight of the basic minimum in comparison to super-minimum valued project-improvements.

4.8. CONCLUSION

This chapter has addressed the first stage of the problem of weight. Doing so is a grim job. Evaluating the relative goodness of the basic minimum in comparison to other benefits, especially to benefits for people who are very poorly-off, is enough to make one's stomach turn. But the unenviability of this inquiry is no reason for it to be ignored.

However, the views I advocate here reflect at least one feature of the more traditional, overriding, moral weight of the basic minimum. Remember that *Guarantee* and *Maximize* both insist that there is an overriding reason to promote the achievement of the basic minimum. Insofar as this reason is *overriding*, it must be morally decisive with respect to the reasons to promote sub-minimum achievements. And though the view I advocate here says nothing – yet – about moral weight, it does say something similar when it comes to *evaluative* weight: the basic minimum lexically dominates sub-minimum goods. However, my view tempers the overriding approach by adopting a prioritarianesque weight of the basic minimum in comparison to super-minimum valued projects. I do not claim that the achievement of the basic minimum will trump all welfare benefits above the minimum, though they are comparatively strongly weighted.

Before I move on, I want to make one brief comment concerning an important implication of the axiology I advocate here. If my proposal is correct, the acceptance of a basic minimum is compatible with a very wide range of substantive moral and political theories. This result is significant.

Previous writers on the topic of a basic minimum have assumed that the commitment to a basic minimum is beyond the reach of, e.g., utilitarianism. Richard Miller, for instance, writes that commitment to a basic minimum is, for those who accept it, "a crucial nonutilitarian precondition for mutually respectful citizenship."[47] However, a commitment to a basic minimum need not be nonutilitarian. *Prioritarianesque* and *Lexical* are compatible with the claim that impersonal value is maximized by maximizing aggregate human welfare; no other values need operate at the impersonal domain than human welfare itself. If this is correct, act-utilitarianism (which joins a commitment to consequentialism with a commitment to the claim that impersonal goodness is a function only of aggregate welfare) will hold that the basic minimum must take lexical priority to sub-minimum states, and "prioritarianesque priority" to super-minimum projects. If so, act-utilitarianism accepts a strong basic minimum, indeed. Of course, these facts neither support, nor cast aspersions on, the axiology I adopt here. But it is simply worth noting that the view I endorse shows that a utilitarian need not reject commitment to a basic minimum even if we insist that moral facts go no further than the promotion of aggregate welfare.

The goal of this chapter has been to articulate a thorough axiology of the basic minimum that, along with the view I advocate in Chapter 5, provides a satisfying solution to the problem of weight. Of course, the argument for my view has very often relied on my own considered judgments, or on evaluative propositions that simply seem right to me. Not all readers will march with me in lockstep. And though I regard the overall picture as attractive, I should note one more time that this chapter is simply one module in my overall welfarist approach to the basic minimum. Indeed, it is the module that I take to be most easily jettisoned. None of my arguments going forward will rely on this *particular* axiology. Nevertheless, whether one accepts my theory of the comparative intrinsic value of the basic minimum or not, one should have very good reason to adopt a *teleological* approach to the second stage of the problem of weight, outlined and defended in the next chapter.

[47] Miller (2010), 50.

CHAPTER 5

Against rights

The previous chapter offered an account of the relative intrinsic value of the basic minimum. This is the first stage of my solution to the problem of weight. We must now proceed to the second stage: how, if at all, does the comparative goodness of the basic minimum influence the comparative moral importance of the basic minimum? My proposal is simple: the comparative moral importance of the basic minimum just *is* the comparative intrinsic value of the basic minimum. In other words, the morality of basic minimum-promotion is teleological: we should promote the basic minimum only when it is best to do so. Put together with the axiology I defend in Chapter 4, this approach offers an account that approaches an overriding view without the excesses on display in *Tsunami* and *Severe Disability*.

Against this view is set a supposition made by many political theorists that the basic minimum is the object of a moral *right*, which itself implies a stronger reason to promote the basic minimum than would my approach. Most of this chapter responds to this popular, though I believe mistaken, view. Though a rights-based approach is not the only alternative to a teleological view, the problems for rights-based approaches should be widely worrisome.

This chapter is organized as follows. In §5.1 I present, and offer some brief considerations in favor of, a teleological approach to the basic minimum. However, in defending teleological approaches to any domain, most of the action is in the rejection of competitors, the most important of which I introduce in §5.2: that the basic minimum should be the object of a right. In §5.3, I argue that no rights-based view can escape the problems of *Guarantee* or *Maximize*, or avoid collapse into a teleological approach. In §5.4, I offer one important way in which the language of human rights might be morally appropriate even if we accept a teleological approach to the morality of the basic minimum. In §5.5, I discuss one important limit of the approach I offer here.

5.1. THE TELEOLOGICAL VIEW

As so far outlined, the basic minimum is a prominent feature of the good. The basic minimum has a distinctive axiological structure, taking lexical priority to sub-minimum benefits, and strong, but not lexical, priority to super-minimum project-improvements.

But the problem of weight is not yet solved. Recall that the problem of weight does not concern the axiological structure but rather the *moral* structure of the basic minimum: how are we to *morally* weigh the promotion of the basic minimum against non-minimum states? It seems to me that the obvious starting point is

The Teleological View: For any two goods *p* and *q*, one has greater reason to promote *p* rather than *q* if and only if the promotion of *p* promotes the value of resulting states of affairs to a greater extent than the promotion of *q*.

As a solution to the problem of weight, *The Teleological View* holds that the moral weight of the basic minimum in comparison to other valuable states is simply given by the comparative value of these states. In any circumstance in which one could either promote the basic minimum or promote some other valuable state, one should promote the basic minimum when and only when promotion of the basic minimum is *better* than promotion of other states.

A feature of *The Teleological View* is worth noting. In keeping with the limitation of BM3, *The Teleological View* governs only the moral reasons that urge us to adopt a certain moral *stance* toward the basic minimum, viz., the stance of promotion. *The Teleological View* says nothing about whether we may have moral reasons to adopt alternative stances (such as, for instance, the stance of preservation, or "honoring"), nor does *The Teleological View* say anything about the comparative moral weight of reasons to adopt alternative stances toward the basic minimum, or the comparative weight of a reason to promote the basic minimum against reasons to adopt such alternative stances. Though *The Teleological View* is compatible with a thoroughgoing act-utilitarianism (see §4.8), it is also compatible with moral views that limit the pursuit of valuable consequences in important ways.

The argument for *The Teleological View* is relatively straightforward. Step one is to show that there is at least *a* reason to treat the basic minimum with moral weight that corresponds to its relative intrinsic goodness. But this is easy to show. There is good reason, independent of the existence of the basic minimum, to believe that there is a moral reason to promote intrinsic impersonal value. Indeed, no sane moral view will reject a moral reason to do so. As John Rawls writes: "All ethical doctrines worth our attention take consequences into account in judging rightness. One which did not would simply be irrational, crazy."[1] Rawls is correct. Though many moral views will constrain a reason to promote the good in certain ways, it is uncontroversial to believe that there is such a reason. This can be illustrated by means of an easy example. Imagine that one is faced with two actions ϕ and ψ. Imagine also that ϕ and ψ are otherwise morally identical, but for the fact that ϕ-ing produces a slightly better state of affairs than ψ-ing. If everything else is equal, it would seem morally irresponsible to ψ. If so, there is good reason to believe that, in any trade-off, there is at least *a* reason to morally weigh various goods according to their relative intrinsic goodness.

Step two is that there are no moral reasons that would have us treat the moral weight of the basic minimum as more or less significant than its relative intrinsic goodness (at least in terms of the stance of promotion). This is a little trickier to establish. Given the space allotted here, I will not come close to showing that there could be *no* reason to promote the basic minimum beyond the reason to promote the good. However, I will argue against what I take to be the most important deviation from *The Teleological View*. Many who think about the moral structure of a basic minimum would reject *The Teleological View* because they are committed to the view that the basic minimum should be the object of a moral right. Hence the remainder of this chapter will attempt to shed doubt on the existence of such rights. If I can show that a rights-based approach to the morality of the basic minimum fails, this should be a strong (though defeasible) reason to accept *The Teleological View*. With that, I shall remain content.

5.2. INTRODUCING RIGHTS[2]

A rights-based approach to the morality of a basic minimum is widespread: Henry Shue, David Miller, Thomas Pogge, Nicole Hassoun, James Nickel, and James Griffin[3] (among many others) all argue that the fundamental moral structure of the basic minimum must be put in terms of a human

[1] Rawls (1971), 30.

[2] Some of the groundwork for §§5.2–5.4 is laid in Dorsey (2005). In that paper, I end up advocating a view similar to *Maximize*, but have since thought better of it, in favor of *The Teleological View*.

[3] Shue (1981), Miller (2007), Pogge (2001), Hassoun (2009), Nickel (2007), and Griffin (2007).

right, viz., that whoever lacks the basic minimum has a *right* to it or, at least, the necessary means to it.

Typically, a rights-based approach will insist that rights generate not only *a* moral reason to promote the achievement of the basic minimum for those who fail it, but will insist that rights give rise to reasons that are morally overriding – or, at least, morally decisive with respect to the reason to promote value. As Dworkin notes, rights *trump* utilities.[4] And though whether rights are *always* morally decisive with respect to the promotion of the good is open to dispute, moral rights will at least in many cases be morally overriding. If so, a rights-based approach will provide a very different account of the moral weight of the basic minimum than *The Teleological View*. For a rights-based approach, the basic minimum has moral heft that goes beyond its intrinsic value.

There are two different types of moral right that I wish to keep separate. Often the distinction to which I point is put in terms of "negative" and "positive" rights, though this language is to some degree misleading.[5] To explain what I mean, consider that one can either *maintain* the basic minimum, or one can *fail* the basic minimum. The first sort of right, possessed by those who do not maintain the basic minimum, is a "benefit right" – a right *to be provided* the basic minimum.[6] The second sort of right, possessed by those who maintain the basic minimum, is hereby dubbed a "non-harm right," a right of those who have the basic minimum not to have the achievement of the basic minimum traded-off for the sake of overall goodness.

Non-harm rights to the basic minimum are compatible with *The Teleological View*. *The Teleological View* governs only the relative weight of reasons to promote the basic minimum in comparison to reasons to promote non-minimum states. According to *The Teleological View*, one has a moral reason to promote the basic minimum if and only if doing so increases the value of resulting states of affairs. But a non-harm right is not properly construed as delivering reasons to promote the basic minimum, but rather to *preserve* – or, recalling Pettit's terminology, to "honor" – the achievement of the basic minimum. Hence *The Teleological View* is compatible with the claim that a reason to promote value can be overridden by a reason to

[4] Dworkin (1984).

[5] For instance, it is often claimed that a negative right is a right that entails a duty in others to *refrain* from certain actions, but a positive right is a right that entails a duty in others to *perform* certain actions. Of course, for my purposes this is misleading. One might, to best promote the achievement of the basic minimum, be required to refrain from acting rather than acting.

[6] My terminology here overlaps with terminology accepted by Oswald Hanfling in Hanfling (2006), 64.

honor, or to preserve, the basic minimum or any other valuable states. Given their compatibility with *The Teleological View*, I lay aside non-harm rights here. Hence, when I refer to "rights" or a "rights-based approach" to the basic minimum, I refer to benefit rights, or an approach that characterizes reasons to promote the basic minimum at least partially in terms of benefit rights, which *The Teleological View* denies.

I think the suggestion that the moral importance of the basic minimum should be understood in terms of benefit rights is misguided, and I will argue against the existence of such rights here. My general strategy is as follows. As we have so far seen, no plausible moral theory can reject reasons to promote value, or to do what's best. But if this is the case, those who believe that rights exist must show that the structure of morality insisted upon by a rights-based view cannot be accommodated by a view that rejects any reference to rights. My argument, in essence, boils down to an appeal to parsimony. Because a teleological approach to the basic minimum is comparatively parsimonious, a rights-based approach must justify its insistence that rights exist by showing that the rights-based approach delivers different – *and better* – verdicts than *The Teleological View*. I argue that any such attempt is doomed to failure.

One further point is worth mention before I begin my critical discussion of rights-based views. I am interested only in particular methods of understanding a right *to the basic minimum*. Some of the views I consider will deny that a right to the achievement *of a valued project* exists, insofar as other theorists have a different understanding of the basic minimum. However, I do not rest any of my coming discussion on WBM (or WBM2), i.e., the view that the basic minimum is the achievement of a valued project (or, if one accepts WBM2, the achievement of a valued project of sufficient preference-independent value). Rather, I insist that any plausible rights-based approach to the basic minimum must eventually evaluate the moral import of the basic minimum by its comparative intrinsic goodness – whatever this is – leaving their views simply equivalent to a teleological approach to the basic minimum, as outlined in *The Teleological View*.

5.3. BENEFIT RIGHTS

Any approach to the moral importance of the basic minimum in terms of benefit rights must avoid problems that felled *Guarantee* or *Maximize*. But, at least initially, this challenge seems overwhelming. To see this, consider Shue's account of the essence of a benefit right:

Being socially guaranteed is probably the single most important aspect of a standard right, because it is the aspect that necessitates correlative duties. A right is ordinarily a justified demand that some people make some arrangements so that one will still be able to enjoy the substance of a right if – actually, *especially* if – it is not within one's own power to arrange on one's own to enjoy the substance of the right. Suppose people have a right to physical security. Some of them may nevertheless choose to hire their own private guards, as if they had no right to social guarantees. But they would be justified, and everyone else is justified, in demanding that somebody somewhere make some effective arrangements to establish and maintain security.[7]

Shue's account of rights is similar to Nussbaum's *Guarantee*. At least as stated, Shue's account appears to have the following two features: first, all individuals have a right to the basic minimum, and second, the provision of that to which A has a right must be a social guarantee: if A has a right to p, A's non-possession of p is incompatible with the fulfillment of the moral obligations of those against whom A has the right. But if A's right to the basic minimum requires a social guarantee, this appears to generate precisely the problems that felled Nussbaum's approach. Recall *Tsunami*. Surely, in this case, one behaves morally appropriately in granting the basic minimum to more rather than fewer when not all can be granted the basic minimum. But this is incompatible with Shue's view. On Shue's approach to rights, one has a moral obligation to guarantee the basic minimum to all who fail to maintain it, despite the fact that, in this case, this cannot be done. Indeed, Shue's approach has a problem not just with *Tsunami*, but also with *Severe Disability*. Because the basic minimum is socially guaranteed, one is morally required to promote the basic minimum for an individual who can achieve it only at exorbitant cost.

So far my critique of Shue's approach has been a bit unfair. Most who posit benefit rights do so in a way that is more complex than the simple account sketched above. Two potential qualifications are worth consideration here. First, Shue himself holds that a right to the basic minimum does not entail that one must be provided whatever is required to maintain the basic minimum, but rather one must be provided protection from "standard threats" to the basic minimum. The standard threats approach is considered in the next section. The second possibility differs from *Guarantee* in the following way: though one has a moral reason to respect rights to the basic minimum, rights are limited by certain "practical considerations." The "practicalities" approach is advocated most forcefully by David Miller, and will be considered in §5.3.2.

[7] Shue (1981), 16.

5.3.1. Standard threats

Recall the problem facing Shue. *Guarantee* is too strong; hence if any rights-based view faces the same problems as *Guarantee*, this view is also too strong. And, at least on the face of it, a benefit right to the basic minimum faces these problems. But according to Shue, he is

> not suggesting the absurd standard that a right has been fulfilled only if it is impossible for anyone to be deprived of it or only if no one is ever deprived of it. The standard can only be some reasonable level of guarantee. But if people who walk alone after dark are likely to be assaulted, or if infant mortality is 60 per 1000 live births, we would hardly say that enjoyment of, respectively, security or subsistence had yet been socially guaranteed. It is for the more precise specification of the reasonable level of social guarantees that we need the final element in the general structure of moral rights: the notion of a standard threat. . . . [T]he social guarantees required by the structure of a right are guarantees, not against all possible threats, but only against what I will call standard threats.[8]

Shue's suggestion is initially compelling: *Guarantee* seemed problematic in light of the fact that not all persons will be able to achieve the basic minimum, or could achieve the basic minimum only at absurd cost. As Shue notes, however, if a benefit right to the basic minimum only provides a reason to protect persons from standard threats, this might alleviate the worry about *Severe Disability*. Indeed, Shue claims that a right to the basic minimum should not include a right to "open-heart surgery," let alone complex and costly medical procedures that are yet to be developed.[9] This seems to allow the possibility that, consistent with justice or the fulfillment of one's moral obligations, some might fail the basic minimum in a way that does not imply moral failure. Of course, the standard threats approach requires a guarantee: a guarantee of protection against standard threats. But this guarantee would be to states of affairs that are not, one might think, unduly burdensome or that succumb to problems faced by *Guarantee*.

But which threats are "standard"? Does protection from standard threats include provision for protection against tsunamis, hurricanes, and other natural disasters, which are, no doubt, threats to one's achievement of the basic minimum? If so, the problem with *Guarantee* arises again. Even in cases of resource abundance, protecting all persons from the devastating effects of tsunamis, earthquakes, etc., is simply impossible. One might instead reject the idea that a tsunami or any other such natural disaster is a standard threat to subsistence and security. But on what grounds?

8 Ibid., 17, 29. 9 Ibid., 23.

Whether a hurricane is a standard threat to one's subsistence and security surely depends upon where one is. A hurricane is not a standard threat to one's subsistence in Edmonton, Alberta. But it surely is a standard threat to one's subsistence in Kingston, Jamaica, or Biloxi, Mississippi. If so, it would appear that any attempt to rule out, say, hurricanes or other natural disasters from being standard threats is simply arbitrary. In any event, without a proper theory of what makes a threat "standard," Shue's account is hard to evaluate in light of the failure of *Guarantee*.

But leave this aside. Let's assume a plausible theory of "standard" threats can be found. A serious problem remains. No matter *what* conception of "standard threats" one holds, the standard threats approach does not avoid the most serious problem confronted by *Guarantee*: because each person is *guaranteed protection from standard threats*, any particular society that lacks sufficient power (for whatever reason) to provide all persons protection from standard threats to the basic minimum will violate the rights of those who cannot be granted protection from standard threats. On Shue's model, a right is a *social guarantee*. But any guarantee can at least in principle require expenditures of resources, say, that not all will have available. How the guarantee is specified is irrelevant. To guarantee protection from standard threats will occasionally require resources or other powers that might simply be unforthcoming or unavailable. In such cases, failure to provide protection against standard threats is a failure of morally overriding reasons despite the fact that moral or political agents might have done the best they could. This position is unacceptable.

But even if we accept the claim that the standard threats approach alleviates the problems with *Guarantee*, Shue's approach is independently implausible. Take two people, A and B. Assume that A lacks *p* (the lack of which, assume, is a standard threat to the basic minimum), B lacks *q* (the lack of which is not a standard threat). However, also assume that A is not threatened with the lack of a basic minimum. In other words, assume that for whatever reason, A's failure to obtain *p* will never lead to A's failure of the basic minimum, despite the fact that a lack of *p* is a *standard* threat to the basic minimum. B's achievement of the basic minimum *is* threatened by the lack of *q*, though this threat is non-standard. Assuming that the right to protection against standard threats is morally overriding, A must be provided *p* before B receives *q*. But this is surely the wrong answer. Providing *p* for A will have no effects whatever on A's achievement of the basic minimum. Providing *q* for B will have profound effects; doing so will allow B to achieve the basic minimum. Hence it would seem that the obligation to provide protection against at least one of B's non-standard threats is of greater moral weight than the obligation to provide protection against A's standard threats to the achievement of the basic minimum. Hence it seems wrong to say that if there is a right to the basic minimum, it is a right to protection from *standard threats* to the basic minimum. If B's claim is morally prior – as it surely is – the standard threats approach fails.

Furthermore, the standard threats approach seems in tension with Shue's own justification of rights to the basic minimum (or that which he defines as the basic minimum). When it comes to a right to subsistence, Shue writes:

> No one can fully, if at all, enjoy any right that is supposedly protected by society if he or she lacks the essentials for a reasonably healthy and active life. Deficiencies in the means of subsistence can be just as fatal, incapacitating, or painful as violations of physical security. The resulting damage or death can at least as decisively prevent the enjoyment of any right as can the effects of security violations. Any form of malnutrition, or fever due to exposure, that causes severe and irreversible brain damage, for example, can effectively prevent the exercise of any right requiring clear thought and may, like brain injuries caused by assault, profoundly disturb personality. And, obviously, any fatal deficiencies end all possibility of the enjoyment of rights as firmly as an arbitrary execution.[10]

Shue justifies an interest in subsistence and physical security in the same way: without subsistence, very little else is possible. For Shue, the all-encompassing effects of a lack of subsistence render it the subject of social guarantees. But this principle is in tension with the insistence that persons only have rights to be protected against *standard threats* to the basic minimum. Some persons will fail to achieve subsistence (or whatever it is that constitutes a basic minimum) as a result of non-standard threats. Insisting that people have only a basic right to protection from standard threats seems to place greater moral weight on the subsistence of those who are threatened in standard as opposed to non-standard ways. After all, all persons who fail subsistence fail to possess the ability to follow through on other rights, goals, or opportunities. The mere fact that the achievement of the basic minimum is threatened in a standard as opposed to a non-standard way seems to make very little difference to whether one can fulfill one's rights, or pursue other states one regards as valuable.

The above problems seem to me decisive against any standard threats approach. However, there is some possibility that I have committed Shue to a position he does not hold. Though he does not develop the thought in

[10] Ibid., 24–5.

any detail, at one point Shue claims that "[m]any causes of death and illness are outside the control of society, and many deaths and illnesses are the result of very particular conjunctions of circumstances that general social policies cannot control."[11] One interpretation of Shue's remark is as follows: a "standard threat" is not determined relative to some more or less absolute theory of what makes a particular threat standard as opposed to non-standard. Rather, a standard threat just *is* a threat that a particular society has the power *to control*. This approach solves a number of problems. First, if social institutions must only guarantee that they will protect against what they *can* protect, the standard threats approach avoids the problematic suggestion that justice is simply beyond the bounds of societies in the midst of natural disasters, for instance. Second, if standard threats are those that can be controlled, it would appear that there is no motivation to grant non-standard threats moral priority – non-standard threats cannot be controlled.

Though this possibility fruitfully solves some problems with a standard threats approach, problems remain. Most importantly, this interpretation of the standard threats approach can no longer adequately address *Severe Disability*: because Elise's achievement of the basic minimum is *under the control* of her political society, the standard threats approach – as so interpreted – would entail a morally overriding reason to promote her achievement of the basic minimum despite its astronomical cost to the welfare of others. But this should be rejected. It must be the case that the basic minimum is morally fungible against non-minimum states, including super-minimum states. If Shue's standard threats approach avoids the problems of *Guarantee*, it cannot avoid the problems of *Maximize*.

5.3.2. Practicalities

The standard threats approach cannot salvage benefit rights to the basic minimum. As articulated by Shue, this view either succumbs to the problems that face *Guarantee* or those that face *Maximize*. However, another approach has been offered by James Griffin and David Miller. According to Miller:

> human rights, precisely because they are liable to place others under obligations of justice to fulfil them, have to take account not only of the interest of the right-bearer but also the interests of those whose behaviour would be constrained by the existence of a right. Theories of human rights characteristically attempt to do

[11] Ibid., 25.

this by incorporating a practicality requirement into the existence conditions for a right . . . By appealing to practicalities we ensure that rights claims do not exceed what it is feasible for a particular society at a particular point in its development.[12]

According to Griffin, the existence of any particular right "must depend, to some extent, upon its being an effective, socially manageable claim on others."[13] If the existence of rights depends on their being a practical, manageable claim on others, benefit rights to the basic minimum might very well avoid the problems faced by *Guarantee* and *Maximize*. One might think that in both *Tsunami* and *Severe Disability*, to guarantee the achievement of the basic minimum to all is not practical; in the former because it is not possible, in the latter because one cannot do so at reasonable cost.

To properly evaluate this approach, however, we must have an answer to the following question: to what extent might the fulfillment of a right to the basic minimum be "impractical" or "unmanageable"? In discussing this question, I think it is worth distinguishing three "levels," as it were, of impracticality that might limit the existence of a right to the basic minimum:

1. *Impossibility:* A's right to the basic minimum does not exist in cases in which to provide the basic minimum for A is not possible.
2. *Costliness 1:* A's right to the basic minimum does not exist in cases in which to provide the basic minimum for A would be costly in terms of the promotion of the basic minimum for others.
3. *Costliness 2:* A's right to the basic minimum does not exist in cases in which to provide the basic minimum for A would be costly in terms of the promotion of non-minimum states for others.

What is Miller's method? First, it is relatively clear that Miller accepts *Impossibility*. Miller insists that rights can be limited if "[w]hat is needed [for the procurement of the object of a right] cannot be provided by human agency. Consider diseases for which there is at present no known cure, such as several forms of cancer . . . [I]t makes no sense to say that they have a right to this [non-existent] form of medical aid. Or to put it differently, their general right to medical treatment does not include, at present, a right to the specific treatment that would halt the cancer."[14]

Accepting *Impossibility* does very little to solve the problems that felled *Guarantee*. In *Tsunami*, each person (A–F) *could* be assisted. Assisting every individual person is possible, hence anyone who is not assisted maintains a right to the basic minimum, so long as one accepts only *Impossibility*

[12] Miller (2007), 185–6. [13] Griffin (2001), 315. [14] Miller (2007), 186.

as a method of constraining the existence of rights as a result of practical considerations.

Hence to avoid the problems of *Guarantee*, Miller must accept – at least – *Costliness 1*. In *Tsunami*, granting the basic minimum for any given individual is costly in terms of the basic minimum for others: only five of six can achieve it. Hence there can be no guarantee of the basic minimum, and hence there need be no moral failure in this case if one person fails the target threshold. Does Miller accept *Costliness 1*? It would appear not. Miller writes, for instance, that: "[r]esource scarcities mean that not all needs of a certain kind can be fulfilled simultaneously. Under this heading I want to consider cases in which it is feasible to fulfil the needs of each person taken separately without imposing obligations on others that are either impossible to fulfil or that violate their own rights, but in which this cannot be done for all taken together."[15] Although Miller feels the pull of the suggestion that we would not want to "say in such cases that when we distribute our limited supply of food in the morally best way, we are at the same time infringing a multitude of obligations to all those who get less than they need," he believes that limiting the moral force of rights in this case is problematic. Hence Miller appears to believe that we should not accept either *Costliness 1* or *Costliness 2*. Hence, it would appear, Miller's view succumbs to problems inherent in *Guarantee*, providing us with reason enough to reject Miller's approach.

I should take a moment to consider Miller's argument that limiting the force of benefit rights in cases in which they could not be fulfilled for all is problematic. First, Miller notes that limiting the force of benefit rights requires us to come up with some prior account of the moral reasons involved, and to limit the force of rights in accordance with those moral reasons.[16] Miller holds that there are two problems with doing this. First, any such account of moral reasons that govern distribution in cases in which not all can be helped is bound to be controversial. But, says Miller: "Human rights, by contrast, are supposed to set minimum standards of treatment for human beings that are incontestable – as I have argued, the requirements of a minimally decent life for human beings in any society can be established objectively, in principle anyway. To limit human rights by reference to controversial principles of distributive justice therefore seems a mistake."[17] But this line of reasoning is not compelling. When not everyone can be granted the basic minimum, there still remain important moral questions. Do we maximize? Do we provide for the better-off? Worse-off? And to what

[15] Ibid., 190. [16] Ibid., 192. [17] Ibid., 193.

extent? And though the answer to such questions may well be controversial, this shouldn't lessen their importance; there are surely morally better or worse ways of answering such questions unless we simply choose to adopt a position of moral skepticism. But if we agree that there are morally better and morally worse ways to respond to cases in which not all can be granted the basic minimum, it seems wrong to say that those who answer those questions in the best way still fail to conform to their moral obligations. Though incontestability is surely desirable, committing ourselves to the claim that individuals have failed morally when they could not have done better is too high a cost to pay.

Second, Miller writes that: "The purpose of human rights is not simply to guide the behaviour of those who have to deal directly with people whose human needs are not being met. They can also be used to set targets for governments, international organizations, etc. From this perspective, it may be important to state that scarcity itself may constitute a human rights violation where it can be prevented by human agency . . . For this we need a conception of human rights that is *not* sensitive to the quantity of resources available to a society at any given moment but is based directly on human needs understood as requirements for a minimally decent life."[18] Miller is surely correct that we do not want to index rights to the basic minimum to the *tout court* availability of resources; after all, sometimes resource scarcity can be the fault of those in charge. But this does not imply that we should refuse to say that the moral force of human rights must not be limited by *Costliness 1*. After all, even if we accept *Costliness 1*, we can also say that a political society failed in its obligations *if its resource scarcity could have been prevented*. (Indeed, Miller's important insight here is fully compatible with *The Teleological View*, which rejects rights altogether.) The problem with rejecting *Costliness 1*, or adopting the strong account of human rights Miller prefers, is that it would imply that political society failed in its obligations in cases of resource scarcity it *could not* have prevented. *This* conclusion is untenable, as shown in *Tsunami*. Furthermore, in cases in which resource scarcity could have been prevented, we should distinguish two actions: first, the failure to prevent it (which is surely a failure of justice), and, second, adopting a distributive scheme *given* the (preventable) resource scarcity. Miller's approach holds that no one can distribute resources in a morally appropriate way if that distributive decision is causally downstream from a previous morally inappropriate act. But this lumps together two separable actions, and is implausible to boot; even though I may have, in a morally

[18] Ibid., 193.

inappropriate way, failed to prevent this resource scarcity, I can still, in a morally appropriate way, do the best I can under resulting conditions of scarcity.

So I think, if Miller's view is committed to the rejection of *Costliness 1* and *Costliness 2*, it should be rejected. But my interpretation of his view is complicated by the following. Miller also argues that considerations of practicality limit the extent to which one possesses a right insofar as the achievement of the basic minimum for any particular person is threatened by various medical needs, including, for instance, a need for a kidney or liver transplant. In this case, Miller writes, people have a right to refuse to give up their livers or kidneys, even though doing so would not threaten their achievement of the basic minimum, and would promote the achievement of the basic minimum overall. Taking Miller's claim at face value, he seems to claim that there are other goods against which the achievement of a particular right may be balanced, and hence that non-minimum states can render the fulfillment of any given right to the basic minimum too costly. It would appear that Miller refuses to accept *Costliness 1*, but accepts *Costliness 2*. But this is a strange combination of views. How could it be that the achievement of non-minimum goods is sufficient to render the achievement of the basic minimum impractical, but the achievement of the basic minimum itself – which is morally more important (given BM3) – cannot?

However, I think Miller has something else in mind. Miller seems to insist that the existence condition of rights fails to hold when "[o]bliging others to provide what is needed would violate their own human rights. I am thinking here of cases in which the need is such that to meet it would place demands on others that they have the right to refuse, even though they might choose voluntarily to supply what is needed."[19] The fact that A's right to the basic minimum does not outweigh the interest others have in keeping their kidneys "stems from the human right to bodily integrity: in order to live a decent life, we must have assurance that our bodies will not be used in significant ways without our consent, even for the benefit of others . . . Before a need can ground a right, we have to know that the proposed right would not impose obligations on others that would necessarily violate their own human rights."[20]

The best way of interpreting Miller's intuitions is by way of a fourth possible practical limitation of the existence of benefit rights:

[19] Ibid., 187. [20] Ibid., 187–8.

4. *Non-Harm Preservation:* A's right to the basic minimum does not exist in cases in which to provide for A's basic minimum would require the violation of the non-harm rights of others.

I have no problem (or, at least, no problem I'll get into here) with *Non-Harm Preservation. Non-Harm Preservation* is not inconsistent with *The Teleological View.* But it does little to salvage the practicalities approach: in at least some cases, the practicalities approach will succumb to the same problems that felled *Guarantee.*

One final word on the practicalities approach. Because Miller rejects *Costliness 1*, his view cannot adequately address *Tsunami.* But unlike Nussbaum, Miller actually attempts to respond to the various "practical questions" that such a position leaves open. In so doing, Miller offers a more complex view than Nussbaum's sparse specification of *Guarantee.* This complexity is worth examining in greater detail. Miller writes:

> Typically . . . a human right will bring with it "successive waves of duty" – the primary duty not to violate the right directly being followed by various duties to ensure that the right is not infringed in indirect ways. Thus corresponding to the right to food is first the duty not to snatch food out of the mouth of the starving person, and then various duties to ensure that the conditions that lead to starvation in the first place do not materialize. Even in cases where because of scarcity we cannot meet our direct obligation to protect A's right, we can still act on background duties that make it more likely that the right will be fulfilled in time.[21]

According to Miller, even when one has violated one's moral obligations – behaved unjustly – one can still "act on background duties that make it more likely that the right will be fulfilled in time." In this way, Miller offers a concrete answer to the "practical questions" on which Nussbaum was silent. But this does little to alleviate the problems with his view. It is unclear that every case of B's failure to fulfill his obligations to protect A's right to *p* can be responded to by making it more likely that the right will be fulfilled in time. Certainly cases arise in which for any given individual whose right to *p* is violated, her right cannot be fulfilled "in time," because the fulfillment or non-fulfillment of the right means the difference between life and death. In addition, there is no guarantee that, for any given society, such ancillary rights can be established for all: even in cases in which one fails one's obligations to establish the basic minimum for some range of people, there is no guarantee of sufficient resources to allow all rights to be fulfilled "in time." If I fail to establish the basic rights of fifty people, and

[21] Ibid., 193–4.

I have resources only to make it more likely that the rights of twenty-five people will be established "in time," I have failed even if I have done all I can when it comes to the promotion of the basic minimum, not just now but in the future. This position is no more acceptable than *Guarantee*, and still leaves open practical questions that deserve an answer.

5.3.3. A general argument against benefit rights

My discussion might give rise to the following complaint. So far, I have interpreted the various rights-based approaches to a basic minimum in ways that are specific to the thinkers who advocate them. For instance, I interpreted the standard threats approach – as per Shue's writing – as insisting on a social guarantee of protection against standard threats to the achievement of the basic minimum. I have interpreted a "practicalities" approach in Miller's very specific way, accepting *Impossibility*, but rejecting *Costliness 1*, and *Costliness 2*. But *surely* there are more charitable accounts of a rights-based approach to the basic minimum. Surely, for instance, there is the possibility that one might accept a standard threats approach, but reject the claim that rights are a social guarantee. Surely, for instance, one might accept not just *Impossibility*, but also *Costliness 1* and *Costliness 2*. My rejection of the approaches taken by Shue and Miller do not exhaust the important permutations of a rights-based approach to the basic minimum.

In this section, I offer a more general argument against a rights-based approach. The argument runs as follows. As we have seen so far, any such approach must avoid *Guarantee*. Hence, in so doing, it must weaken the moral importance of the basic minimum in comparison to *Guarantee*. But a good place to begin in considering ways in which such a view might be weakened are by considering *Impossibility*, *Costliness 1*, and *Costliness 2*. First, if such a view accepts *Impossibility*, but not *Costliness 1* or *Costliness 2*, this view succumbs to the problems that felled *Guarantee*. In *Tsunami*, for instance, though it is impossible to grant the basic minimum to all, it is possible to grant *any given person* the basic minimum, and hence not doing so remains (unacceptably) a failure of justice.

Second, if a rights-based view weakens the moral force of the basic minimum by accepting *Costliness 1* but not *Costliness 2*, this approach to benefit rights is equivalent to *Maximize*: the moral force of the basic minimum is limited, but limited only to the extent that the promotion of A's basic minimum would interfere with the promotion of the basic minimum for others. This view has clear problems with *Severe Disability*.

The basic minimum obviously *can* be outweighed by a sufficient amount of non-minimum states.

If a rights-based approach accepts all three methods of limiting the existence or moral force of the basic minimum, and allows that rights to the basic minimum can be limited given the cost to others in terms of non-minimum states, we are met with an obvious question. How is the promotion of the basic minimum to be weighted against non-minimum states? When does the achievement of non-minimum states become too costly in comparison to the achievement of the basic minimum? And it seems to me that an obvious, and perfectly natural, answer is to compare the overall goodness of the basic minimum to the overall goodness of non-minimum states. But if a rights-based view weakens the moral force of the basic minimum in this way, it cannot distinguish itself from *The Teleological View*.

To deny the force of this argument, one must offer a principled approach to the relative moral force of the basic minimum that accepts *Impossibility*, *Costliness 1*, and *Costliness 2*, but that does not morally weigh the basic minimum exactly as *The Teleological View* does. But coming up with a principled reason to depart from *The Teleological View* is difficult. After all, *The Teleological View*, and views that simply boil down to *The Teleological View*, have a clear and obvious rationale: the comparative moral force of the basic minimum, whether this is in terms of a right or not, is determined by the comparative intrinsic value of the basic minimum. Any deviation from this proposal must offer a similar, and similarly strong, rationale.

Of course, alternative rationales exist: there are recognized, non-arbitrary, deontic principles of the moral weight of competing benefits that might help govern the comparative moral importance of the basic minimum and that do not simply boil down to *The Teleological View*. Four seem worth consideration here (obviously, these options are not exhaustive, but seem to me to capture the most plausible non-teleological principles by which one might weigh the competing moral importance of the basic minimum against non-minimum states):

1. *Deontic Egalitarianism:* the comparative moral importance of the basic minimum is determined by the equality of the resulting state, not the intrinsic value of the resulting state.
2. *Deontic Leximin:* the comparative moral importance of the basic minimum is determined by the position of the worst-off in the resulting state (lexical priority), not the intrinsic value of the resulting state.

3. *Deontic Crispian Sufficientarianism:* the comparative moral importance of the basic minimum is a function of three factors: a weighted sum of all benefits (lexical priority) for those below a line of "sufficient goodness," a weighted sum of benefits strictly among those below the line of "sufficient goodness" (non-lexical priority for the worse-off), and a sum of benefits for those strictly above the line of "sufficient goodness" in the resulting state, not the intrinsic value of the resulting state.
4. *Deontic Prioritarianism:* the comparative moral importance of basic minimum is determined by a weighted sum of benefits (non-lexical priority for the worse-off) in the resulting state, not the intrinsic value of the resulting state.

Before considering these views individually, it is worth noting that there is always at least one reason to reject deontic principles that override a teleological approach to moral obligation. Each of these principles license a moral requirement to act in ways that result in states of affairs that are *worse* than they otherwise would have been had one adopted a teleological approach. Of course, to say that this by itself is reason enough would obviously be question-begging. However, it is worth noting that there is at least *one* important moral reason that tells against each of them: the moral reason to promote the best states of affairs.

With this in mind, take *Deontic Egalitarianism.* This view would insist that though people have a right to the basic minimum, this right generates an obligation to promote the basic minimum only to the extent that doing so increases equality (perhaps weighted against overall welfare, or admitting welfare as a tie-breaker, etc.). However, this view seems to provide the wrong answers. First, one could imagine a state of affairs in which virtually everyone lives extremely good lives, save A, who fails the basic minimum. To provide the basic minimum for A would make the state of affairs much more unequal, but only by *increasing* the well-being of a number of persons already well-off. Assuming that inequality is increased enough, this would seem to generate the implausible verdict that the basic minimum should not be granted in this case. Furthermore, one could imagine that very many people are equally poorly off, and that one could grant the basic minimum to many, but in a way that would increase inequality (though it wouldn't affect the well-being of those who wouldn't be granted the basic minimum). Again assuming that inequality is increased enough, it would seem that balancing the competing demands of the basic minimum and equality would render sufficient reason not to grant anyone the basic minimum in this case. Again, this is an incorrect answer. (One might choose to accept a deontic version of any of the various variants of egalitarianism, i.e., Paretian or conditional egalitarianism, for instance. But I can see no reason to believe that a deontic version of these views would be able to avoid the moral analogue of the seriously problematic implications that plagued axiological interpretations of these views.)

Second, one might accept *Deontic Leximin*, and hold that though people have a right to the basic minimum, this right entails an obligation to promote the basic minimum if and only if the least well-off are benefited by so doing. But this view fares little better. This view would generate the problematic verdict that the reason to assist any worse-off person is morally decisive with respect to the moral reason to promote the basic minimum. Strictly interpreted, this view would eliminate the moral possibility of upward distribution (which is essential, given BM3). But even if we sidestep this problem (say, by focusing only on the distribution of valued projects), it is far too strong: the achievement of the basic minimum, in this case, is morally overriding in comparison to super-minimum states, and *Severe Disability* seems to loom large.

Like *Deontic Leximin*, *Deontic Crispian Sufficientarianism* is plagued by the same problems that plagued its axiological cousin. This view must hold that the basic minimum takes lexical priority to any benefits for individuals above the relevant threshold *l*. But any such *l* seems to succumb to problematic sequence arguments – or, at least, moral versions of them – as explored in the previous chapter, which ended up destabilizing the position as a whole. (Surely there is a sequence of people A–Z, from worst-off to best-off, each better-off than the next by a marginal amount, such that sufficient magnitude project-improvements for any given individual in the sequence is sufficient to *morally* outweigh any magnitude of valued project-improvement for the next-worse-off person.) Hence it seems to me that *Deontic Crispian Sufficientarianism* cannot be plausibly accepted.

The final possibility is worthy of more careful examination. One might accept *Deontic Prioritarianism* and claim that a moral right to the basic minimum entails that a reason to promote the basic minimum, while itself of significant moral weight, is more heavily weighted against the moral reason to promote the interests of the better-off, less heavily weighted against the interests of the worse-off. On this view, the interests of the worse-off get a "moral boost" in comparison to the interests of the better-off. This rights-based proposal would yield a view that does not simply reduce to *The Teleological View*: whatever axiology one accepts, there is always *greater* reason to promote the interests of the worse-off than the better-off than is claimed by a teleological approach.

Deontic Prioritarianism is a perfectly coherent, and indeed plausible, method by which a rights-based view might accept *Impossibility*, *Costliness 1*, *Costliness 2*, and avoid arbitrariness. However, to accept *Deontic Prioritarianism* as an alternative to *The Teleological View* seems an awkward position. The chief reason is the availability, and comparative plausibility, of prioritarianism as an axiological, rather than deontic, view. Though I don't wish to rest an argument for *The Teleological View* on the acceptance of my specific approach to the axiology of the basic minimum, it does seem that a prioritarian approach to equivalent welfare benefits is plausible. Take, for instance, the following two states of affairs. In S1, A has five hedons, B has 10 hedons. In S2, A has 7 hedons, B has 7 hedons. I find it overwhelmingly plausible to believe that S2 is better. And if this is the case (and if this isn't to be explained by a commitment to egalitarianism) axiological prioritarianism is plausible. Furthermore, there's reason to believe that prioritarianism's natural expression is as an axiological, rather than deontic, position. The most powerful reason to treat benefits for the worse-off as of greater moral priority seems, simply, to be that it is *better* to do so. As Nils Holtug writes: "Like the egalitarian, we should characterise the prioritarian in terms of her commitments with respect to intrinsic value. We should require that she favours giving priority to the worse off not (only) because doing so will tend to further some other goal of hers, say, fraternity or political stability, but (at least in part) because she holds that, everything else being equal, an outcome in which a benefit falls at a lower level is *intrinsically* better than an outcome in which an equal benefit falls at a higher level."[22]

Of course, one could say, with Richard Arneson, that "[t]he root idea of prioritarianism is that one ought as a matter of justice to aid the unfortunate, and the more badly off someone is, the more urgent is the moral imperative to aid."[23] But there is no reason to favor a particularly deontic expression of this "root idea" in comparison to an axiological version of prioritarianism combined with *The Teleological View*. Any rationale that could be offered to treat the interests of the worse-off with moral urgency (on grounds of, say, fairness, reciprocity, "fraternity," or "political stability," or any other) could be equally managed by *The Teleological View*.

Thus if axiological prioritarianism is plausible – and it seems that it is – *Deontic Prioritarianism* is rendered otiose by *The Teleological View*. But not just otiose! Accepting *Deontic Prioritarianism* in the face of a prioritarian axiology would grant *additional* priority to the worse-off, beyond that

[22] Holtug (2007b), 132. [23] Arneson (2000d), 343.

which is required to account for whatever rationale one might offer for its acceptance, in a way that *worsens* the value of resulting states of affairs. But if this is correct, a rights-based approach plus *Deontic Prioritarianism* seems to have no real advantages, and an important disadvantage, in comparison to *The Teleological View* assuming we accept axiological prioritarianism (which seems, in any event, a natural corollary to the prioritarian idea). *Deontic Prioritarianism* is thus no savior for a rights-based approach to the basic minimum.

What is the result of all this? Any very strong conclusion drawn here is bound to be speculative insofar as I have considered only a narrow range of potential deontic principles that could support a rights-based solution to the problem of weight. Indeed, there could be any number of other non-arbitrary deontic principles of distribution I have not considered, some of which may even be plausible. However, the problem displayed by *Deontic Prioritarianism* should be widely worrisome: any acceptable rights-based view that rejects the problematic implications of *Guarantee* and *Maximize* will have a very difficult time offering a rationale that could not also be accommodated by a teleological approach, which is independently plausible, comparatively parsimonious, and supported by additional reasons not to worsen the intrinsic value of resulting states of affairs. I conclude that in the face of *The Teleological View*, there is no reason to suppose that benefit rights exist.

5.3.4. *Parsimony Reconsidered*[24]

So far, I have claimed that benefit rights either display the same problems as *Guarantee* or *Maximize*, or are rendered otiose by *The Teleological View*. However, some hold that an appeal to parsimony is not as decisive as I claim. It might be that rights have a role to play even if a rights-based account of the morality of the basic minimum is equivalent to *The Teleological View*. And the role is this: rights seem to have a form of interpersonal moral heft that non-rights-based views lack. Rights, some have argued, allow those who fail the basic minimum to claim that the achievement of the basic minimum is owed *to them*, rather than simply as a biproduct of the promotion of the good.[25] In other words, rights are required to say that, when someone does not grant A the basic minimum, they have *wronged* A. Allen Buchanan puts the matter this way:

24 I'm grateful to Fred Harrington and David Reidy for stimulating conversations on this topic.
25 Harrington (MS), Feinberg (1970), 245.

The judgment that you have violated my right and thereby wronged me has certain implications which the judgment that I have failed to give you something you ought to have, or failed to treat you as you ought to be treated, does not have . . . The judgment that you have wronged me implies a presumption that you ought to provide restitution, compensation, or at least apologies *to me*. This is not the case if you merely fail to fulfill a non-rights-based requirement, such as a duty of beneficence. If your duty toward me has a correlative right, then your failure to fulfill that requirement *changes your moral (or legal) relationship to me* in ways in which your failure to fulfill a non-rights-based requirement does not.[26]

If B has a duty to promote A's basic minimum, on *The Teleological View*, B has this obligation only in virtue of the fact that A's achievement of the basic minimum would be a good thing. But this fact seems to entail that B does not *owe* the basic minimum to A – the achievement of the basic minimum is not A's "due." Furthermore, B's failure to promote the basic minimum for A does not change B's moral relationship to A; B has not wronged A. B has merely failed in his moral requirement to promote the good.

But it is worth wondering what all this amounts to. What does it mean to say that B's promotion of A's basic minimum is owed to A as A's due? What does it mean to say that B *wrongs A* in not promoting his achievement of the basic minimum? And why can't *The Teleological View* accommodate this?

Because we are assuming that the rights-based view in question is extensionally equivalent to *The Teleological View*, any difference between *The Teleological View* and a rights-based view must be in the *explanation* of the moral reasons in question. If so, accommodating the interpersonal heft of rights-claims must be accompanied by a particular explanation of moral requirements to promote the basic minimum. In short, A, or some particular property of A, must explain, or be the source of, B's duty to promote A's basic minimum. If A is the source of B's duties, we can begin to see how B's promotion of A's basic minimum is owed to A. Insofar as A is the *explanation* of B's moral obligations, this establishes a particular, morally relevant, relationship between A and B, the breach of which is sufficient to, as Buchanan puts it, change this relationship "in ways in which [the] failure to fulfill a non-rights-based requirement does not."[27] Thus if a plausible rights-based view can accommodate the claim that the right-holder is the

[26] Buchanan (1984), 74.

[27] See Harrington (MS). Buchanan argues that characterizing A as the "source" of B's duty to ϕ is insufficient (see Buchanan (1984), 74). A could be the "source" of a duty of beneficence, while admitting there is no right to such beneficence on the part of A. However, this analysis sounds wrong to me; if we can say that A is the "source" of B's duty to ϕ, this is sufficient to establish

source, or explanation, of corresponding obligations in others, I see no reason to bar it from the claim that it can accommodate the important interpersonal features of morality.

I am willing to grant that a non-rights-based view cannot accommodate the claim that A is the "source" of B's moral obligations. Unfortunately no plausible rights-based view can accommodate it, either. My argument runs as follows: any moral view (rights-based or not) that is coextensive with *The Teleological View* is going to posit a particular moral obligation to which B must conform when and only when *The Teleological View* does so. But such a view is compatible with the claim that right-holders are sources of duties only if this obligation is plausibly *explained* by A, or some particular property of A, rather than the promotion of the overall good. But no moral theory can just *say* that B's obligation is explained by particular properties of A. This claim must be the product of independent argument, especially in light of the moral obligations this view posits. Hence for a rights-based view to plausibly support the claim that A is the source of B's duties or obligations, it must be the case that some property *p* of A provides a *good* explanation of B's moral obligations.[28] But any explanation of B's obligation to promote A's basic minimum that goes beyond the promotion of the overall good is a *worse explanation* than an explanation of B's obligation that makes reference only to facts about value.

This can be seen simply by examining the standards of good explanation in any domain. The teleological explanation is parsimonious: it relies only on properties that we have independent reason to believe are morally relevant. The A-based explanation is bloated: it offers normatively relevant properties that go beyond what is necessary to explain B's obligation. If we accept a view that is extensionally equivalent to *The Teleological View*, the reason to promote value *fully explains* B's obligation. Hence there is no call to believe that particular morally relevant properties of persons play

an important normative relationship between A and B, such that, were B not to ϕ, B violates the "terms," as it were, of this relationship. I can see no reason, then, to believe that if A is the genuine source of B's duties, A cannot claim to be wronged, were B not to fulfill his obligation to ϕ. However, as I shall argue below, no matter what source, or explanation, of duties is posited by a rights-based view, it is problematic in the face of an alternative, teleological, explanation.

28 One might object that it is not just B's obligation that should be explained, but also the fact that this obligation is *owed to* the right-holder. But this is to put the cart before the horse. What it means to say that something is *owed to* the right-holder, as we've so far seen, is that the right-holder is the source of such an obligation. But this boils down to an explanatory principle: A explains B's obligations. But if A is a *worse* explanation of B's obligations than some other explanatory principle, it is plausible to say that A does not explain B's obligations, and hence that A is not the source of B's obligations, and hence that B's ϕ-ing is not A's "due."

any role in explaining obligations. The explanatory principle on which this argument for a rights-based view relies fails. We *could* accept the explanatory claim if we are willing to accept a rights-based view that is not coextensive with *The Teleological View*. But this possibility is problematic for reasons already explored. *Once we have adopted a rights-based view that is coextensive with* The Teleological View, *we reject any previous claim we had to accommodate the right-holder* qua *source of obligations*. Given the failure of views that are *not* coextensive with *The Teleological View*, we no longer have any claim to explain these moral reasons in a way that would allow us to claim that any particular treatment is A's "due."

My argument here might be put formally:

1. To accommodate the claim that B's ϕ-ing is A's due, A must – at least in part – be the source of B's duty to ϕ.
2. A is the source of B's duty to ϕ if and only if some morally relevant property p of A explains B's duty to ϕ.
3. For any view that is coextensive with *The Teleological View*, B's duty to ϕ can be fully explained by reasons to promote the good.
4. If B's duty to ϕ can be fully explained by reasons to promote the good, there is no reason to believe that a morally relevant property p, possessed by A, is necessary for an explanation of B's duty to ϕ.
5. Hence, for any view that is coextensive with *The Teleological View*, p, possessed by A, is a comparatively poor explanation of B's obligation to ϕ.
6. Hence, for any view that is coextensive with *The Teleological View*, no facts about A explain B's duties.
7. Hence, for any view that is coextensive with *The Teleological View*, A is not the source of B's duty to ϕ.
8. Hence, for any view that is coextensive with *The Teleological View*, B's ϕ-ing is not A's due.

To sum up, it seems to me that the insistence on rights, or the right-holder, as a source of duties does nothing to salvage the efficacy of rights-claims if we have already assumed that, e.g., *Maximize* or *Guarantee* are unacceptable. Once these views are rejected, one is forced to admit that the best explanation of the moral significance of the basic minimum does not appeal to benefit rights.

5.4. RIGHTS: AN ECUMENICAL COMMENT

There is little reason, in the face of the welfarist approach I propose here, to believe that benefit rights to the basic minimum exist. *The Teleological View* seems perfectly suited to the job of accounting for the moral importance of the basic minimum.

But I think there is room for an ecumenical comment. There is good reason to believe that an approach that deals in human rights is an important tool in the promotion *of the good*, and with it, the achievement of the basic minimum for more rather than fewer. Insistence that individuals have a right to the basic minimum is likely to generate public support, and to do more good, than alternative methods of framing our moral obligations. Given the importance of the basic minimum, it seems as though we might, for public policy purposes, insist that the basic minimum is a requirement of basic justice or moral decency – without committing ourselves to believing that such a right governs the actual moral structure of the basic minimum.

Part of what motivates this comment is the fact that *talk* of human rights has tremendous currency on the world stage. Bodies most responsible for the welfare of the worst-off cast their appeals in the language of human rights. The United Nations' chief office of humanitarian concern, for instance, is the United Nations Human Rights Council. *Talk* of human rights now is ubiquitous, and it seems quite plausible to say, with Charles Beitz, that "'human rights' names not so much an abstract normative idea as an emergent political practice."[29] In this way, when discussing the nature of human rights, "we take certain basic facts about the world's political structure as fixed and consider the purposes of a practice of human rights within this structure."[30] In other words, we accept that there are certain features of the political and moral world we inhabit, and we take the rhetoric of rights to be the fundamental means by which to navigate this world. *The Teleological View* is perfectly compatible with this approach to thinking about human rights, without embracing the claim that human rights are *per se* factors in determining our moral reasons.

Indeed, this point is noted by Nussbaum. Though Nussbaum rejects the normative force of rights, she insists that talk of human rights is important for four reasons. First, she holds that an appeal to human rights "reminds us that people have justified and urgent claims to certain types of treatment, no matter what the world around them has done about that."[31] Second, an appeal to human rights – compared to a direct appeal to human capabilities or welfare – "is more rhetorically direct. It tells people right away that we are dealing with an especially urgent set of functions, backed up by a sense of the justified claim that all humans have to such things,

[29] Beitz (2009), xii. [30] Ibid., 128. [31] Nussbaum (2000), 100.

by virtue of being human."[32] Third, Nussbaum writes that "the language of rights . . . helps us to lay extra emphasis on the important fact that the appropriate political goal is the ability of people to choose to function in certain ways, not simply their actual functionings."[33] Fourth, "the language of rights preserves a sense of the terrain of agreement," in cases in which "we disagree about the proper analysis of rights talk."[34] In this sense, Nussbaum believes that the language of rights can spur political action even "where the claims of utility, resources, and capabilities are still being worked out."[35]

I think that the third role for rights talk should surely be disputed. Indeed, if my welfarist approach is correct, the emphasis on capabilities and choice rather than actual functionings is not to be encouraged. (Although, to my mind, it is difficult to see why a rights-based approach should emphasize choice rather than specific functionings, it would depend, obviously, on what the right is a right *to*, i.e., a right to some set of choices, or some set of functionings.) However, the other three points seem important to note: rights-talk can be an important tool in the establishment of any basic minimum. Thus political precedent and salutary effects seem to me good reasons not to simply jettison rights *talk* for talk of overall good or the promotion of human well-being. Doing so is likely to achieve less good than we might otherwise have in insisting on human rights, and is likely to erase whatever progress a political approach to human rights has in establishing good quality lives for the disadvantaged. However, there is a difference between embracing rights *talk* and embracing *rights*. For the reasons I have so far noted, I do not believe there is any reason to admit the existence of rights in an explanation of the moral reasons to promote a basic minimum. Nonetheless, if we take the importance of rights to be confined to the importance of reference to rights in political or social dialog, it surely has a place in our moral and political theory.

However, insofar as the appropriateness of rights-language is, as it were, *just talk*, I have shown that no rights-based approach to the morality of basic minimum promotion is acceptable. This is a significant result for the defense of *The Teleological View*. Though I have discussed only rights-based deviations from *The Teleological View*, my arguments here should be widely worrisome for its opponents. Any view, rights-based or not, must justify a deviation from considerations of the value of resulting states of affairs in determining the relative moral weight of the basic minimum. However, I have shown that if such views are not to collapse into *Guarantee*

[32] Ibid., 100. [33] Ibid., 101. [34] Ibid. [35] Ibid.

or *Maximize*, there is much pressure indeed to simply accept a view that collapses into *The Teleological View*.

5.5. HONORING AND OTHER MORAL STANCES: SOME SCHEMATIC COMMENTS

The Teleological View is limited. Though it provides a relatively clear account of the relative moral weight of the basic minimum when it comes to the stance of promotion, it says little about the relative moral weight of the basic minimum when the promotion of the basic minimum must be weighed against the *honoring* of non-minimum states, or, indeed, the honoring of the basic minimum itself. But this is quite a limitation! After all, one might think, there is rarely an opportunity to promote the basic minimum that does not harm others, whether in terms of non-minimum states, or the basic minimum itself.

Of course, *The Teleological View* could be expanded. One might accept:

The Teleological View 2: For any moral stance *S*, one has reason to adopt *S* toward any valuable state of persons *p* if and only if doing so maximizes the value of resulting states of affairs.

The Teleological View does not reject the existence of reasons to honor particular valuable states of persons, nor does it assign a relative weight to these potential reasons. But *The Teleological View 2* holds that the relative weight of *any* stance one might take toward the basic minimum or any other valuable state of persons is simply governed by the value of the resulting states of affairs.[36]

I am attracted to *The Teleological View 2. The Teleological View 2* seems to adequately represent a number of initially intuitive thoughts about the nature of the basic minimum. For those who accept the existence of the basic minimum, as noted in the previous chapter, it is natural to believe that the moral weight of the basic minimum should be very strong – or, at least, as strong as it can be without accepting *Guarantee* or *Maximize*. If so, one would expect that there should be no hesitation to trade-off super-minimum goods for some to promote the basic minimum for others, at least within the bounds of overall good-promotion. Limiting the promotion of the basic minimum with reasons to honor non-minimum states further weakens the moral importance of the basic minimum, taking us further

[36] Even *The Teleological View 2* is not a version of full-blown consequentialism; one might still accept reasons, say, to promote or preserve things like culture, community, democracy, etc., that go beyond valuable states of persons.

than is warranted from an overriding approach. In addition, limiting the moral force of the basic minimum by recognizing reasons to honor the basic minimum itself seems to me to end up with an undesirable result: fewer, rather than more, will achieve the basic minimum. (Of course, these considerations simply pound the table in favor of *The Teleological View 2*; I do not pretend to consider any number of potentially convincing arguments in favor of a stance of honoring, whether for non-minimum states or the basic minimum. I merely report that which I find plausible, and why.)

However, the extent to which one accepts *The Teleological View 2*, or limits the promotion of the basic minimum by, e.g., reasons to honor valuable states of persons, obviously depends on whether one believes the stance of honoring is or can be a morally appropriate stance to adopt. Insofar as this is a deep and complex question, the answer to which would go most of the distance toward solving the centuries-long dispute between consequentialists and non-consequentialists, it is *far* beyond the purview of this book to answer. However, I do want to say a few words about the method by which one might weigh various reasons to honor versus reasons to promote the basic minimum or non-minimum states, assuming one accepts such reasons. It seems right to me to say that whatever reasons one might have to honor a particular state p should be indexed, at least in part, to the relative welfare value of that state. If p is more important in terms of welfare value than q, it seems that any reason to honor q must be outweighed by a reason to honor p. Hence, looking strictly at the comparative weight of reasons to honor states of persons, it does seem to me that the relative intrinsic value of these states provides a rough guide. But if this is correct, one can determine the *relative* weight of reasons to promote in comparison to reasons to honor by determining the relative moral weight of *honoring* some particular state p against the relative moral weight of *promoting* p. If honoring p is morally prior to promoting p, one would expect that the extent to which honoring p is morally prior to promoting p will provide a "moral multiplier," e.g., that the moral reason to honor p is twice (or thrice, or whatever) the moral importance of the moral reason to promote p. If this is right, this moral multiplier could be applied to the relative intrinsic value of p and q in determining the relative moral weight of the reason to honor p rather than to promote q. If p is 3x better than q, and the honoring of p is 2x the moral importance of the promotion of p, then the honoring of p is 6x the moral importance of promoting q, and so forth.

Of course, this is all very schematic and artificial. Furthermore, additional normative dimensions may be relevant which would alter any potential "moral multipliers." I hesitate to say more simply because I do not wish to commit to any one way of judging the relative merits of honoring versus promoting. To offer my own view, there can be no such difference, and hence there is no more reason to honor *p* than to promote *p*. But others may very well disagree; I thus leave the precise relative weight, or "moral multiplier," to those who would accept differential reasons to honor rather than to promote. Nevertheless, it should be relatively clear that the axiology of the basic minimum – and hence the solution to the problem of weight as I define it – is relevant in any such inquiry.

5.6. CONCLUSION

In this chapter, I have argued against benefit rights to the basic minimum and in favor of *The Teleological View*. This solves the problem of weight. Though I have left open the possibility that there is more to morality than the promotion of the good, once the structure of human well-being – including the relative weight of various goods – is fully understood, there is good reason to believe that we need look no further than a standard utilitarian, consequentialist account of moral or political obligation to end up with a basic minimum that is not only plausible in itself, but that conforms to the conceptual requirements of any basic minimum identified by BM3 (and, indeed, comes reasonably close to the traditional, and plausible, overriding approach without falling victim to its problems, on display in *Tsunami* and *Severe Disability*).

This, however, does not conclude the book. I have so far not discussed a range of objections to a welfarist approach to the basic minimum. Insofar as I have been saving the best for last, however, the next, and final, chapter will discuss six reasons that have compelled some thinkers to reject welfarism as an approach to the basic minimum, disadvantage, or political morality more generally.

CHAPTER 6

On objections to welfarism

My approach to the basic minimum is now fully on the table. I have argued in favor of WBM (of the claim that the basic minimum is the achievement of a valued project) against non-welfarist conceptions of the basic minimum. I argue that *Lexical* and *Prioritarianesque* properly characterize the comparative intrinsic value of the basic minimum against non-minimum states, and that when combined with *The Teleological View* provide a thorough (and, I humbly submit, attractive) solution to the problem of weight.

However, I recognize that the reader may have grown impatient. After all, there are a number of well-known (and well-worn) objections to welfarism I have not yet discussed. The time has come to reckon with them. The final chapter of this book thus responds to a number of classic (and not-so-classic) objections to a welfarist approach to the basic minimum, or, indeed, to morality (especially political morality) in general. There are six objections to be discussed.

The first – in §6.1 – notes two problems for welfarist approaches to political morality: the problems of expensive and offensive tastes. In §6.2, I consider an objection that might motivate a return to the capabilities approach: the objection from imprudent choices. Incidentally, my response to the objection from imprudent choices will help motivate a further response to *some* forms of the objection from expensive and offensive tastes. In §6.3, I address an objection to a welfarist view on grounds of respect for persons. §6.4 is devoted to a discussion of a relatively recent argument against welfarism by Jonathan Wolff and Avner De-Shalit. Wolff and De-Shalit claim that welfarism inappropriately implies that any disadvantage can be compensated with *cash*. In §6.5, I discuss a classic objection to welfarism, in a form stated by David Braybrooke, that welfarism is unworkable given the problems welfarist views face in being put into practice. Finally, in §6.6, I discuss a second objection from Wolff and De-Shalit, viz., that the basic minimum must include not just the achievement of a particular state (such as a valued project), but the *secure* achievement of that state. §6.7 concludes not just this chapter, but also the book as a whole.

6.1. EXPENSIVE AND OFFENSIVE TASTES

A welfarist approach to the basic minimum must contend with a number of traditional objections to a welfarist approach to political morality, the most important of which concerns the problem of *expensive* tastes. Roughly speaking, this objection takes the following form: because, according to WBM, the basic minimum is in part constituted by the satisfaction of (the right kind of) preferences, the achievement of a sufficient level of well-being will in some cases require the satisfaction of preferences that we do not regard as essential to the achievement of the basic minimum. If this is the case, WBM fails; WBM sets a basic minimum that is (or can be) far *too high*. The classic statement of the expensive tastes objection is stated here by Dworkin:

> Imagine that a particular society has managed to achieve equality of welfare in some chosen conception of that ideal. Suppose also that it has achieved this through a distribution that in fact (perhaps just by coincidence) gives everyone equal wealth. Now suppose that someone (Louis) sets out deliberately to cultivate some taste or ambition he does not now have, but which will be expensive in the sense that once it has been cultivated he will not have as much welfare on the chosen conception as he had before unless he acquires more wealth. These new tastes may be tastes in food and drink: Arrow's well-known example of tastes for plovers' eggs and pre-phyloxera claret. Or they may (more plausibly) be tastes for sports, such as skiing, from which one derives pleasure only after acquiring some new skill; or, in the same vein, for opera; or a life dedicated to creative art or exploring or politics. Can Louis be denied extra wealth, taken from those who acquire less expensive tastes (or simply keep those they already have), without contradicting the ideal of equality of welfare that his community has embraced?[1]

One problem. Dworkin's version of the problem of expensive tastes explicitly discusses a position that insists upon a welfarist treatment of egalitarianism, or "equality of welfare." My view rejects egalitarianism. Nevertheless, my view faces a problem in the same rough neighborhood. On my view, the basic minimum is construed as the achievement of a valued project. But *expensive projects* of this kind are certainly not necessary for the achievement of the basic minimum. If so, the basic minimum is not adequately captured by WBM.

[1] Dworkin (2000), 49–50.

One response might be to note that though expensive tastes may be a problem in principle, its scope as a problem in fact is limited. Recall that to achieve or fulfill a valued project, the maintenance of this project must help to explain one's assessment that one's life is worth living. But virtually any person will value (in my sense) *maintaining a loving relationship*, or *supporting a family* under conditions of moderate autonomy. Virtually no person will fail to value more modest projects, despite, perhaps, being willing to trade these modest projects for projects that are more expensive. The general point here is that even if a person *strongly desires* and *seeks to pursue* champagne wishes and caviar dreams, there will be a great many *cheap* projects that are valued by almost any person. Hence because the achievement of the basic minimum requires that only *some* valued project be achieved, a welfarist basic minimum is far less vulnerable to the objection from expensive tastes.

In this way, WBM can accommodate worries about people like Louis. But imagine the following person:

Robin: Robin sets out to deliberately cultivate *only* tastes in luxury goods, such as champagne and caviar, and expensive projects, such as becoming a global jetsetter. Furthermore, though the achievement of Robin's basic minimum would not hamper the achievement of anyone else's basic minimum, providing for Robin's achievement of his expensive global projects would conflict with the provision of non-luxury, but also *non-minimum*, projects for others.

Robin's valued projects are expensive, as a result of his own cultivation. But the problem with Robin is not that he *has* champagne wishes and caviar dreams (don't we all?), but that he *doesn't* have Spanish plonk wishes and cocktail nuts dreams: he refuses to value any but the most costly global projects. Here it would seem that WBM has a problem. Given his values, it just seems wrong to say that the maintenance of a valued project is necessary for Robin to maintain the basic minimum. Maybe he could achieve some other project which, though he doesn't strictly value it, is good enough – intuitively speaking – to constitute Robin's achievement of the basic minimum. If so, Robin could fail to be, e.g., a global jetsetter without *thereby* failing to maintain the basic minmum.[2]

Before I respond to this objection, Robin's case requires some further examination. What is it about Robin's tastes that renders them unfit to

[2] Note that this objection cannot be avoided by opting for WBM2 rather than WBM. WBM2 requires that a project of preference-independent value be *valued* for it to constitute the basic minimum. But if a person values only expensive projects the fact that they must also be of preference-independent value does little to solve the problem of expensive tastes.

characterize a minimum threshold? Answering this question turns out to be more difficult than is often thought. If we believe that Robin's case presents a problem for my approach, it cannot simply be on the basis of the *expense* of his project. For instance, imagine a disabled person, Jackie, whose achievement of a valued project is or would be substantially expensive compared to individuals that are able-bodied. For Jackie, we should certainly not conclude that the fact that his achievement of a valued project is expensive entails that this valued project would be "too high" for the basic minimum.[3] Rather, it seems quite appropriate that the achievement of a valued project for Jackie is no less important than any other welfare good for anyone else, consistent with the relative weight of the basic minimum.

Thus some instances of expensive tastes are problematic for WBM, others are not. What is the difference? If not expense *per se*, what about Robin's preferences renders his case so problematic? One possibility might make reference to the *content* of these projects: Jackie's preferences are important to take into consideration because it would seem that his preferences may be for activities or projects that *seem* required to maintain the basic minimum. But being a global jetsetter certainly goes beyond the maintenance of the basic minimum. Robin could achieve the basic minimum with a less expensive project. Thus the problem is not that Robin's tastes are *expensive*, it is that they are *expansive*: he values only things that go wildly beyond what is necessary for the basic minimum. Hence there is very little reason to treat his champagne wishes and caviar dreams as essential to his achievement of the basic minimum.

But I don't think this works, either. Expansive projects can, for at least some people, constitute the basic minimum. Imagine that a further individual (Randy) has exactly Robin's preferences, but not as a result of his own cultivation. Randy's conception of the good is no fault of his own. Imagine now that though Randy possesses a set of more "basic" global projects, he still fails to live a life of valued, self-directed meaning. In this case, I think it is not implausible to believe that Randy fails the basic minimum. He is, in a very real sense, disabled: unable to value that which would be easy, for him, to get (or easy, for us, to give). Though his preferences are "expansive," they do not seem to cause any problem for WBM. After all, Randy still lacks a life of valued, self-directed meaning; one would certainly

[3] See, for instance, Nussbaum's moving discussion of the requirements of justice as concerns persons with disabilities; Nussbaum (2006), ch. 3.

say that his life is broadly speaking a failure, despite the fact that he values only those projects most would regard as *de luxe*.

Hence I do not think that the problem of expensive tastes, or the distinction between Robin and Jackie, should be understood along the dimension of that which is expansive rather than non-expansive. But then where's the problem? One might put this more pointedly: if Randy, in failing to achieve a valued project, fails to achieve the basic minimum, we must also say, of Robin, that his projects are also essential to his achievement of the minimum threshold. WBM is under no threat from the problem of expensive tastes.

Not so fast. There is at least one difference worth exploring: Robin's projects are expensive as a result of his own cultivation.[4] Robin's tastes – like Louis's – are deliberately cultivated in a way that makes them difficult to satisfy. The disabled person has no control over the expense of his projects: they are expensive simply because he is disabled.[5] If a person with expensive (or expansive) tastes fails to have control over the expense (or expanse) of his preferences, we should not distinguish his preferences from those of the disabled person. However, *if* such a person has control of his preferences and chooses instead only to value expensive projects, it would appear much more problematic to insist that the maintenance of such projects is essential for the basic minimum. Pretheoretically, this seems a sound method of differentiating Robin's project – which is not essential to Robin's achievement of the basic minimum – from Randy's project – which is. WBM, once again, faces a serious, and principled, objection.

But if *this* is the problem of expensive tastes, the view I advocate here has a natural solution. For WBM to be threatened by the problem of expensive tastes, it must be that WBM holds that individuals with cultivated expensive tastes nevertheless require the achievement of those expensive tastes to maintain the basic minimum. But WBM explicitly rules out cultivated expensive tastes: these tastes, given PC, will not constitute a given person's *genuine values*. To put this more provocatively, expensive tastes, or, at least, expensive tastes that are problematic for our purposes here, are best described as a form of shallow adaptation; a refusal to value not those things that are beyond one's reach, but a refusal to value things that seem to one not to have certain other desirable characteristics, such as the requisite degree of luxury or social status. Indeed, this can be seen

[4] Indeed, this thought is reflected in Rawls's own treatment of expensive tastes. See "Social Unity and Primary Goods" in Rawls (1999), 369–70.

[5] I do not wish to wade into metaphysical discussions of the nature of control here; I will simply assume some or other intuitive understanding of this idea.

by looking more closely at Randy and Robin. Randy's valued project, it seems natural to say, is essential to his achievement of the basic minimum because Randy's expensive tastes are deeply and genuinely *his*. Robin's tastes, given their artificial cultivation, are more like Erin's preferences after her strategic adaptation: they do not plausibly reflect his conception of the good.

Imagine what must be the case for a person to have control over the refusal to value a given project. To be in control of one's preferences requires it to be the case that, *but for this choice*, the person in question would have valued *p*. But this sort of choice just is an example of shallow adaptive preferences. Given that all conceptions of the good are fully tested against *all possible value data* and revised accordingly, preference coherentism blocks the cognitive conditions that yield development of problematic forms of expensive tastes. A value datum that is used to evaluate a particular project, or a particular life containing such a project, contains a judgment of the value of a particular life *only on the basis of experiencing that particular life*, not on the basis of a decision made in one's actual life to commit to expensive projects. The value judgments that one might use to *refuse* to value more basic projects or tastes will be revised when confronted with honestly assessed recalcitrant value data. In this way, a given individual's conception of the good will not be influenced by the particular choice an individual makes in a particular life not to value *p*. If *p* could be valued by A, this will be reflected in the value data, which are used to revise A's (incomplete) conception of the good. Just as PC avoids *downward* adaptation, it avoids *upward* adaptation as well.[6]

At the risk of redundancy, it's worth putting this point in slightly different terms. Imagine what one must do to develop problematic expensive tastes on a preference coherentist scheme. One must believe that certain cheaper projects, first, are not good, or at least not a contributor to a life worth living. But the only way that controllable expensive tastes survive

[6] One might point out that this response says nothing about *deep* adaptation; adaptation that eventually forms a central, unchangeable aspect of a person's conception of the good. Deep adaptation, after all, could be the product of one's own cultivation. However, I think there is a relevant difference between deep adaptation and shallow adaptation in this case: if we assume that Robin's preferences form an essential aspect of his conception of the good – however this has occurred – I doubt we would hold that he could maintain the basic minimum if he doesn't satisfy his expensive tastes. Of course, one might complain that even if his basic minimum requires satisfying his expensive tastes, Robin's deeply adaptive tastes do not take the requisite level of moral priority. However, this problem is different than the problem of expensive tastes as I've defined it here. This doesn't mean it's not a problem, but simply that it takes the same shape – and permits of the same solution – as the problem of imprudence or irresponsibility. This solution will be offered in the next section.

is by surviving complete and honest testing by all metaphysically possible value data. But if failure to value cheap projects survives such testing, it appears substantially implausible to believe that such a person has "control" or a substantial "choice" about the values he or she maintains. It would seem churlish to declare that a person controls their preferences or adopts expensive tastes given the scrutiny to which any evaluative belief is put on a preference coherentist scheme. Looking at Robin's case in particular, Robin might value only jetsetting as a result of a commitment simply to value this particular luxury. But if so, we should expect that this commitment will be revised after complete testing. However, if Robin's failure to value cheaper projects survives this process, it seems inappropriate to believe that Robin's achievement of a valued project does not constitute the basic minimum: the expense of his values are not shaped by culpable adaptation. Robin, in this case, becomes Randy, whose valued project clearly does constitute the basic minimum. Though the problem of expensive tastes might be substantially more problematic for a view with an alternative conception of valuing (such as a desiderative view), preference coherentism is immune.

To sum up: if expensive tastes are to generate a problem for welfarist theories of the basic minimum, they must be non-arbitrarily distinguished from expensive projects for the disabled. In so doing, however, we focus on the notion of *cultivation*. But adaptation to expensive tastes, in a way that seems to cause problems for WBM, is ruled out on a preference coherentist scheme. If value data are evaluated honestly, there is no reason to fear the failure to value *p* when *p could have been* valued. And because WBM relies on PC as a theory of an individual's genuine conception of the good, WBM does not insist, for any person, that the basic minimum can only be maintained by the fulfillment of cultivated expensive (or expansive) tastes. Preference coherentism rules out adaptation, whether adaptation to that which one can get, or adaptation away from that which is easily – and cheaply – available.

An objection to this line of reasoning is worth consideration here. Notice that to alter one's tastes is not the only way in which one can have control over the *expense* of one's tastes. Even if A fails to culpably develop expensive tastes, A can act in such a way that renders A's valued projects *more expensive*. For instance, A can render his valuable projects more expensive not only by altering his tastes, but by – to put the point bluntly – cutting his legs off.[7] In this case, his tastes do not alter. Rather, A's circumstances alter such that his

[7] I appreciate the clarity with which this point was put to me by an anonymous reviewer.

tastes are now *more expensive*, and difficult to obtain. By way of a response, I simply note that this case should be distinguished from the problem of expensive tastes: few would agree that A could maintain the basic minimum with a cheaper, perhaps unvalued, project simply because A cut his own legs off. However, there is a difficult objection to WBM on the horizon that this case is an example of: the problem of "imprudent choices." This problem will be discussed in substantial detail in the following section.

The problem of expensive tastes is often mentioned in the same breath as the problem of *offensive tastes*, or preferences the satisfaction of which might cause harm to others. The problem of offensive tastes is stated most clearly by Rawls, in a complaint about classical utilitarianism:

> In utilitarianism the satisfaction of any desire has some value in itself which must be taken into account in deciding what is right. In calculating the greatest balance of satisfaction it does not matter, except indirectly, what the desires are for. We are to arrange institutions so as to obtain the greatest sum of satisfactions; we ask no question about their source or quality but only how their satisfaction would affect the total of well-being. Social welfare depends directly and solely upon the levels of satisfaction or dissatisfaction of individuals. Thus if men take a certain pleasure in discriminating against one another, in subjecting others to a lesser liberty as a means of enhancing their self-respect, then the satisfaction of these desires must be weighed in our deliberations according to their intensity, or whatever, along with other desires.[8]

To see this point more clearly, consider the following case:

> *Jake:* Jake's sole valued project is to kill those in his community who belong to races that are offensive to him. Given the depth of his racism, all races other than his own are offensive to Jake.

Once again, Jake seems to display *some* problem for WBM, or my welfarist approach on the whole, but it is worth asking what such a problem is. Unlike Robin, it seems implausible to say that Jake could maintain the basic minimum without maintaining a valued project. Though Jake's project is offensive in the extreme, we wouldn't say that without any valued project at all, he does not maintain the basic minimum. If so, we might wonder why there should be any problem with WBM.

But a problem approaches, as it were, through the backdoor. Recall that if a particular state of persons p is supposed to constitute the basic minimum, that state had better have *at least* weak moral priority to other states. But it would seem positively obscene to suggest that the fulfillment of Jake's

[8] Rawls (1971), 30–1.

offensive project should take weak moral priority, say, to a non-offensive super-minimum project. And if Jake's project does not maintain the requisite moral priority, and WBM declares that Jake's project is essential for Jake's basic minimum, WBM fails to be an adequate conception of the concept identified in BM3.

One potential response might run as follows: though WBM may grant Jake's offensive project (at least) weak moral priority, this is not as counterintuitive as may be first believed. After all, the achievement of Jake's project itself is a *moral disaster* when it comes to the project of basic minimum promotion. If we accept the approach I advocate, there will never be overriding reason to promote the achievement of this valued project for Jake, despite the fact that it may very well constitute his basic minimum, and hence may very well maintain strong moral priority to other states. Hence though there may very well be a *pro tanto* reason to promote the achievement of the basic minimum for Jake, there is very little reason to believe that granting the basic minimum to Jake will ever be morally decisive with respect to refusing to grant the basic minimum for Jake. The damage caused by allowing Jake to fulfill his project is simply too great.

But this response is pretty weak. First, though the promotion of Jake's horrific project may never be morally decisive with the refusal to promote this project, there is at least a *pro tanto* reason to promote it; this might be problem enough in itself. Furthermore, and more importantly, whether it would be efficient in terms of the promotion of value to promote offensive versus non-offensive projects depends (a) on the content of those projects and (b) on the proper solution to the problem of weight. Consider, for instance,

Reggie: Reggie's sole valued project is to cause discrete moments of pain, as many as possible, for individuals who are so far below the basic minimum that, for them, the basic minimum could not be achieved.

In this case, Reggie's project seems not to be harmful to those who stand to gain or lose the basic minimum, but is harmful instead to those whose welfare benefits are, at least on my view, *lexically dominated* by Reggie's achievement of the basic minimum. And in this case, it would seem as though if I accept *Lexical* and *Prioritarianesque*, I have no ground to claim that promoting Reggie's mean project would not promote the best overall state of affairs. And hence, given *The Teleological View*, I am committed to the claim that political institutions, and moral agents more generally, ought to do so.

However, there are a number of potential responses to the problem of offensive tastes that I consider here, each of which is sufficient to salvage a welfarist approach.

Response One: The first response is to seek refuge in WBM2. This view would allow us to say that without maintaining a valued project, Jake (and Reggie) could not maintain the basic minimum. But it would also allow us to say that Reggie's project (and, indeed, Jake's) does not maintain sufficient preference-independent value to constitute the basic minimum, and hence that there is no need to insist that it maintains even weak moral priority to other states. Indeed, those who accept the possibility of content-based assessment of valued projects should find this point plausible; Reggie's project here seems sufficiently reminiscent of Rawls's grass counter or Kraut's icicle smasher; projects that are held up as paradigmatically worthless life aims.[9] Of course, this response is not available to WBM. But it is certainly in the spirit of a more general welfarist approach to the basic minimum.

Response Two: The second response would be to say that Reggie's (and Jake's) project *does* constitute the achievement of the basic minimum, but that Reggie's project need not take moral priority to other valuable states. Recall that BM3 insists that the basic minimum only maintains the relevant moral priority *in the general case*. *Reggie* (and *Jake*) seems a sensible case in which to enact the qualifier.

Of course, one might wonder why we are licensed to rule out Reggie's project as maintaining the standard moral priority, in light of the fact that such a project constitutes the basic minimum, and especially in light of the fact that it costs no one anything but their minor satisfactions (which are lexically dominated by the achievement of the basic minimum)? Wouldn't this be to reject my solution to the problem of weight? I explore this point in more detail in the next section, but here's a teaser: WBM, and *The Teleological Approach*, are compatible with a further principle of impersonal value which holds that benefits for individuals with negative traits of moral or prudential responsibility are worth less in comparison to benefits for individuals who lack such traits. Indeed, one might adopt a further principle that limits the value of certain offensive projects, simply given their offensiveness. If so, though Reggie's project constitutes, for him, the basic minimum, it need not be of the same *im*personal value as valued projects that do not display such problematic moral traits.

[9] See Rawls (1971), 432–3; Kraut (1994), 41–2. See also Brink (1989), 227.

6.2. IMPRUDENT CHOICES AND OFFENSIVE TASTES RECONSIDERED

One important objection to welfarist approaches to political morality, or, indeed, to morality generally, arises from consideration of various facts of personal or moral responsibility. To put the matter starkly, why should it be the case that the basic minimum for A is worth so much in comparison to sub- and super-minimum states when A's failure to maintain the minimum could be her own fault? Richard Arneson, in evaluating a welfarist view, writes:

> [E]quality of welfare is a poor ideal. Individuals can arrive at different welfare levels due to choices they make for which they alone should be held responsible. A simple example would be to imagine two persons of identical tastes and abilities who are assigned equal resources by an agency charged to maintain distributive equality. The two then voluntarily engage in high-stakes gambling, from which one emerges rich (with high expectation of welfare) and the other poor (with low welfare expectation). For another example, consider two persons similarly situated, so they could attain identical welfare levels with the same effort, but one chooses to pursue personal welfare zealously while the other pursues an aspirational preference (e.g., saving the whales), and so attains lesser fulfillment of self-interested preferences . . . In [each example] it would be inappropriate to insist upon equality of welfare when welfare inequality arises through the voluntary choice of the person who gets lesser welfare.[10]

Like Dworkin, Arneson refers to a welfarist egalitarianism. However, like the problem of expensive tastes, the objection from imprudent choices also applies to my view. Take, for instance, the following individual:

> *Kenny:* Kenny values only the project of being a successful engineer. Indeed, Kenny has the ability to fulfill this project; he is sufficiently talented and has, or would have, sufficient resources to become educated as an engineer. One day during his education, however, he succumbs to temptation and loses his shirt in a game of high-stakes roulette. Being unable to pay for his education, he fails to become an engineer, and fails ever to maintain any other long-term valued project.

Kenny's failure of the basic minimum in this case is not a result of any disadvantage or disability that the state, or any other moral agent for that matter, could have corrected. Rather, he fails the basic minimum given his own dumb choice: he chose, rather than paying for his education, to gamble his money away. It might be thought that political society, or any other moral agent for that matter, has no further obligations to benefit Kenny, or,

[10] Arneson (1989), 83–4.

at least, no further obligations in strength comparable to the moral weight of the basic minimum as defined here. As with the problem of offensive tastes, this is an objection to WBM through the backdoor. Though it may *seem* as though Kenny's project is required for him to maintain the basic minimum, given that his maintenance of the basic minimum does not maintain the weak moral priority required by BM3 (given his poor choices in the past), it cannot constitute, for Kenny, the basic minimum. WBM, once again, fails.

One obvious response to this problem is to retreat from a welfarist view to a capabilities approach, i.e., something like a "capability for welfare" view of the sort proposed by Arneson, and at which I gestured in Chapter 1.[11] This view has obvious advantages. Anyone who fritters away his or her basic minimum as a result of high-stakes gambling or other forms of imprudent behavior has no call to be supported further: Kenny has, or had, the capability to achieve the basic minimum, but chose not to exercise that capability. Of course, determining when a given individual genuinely has the capability to maintain a valued project or can genuinely be held responsible for imprudent choices will be subject to inquiry, and will await a number of philosophical debates (including, e.g., the nature and possibility of free will). But this proposal, in principle anyway, promises to move past this implausible feature of a welfarist approach.

But I think matters are not so simple. I think that the motivation for a capabilities approach on grounds of imprudence or irresponsibility is less than meets the eye. Given that Kenny *would not* maintain a valued project, why insist even on his *capability* do so? *Ex hypothesi*, any capability granted to Kenny to maintain a valued project is a *mere* capability. But it seems decidedly irrational and wasteful to grant Kenny such a capability in priority to *substantive* capabilities for others. Though a welfarist view may have a problem with imprudent choices, a capabilities approach is no solution.

Some will bite the bullet, and hold that Kenny's valued project *does* maintain weak moral priority, despite his history of imprudence, and despite the cost his imprudence has imposed on others. But even if we reject this bullet-biting response, there is no call to reject the welfarist approach I advocate. A welfarist and teleological approach to the basic minimum can be flexible. Indeed (in the words of Arneson himself), such a view can be "responsibility-catering."[12] Responsibility-catering versions of broadly welfarist theories have a long and distinguished philosophical history. To

[11] Ibid., 85–7. [12] Arneson (2000d), 340.

introduce the view in broad outline, consider the following, from Francis Hutcheson's *Inquiry Concerning the Original of our Ideas of Beauty and Virtue*:

In comparing the moral Qualitys of Actions, in order to regulate our Election among various Actions propos'd, or to find which of them has the greatest moral Excellency, we are led by our moral Sense of Virtue to judge thus; that in equal Degrees of Happiness, expected to proceed from the Action, the Virtue is in proportion to the Number of Persons to whom the Happiness shall extend; (and here the Dignity, or moral Importance of Persons, may compensate Numbers) and in equal Numbers the Virtue is as the Quantity of the Happiness, or natural Good; or that the Virtue is in a compound Ratio of the Quantity of Good, and Number of Enjoyers.[13]

Hutcheson appears to be offering a quasi-utilitarian account of moral virtue. But the most interesting feature of his account for our purposes is the parenthetical: the moral importance of persons may *compensate* numbers, or, in other words, it can sometimes be better to improve the well-being of a virtuous person rather than the well-being of two people of neutral or vicious moral character.[14] Call this proposal

Hutcheson's Move: moral traits of individuals can affect the comparative moral importance of well-being improvements for those individuals.

One version of *Hutcheson's Move* is explored by Arneson. According to Arneson, "luckism"

is the idea that the strength of any moral reasons there might be to alter the condition of some individual for the better or for the worse (if the latter, this is to be done for the sake of improving the condition of other individuals) can be amplified or dampened by some factor involving an assessment of individual responsibility. . . . [T]he moral reasons that favor [a transfer from the better-off to the worse-off] are amplified if the potential beneficiary from this transfer is badly off because she was born into poverty and never had any realistic opportunity to escape it, and lessened if the potential beneficiary is badly off because she squandered the wealth and privileges and opportunities to which she was born.[15]

[13] Hutcheson (1726), 125.

[14] This is to some degree complicated by the preceding paragraph, where Hutcheson praises benevolence toward the evil, but I hereby leave aside exegetical matters.

[15] Arneson (2004), 2–3. Luckism has been explored by a number of authors, including Dworkin (2000), ch. 2, and Temkin (1993), 17–18. These views share the crucial feature of luckism, viz., that disadvantages are more important, from a moral point of view, when these disadvantages are no fault of the person who is disadvantaged.

Luckism is a form of *Hutcheson's Move* that focuses explicitly on imprudent and otherwise irresponsible behavior. But this approach is perfectly compatible with my WBM *qua* basic minimum (as dictated by BM3): though we do not treat Kenny's achievement of a valued project as maintaining weak moral priority to all non-minimum states (including valued projects for the non-imprudent who already maintain the basic minimum, or satisfactions for individuals who lack the basic minimum through no fault of their own), the achievement of a valued project still maintains weak moral priority in the *general* case, i.e., in cases in which the failure of the basic minimum is not a result of imprudent or otherwise irresponsible behavior. For those who find Kenny's case troubling (or the case of the culpably legless, for instance), I hereby license *Hutcheson's Move* (in its "luckist" form) as a fix. WBM does not insist on any conclusion that violates BM3: the achievement of a valued project maintains weak moral priority *in the general case*.

As foreshadowed in the previous section, *Hutcheson's Move* raises an additional question about the stability of the view I advocate. If, as I've defended in Chapter 4, the basic minimum is more impersonally valuable than any other welfare goods, *and*, pursuant to luckism, the basic minimum for Kenny does not take moral priority to all other welfare goods, doesn't this cause problems for *The Teleological View*? Aren't we now judging the comparative moral importance of the basic minimum on the basis of facts (including imprudence or irresponsibility) other than the comparative intrinsic value of the basic minimum?

However, I do not think *Hutcheson's Move* need threaten *The Teleological View*. Different proponents of luckism will interpret the explanation of this weakened moral reason differently. One potential explanation is that the *impersonal value* of a particular welfare good *p* for an irresponsible and/or imprudent person is less than the impersonal value of *p* for a responsible and/or prudent person. In other words, the explanation of the weakened moral importance of Kenny's basic minimum is simply that Kenny's basic minimum, given his history of imprudence, is worth comparatively less. One way to see the plausibility of this proposal might be to consider two possible worlds, W1 and W2, composed of two individuals each, A and B. A is irresponsible and imprudent, B is responsible and prudent. In W1, A is provided with a benefit *p*. In W2 B is provided with the same benefit. One might plausibly say that W2 is better, and hence that responsibility, prudence, etc., are factors in the impersonal evaluation of states of affairs. This proposal is initially plausible, and allows a version of *Hutcheson's Move* even for *The Teleological View*.

Hutcheson's Move fixes the problem of imprudent choices. But an analogue of *Hutcheson's Move* can be marshaled as a supplement to *Response Two* to the problem of offensive tastes. If we are licensed to claim that the imprudence of individuals can affect the extent to which their welfare benefits are impersonally valuable, we are surely licensed to say that the offensiveness of *projects* can affect the extent to which *their* achievement is impersonally valuable. Consider now:

Hutcheson's Move 2: the offensiveness, or other negative moral traits, of global projects can affect the comparative intrinsic value of these projects.

As noted in the previous section, the classic response to the problem of offensive tastes is to note that allowing Jake to achieve his offensive project is likely to do far more harm than good. But for those who seek a more thorough fix (including a fix for the problems on display in Reggie's case), one might accept that facts about the offensiveness of individual projects can influence the extent to which these projects are morally important, or are intrinsically (*im*personally) valuable. Indeed, I think such a move is *prima facie* plausible: leaving all other facts equal, promoting the achievment of an indecent project is worse than a project that is at least neutral when it comes to moral quality. If this is correct, there is little reason to insist that we have even a weak reason to promote the fulfillment of offensive projects (even if we accept *The Teleological View*).[16]

Insofar as *The Teleological View* is compatible with *Hutcheson's Move 2*, *The Teleological View* can sensibly claim that we have only a weakened obligation to establish the basic minimum for Jake, Reggie, and any others who maintain offensive projects. After all, though it may improve Reggie's

[16] This proposal might meet with some resistance. I have so far identified the offensiveness of projects with their poor moral quality. But what about Reggie's project is morally poor? Surely this depends on what moral view we accept. And if we accept *The Teleological View* in combination with *Lexical* and *Prioritarianesque*, we seem committed to the verdict that there is, in fact, *nothing* morally wrong with Reggie's project. One might put this objection slightly differently: the current proposal is circular. It makes reference to the notion of "moral quality" in a specification of moral reasons. But surely the former should await the latter. However, this objection can be sidestepped in any number of ways. One could specify an independent trait of offensive projects like Jake's and Reggie's, e.g., being harmful, or failing respect for persons, etc., and say that projects that display such traits are impersonally less valuable despite the fact that non-harm rights or respect for persons do not by themselves govern moral reasons (i.e., respect for persons could be axiologically, but not morally, important, though they may be morally important as well). Alternatively, one might – in principle, anyway – specify the intrinsic value of individual projects in terms of specifiable *attitudes*, such as reactive attitudes, but deny that such attitudes play any *per se* moral rather than axiological role. "Moral traits" or "offensiveness" needn't refer, specifically, to moral *reasons*, and hence *Hutcheson's Move 2* needn't be circular. (I won't take a stand on such possibilities here; I merely insist that many options are on the table.)

life, the promotion of his offensive project does not improve a state of affairs to the same extent as the promotion of non-offensive projects.[17]

By way of a conclusion to my response to the problem of imprudent choices and offensive tastes, I want to reflect on a general point. In discussing these problems, my response has been simply to assume that they merit response. Some welfarists will disagree. There is surely more to say on the matter than I have indicated and it might very well be that, in the final analysis, the problems of Reggie, Jake, and Kenny present no serious challenge to a welfarist view that rejects any or all of *Hutcheson's Move(s)*. But my strategy here has been simply to stress the *flexibility* of welfarism as a general doctrine. I suggest that even *if* these cases are troubling, WBM can offer principled and independently plausible solutions without giving up the ghost. *Hutcheson's Move* (in any form) is perfectly compatible with my approach to the basic minimum and, interpreted as a claim about impersonal value, is perfectly compatible with a fully teleological solution to the problem of weight. My ambition here is only to stress the ability of a welfarist approach to avoid these problems, not the necessity of so doing. Hence I leave *Hutcheson's Move(s)* as options open for those who are compelled by the problems discussed herein.

6.3. WELFARISM AND RESPECT FOR PERSONS

A fixed point in our judgments about the nature of the basic minimum and its moral importance was noted by Nussbaum in defending the capabilities approach. By way of a refresher, she writes:

> I have spoken both of functioning and of capability. How are they related? Getting clear about this is crucial in defining the relation of the capabilities approach to liberalism. For if we were to take functioning itself as the goal of public policy, the liberal would rightly judge that we were precluding many choices that citizens may make in accordance with their own conceptions of the good. A deeply religious person may prefer not to be well nourished but to engage in strenuous fasting.[18]

Later, she writes:

> [F]or political purposes it is appropriate that we shoot for capabilities, and those alone. Citizens must be left free to determine their own course after that. The

[17] A number of additional topics await a full account of *Hutcheson's Move*(*s*) and their integration into an axiology of the basic minimum, including the discount rate of irresponsible or imprudent behavior, the discount rate of morally unsavory projects, etc. I leave aside this inquiry for another time; the proposals are detailed enough for my purposes here.

[18] Nussbaum, "Women and Cultural Universals" in Nussbaum (1999), 43–4.

person with plenty of food may always choose to fast, but there is a great difference between fasting and starving, and it is this difference that I wish to capture. Again, the person who has normal opportunities for sexual satisfaction can always choose a life of celibacy, and my approach says nothing against this . . . The reason for proceeding in this way is, quite simply, the respect we have for people and their choices. Even when we feel confident that we know what a flourishing life is, and that a particular function plays an important role in it, we do not respect people when we dragoon them into this functioning.[19]

The basic minimum, as I define it here, is compatible with the form of "respect" Nussbaum finds so important. WBM implies no reason to dragoon individuals into lives they do not find valuable. Because any given project must be *valued*, my approach implies no reason to promote the achievement of a state of affairs for any person that this person does not value. Take the religious faster mentioned by Nussbaum above. Plausibly, the religious faster values living according to the principles of his religion under circumstances of fasting and malnutrition. If so, the project of living in accordance with his religious convictions counts as a basic minimum-qualifying valued project. In addition, any project that is obtained in the midst of such force-feeding for the religious faster is unlikely to be valued. Hence there is no pressure given the normative importance of the basic minimum to insist that the faster be force-fed. Fasting, for the religious faster, is an essential part of the achievement of his conception of the good.

However, the situation is a touch more complex than this. As I argued in Chapter 3, we should interpret A's welfare-relevant conception of the good as a set of coherent and complete beliefs about that which is good for A. But if this is correct, there are a number of cases in which p might form a central element of my life plan, without believing that p is, in fact, good *for me*. For instance, I might believe that finding a cure for SIDS is good, and I might choose to dedicate my life to this cause. Nevertheless, I might believe that spending my life pursuing a cure for SIDS is not good for me, but is rather a prudential burden. To put this in terms of Nussbaum's example, the religious faster may choose to fast not because he believes that fasting is good for him. Rather, he might choose to fast because he believes that so fasting is his moral or religious obligation, though bad, in itself, for him. Consider

Steve: Steve believes that he is better-off being fully nourished rather than fasting. But he believes that fasting is his supreme moral obligation, and hence chooses to fast for moral reasons.

[19] Nussbaum (2000), 87–8.

Because he chooses to fast for moral reasons, fasting would not appear in Steve's welfare-relevant conception of the good, and hence, given the moral structure of the basic minimum on my view, there *would* be pressure to insist that he be fed, or compelled to achieve some valued project or other. If we compell Steve to do so, he is more likely to maintain the minimum threshold. On this point, the capabilities approach differs. The capabilities approach indicates only a moral reason to grant the capability for nourishment (or whatever other valuable functioning), not a moral reason to force someone into a state he or she believes is morally impermissible.

To begin my response, I think it is important to stress the fact that even if there is no *in principle* objection to dragooning Steve, there are certainly a number of very strong *in practice* objections to so doing. Dragooning a moral faster into the achievement of a valued project is unlikely to do any good and is likely to do much harm in the meantime. Dragooning a given individual into *any* sort of activity is unlikely to (a) yield a genuine global project or (b) yield a *valued* global project. Though there are certain things that states or other moral agents can do to encourage success at valued projects, these methods will rarely, if ever, include forcing someone into a style of life they would choose – whether for good or bad reasons – to avoid. Few people would *value* the achievement of a global project under threats of force or coercion. Indeed, this point is made most eloquently by Nussbaum: "If people do not have choices, and do what they do because of requirements, their actions may no longer have the same worth, and may in effect be different functions."[20]

But let's leave aside the *in practice* objections to dragooning. My view offers no *in principle* reason not to force people, like Steve, to live lives they do not choose. But this is the right answer. We should take seriously the importance of respecting individuals' choices only if those choices are themselves worthy of respect. Take Steve: if a welfarist approach is correct, Steve's moral belief is irrational, mistaken. Insofar as allowing Steve to fulfill his moral belief would create a worse state of affairs (especially with regard to the achievement of the basic minimum), it is not *worth* respect. The best way to determine when a given individual's choices are worth respect is when these choices either conform to her conception of the good, or conform to genuine moral reasons. And Steve's choices do not do so, at least according to the welfarist approach.

This may sound hard-headed! But before we reject my view in favor of Nussbaum's, however, it is worth wondering the extent to which the

[20] Ibid., 88.

capabilities approach might fail to respect individuals' wider conceptions of the good (including, say, their moral beliefs). Take, for instance:

Henry: Henry's conception of the good includes a commitment to a life of *very limited* capabilities. Henry's choices have been limited since birth, and he has come to embrace a life without, for instance, the capability for play, interaction with the world of nature, or for satisfying relationships with others. He chooses to sabotage any effort to grant him even the capability to engage in these activities.

In this case, either the capabilities approach chooses to insist that Henry maintain the relevant capabilities, or it doesn't. The latter choice seems untenable for a capabilities approach. If the capabilities approach offers no reason to establish these capabilities for Henry, the capabilities approach is once again vulnerable to the problem of adaptive preferences. It might be, for instance, that Henry rejects these capabilities adaptively, and hence the capabilities approach would have no tool for the correction of Henry's adaptive preferences, or reason to pursue any benefits whatever for Henry. Surely this is an unacceptable result, and in strong conflict with the general motivation for any capabilities approach. The right answer, on behalf of the capabilities approach, is to insist that Henry *maintain* these capabilities, despite his rejection of them. But in so doing, the capabilities approach must limit the choices that are worthy of respect; in particular, it must limit respect to choices that are rational *from the perspective of the capabilities approach*. Hence the capabilities approach has no grounds to complain that the welfarist approach I defend here cannot respect the choices of individuals. The welfarist approach and capabilities approach will, of course, differ concerning *which* preferences or choices should and should not be respected. My view argues that preferences should be respected only to the extent that they are compatible with the welfarist approach for which I argue here; Nussbaum will argue that preferences should be respected only to the extent that they are compatible with the capabilities approach for which she argues. But this just *is* a substantive disagreement between the capabilities approach and the welfarist approach concerning which approach forms the best account of a basic minimum, or morally valuable states of persons. Any rejection of a welfarist approach on grounds of a lack of respect for individuals' preferences, then, would appear to simply beg the question against welfarism.

We should be very reluctant to dragoon individuals into lives or activities that they do not value in any respect whatever. Surely if I'm to be dragooned into some life or other, I had better take *some* relevant pro-attitude toward it. Insofar as I accept *The Basic Minimum as Proto-autonomy*, my view does not do this.[21] However, both the capabilities approach and welfarist approach admit (at least in principle) reasons to force individuals not to violate moral reasons implied by those views or jeopardize their own achievement of valued states. The capabilities approach gains no advantage over a welfarist approach on this score.

6.4. THE CASH COMPENSATION ARGUMENT

Jonathan Wolff and Avner De-Shalit have recently offered a novel argument against welfarism that I must consider here. This argument forms part of a treatment of *disadvantage*, rather than the basic minimum; according to Wolff and De-Shalit, well-being cannot form the proper index of what it means for someone to be worse-off than someone else. Wolff and De-Shalit argue that disadvantage is best understood in terms of a revised version of Nussbaum's capabilities approach, i.e., in terms of "genuine opportunity for secure functioning," where the relevant "functionings" include items on Nussbaum's list and a number of important additions.[22]

I won't spend any time criticizing Wolff and De-Shalit's view as a theory of disadvantage, though I believe their approach is problematic for many of the same reasons Nussbaum's approach is problematic. But I do want to briefly consider their rejection of a *welfarist* approach. Wolff and De-Shalit identify welfarism in the following way: "According to the version of welfare theory under discussion here, to be disadvantaged is to suffer from lower levels of preference satisfaction than others, and so disadvantaged people need compensation to bring them to an appropriate level of preference satisfaction."[23] According to Wolff and De-Shalit, this account of a preferentist theory of well-being implies a form of "monism," which they characterize as "comparison monism": "Comparison monism is the view that all goods can be put in a single scale of comparison."[24] To this they contrast "substitution monism": "Substitution monism claims that any good can be substituted for enough of any other, at least before a 'saturation' point kicks in and additional units bring no further satisfaction."[25]

According to Wolff and De-Shalit, all preferentist theories of well-being imply comparison monism. And *if* it is the case that all preferentist views measure well-being simply along the single dimension of preference satisfaction, they are correct. But notice that Strong Strong Subjectivism

[21] There is some question whether the capabilities approach actually violates even this minimal principle: Henry might see *nothing* attractive about a life of broad capabilities. But I'll refrain from pressing this point here.

[22] Wolff and De-Shalit (2007), esp. chs. 1–4. [23] Ibid., 24. [24] Ibid., 25. [25] Ibid.

appears to be the only version of a subjectivist view that implies comparison monism, i.e., that the quality of a given individual's life is to be determined on the overall scale of preference satisfaction this person achieves. Weak Strong Subjectivism implies that a person's well-being needn't always be measured by the extent to which a person satisfies their preferences but perhaps along different scales, such as the dual dimensions of satisfactions and valued projects.

But leave this aside, and concentrate on Strong Strong Subjectivism. Wolff and De-Shalit's argument focuses on the second form of monism, i.e., substitution monism. According to Wolff and De-Shalit, substitution monism is false, and its falsity is also sufficient reason to reject welfarism given that "substitution monism seems implicit within preference based theories of advantage and disadvantage."[26] Again, any non-Strong Strong version of subjectivism has resources to reject substitution monism. Indeed, my own view does so. The basic minimum lexically dominates satisfactions, for instance, hence no amount of satisfactions could make up for the loss of the basic minimum. However, I am willing to put aside what I see as the best account of a welfarist approach for now, and to allow Wolff and De-Shalit the – unargued for and incorrect – premise that welfarist approaches are committed to substitution monism. Why should this pose a problem for welfarism?

According to Wolff and De-Shalit, were substitution monism true, there could be no in-principle objection to compensating any form of disadvantage with *cash*. In other words, because money is ultimately fungible, any person who is worse-off than others could, in principle, be adequately compensated by cash payment. However, according to Wolff and De-Shalit, there are certain instances in which cash compensation is simply not enough to compensate disadvantage. Helpfully, they state their argument formally:

1. In the case of some disadvantages it is appropriate to remedy them with money.
2. If substitution monism is true, and money is appropriate to remedy some disadvantage, then it follows that money, in principle, can remedy all disadvantage.

   But

3. There are cases where money is not an appropriate form of remedy for disadvantage. Therefore
4. Substitution monism is false.[27]

[26] Ibid. [27] Ibid., 26–7.

Given that we have granted the assumption that all welfarist views imply substitution monism, welfarism is also false.

Confining our discussion to Strong Strong Subjectivism (and appropriate versions of Weak Strong Subjectivism), are the premises true? Consider the first premise. For a preferentist is it appropriate to remedy any failure of preference satisfaction with money? Surely not! Failures of preference satisfaction, according to the preferentist, can only be made up for by other instances of *preference satisfaction*. Without attendant preference satisfaction, *money is no compensation at all*. Money may very well be a *means* to preference satisfaction, but money *itself* cannot compensate for the failure of preference satisfaction, unless "to have *x* level of money" is itself preferred for its own sake. Of course, Wolff and De-Shalit surely *mean* that, in at least some cases, money can be used for the satisfaction of preferences that would alleviate disadvantage along a preferentist scale. But the difference is important, as we shall see. But, for now, let us grant this latter claim.

What about premise two? Granting substitution monism, and premise one, can *all* disadvantage be compensated with cash? Consider a person, Jack, who prefers two things in life: the development of a robust collection of Star Wars action figures, and to develop and fulfill a loving relationship with another person, Jill. However, imagine now that because Jill will not consent to be in such a relationship, Jack's second relevant preference will go unsatisfied. However, one might think, *given* substitution monism, because Jack also prefers to collect Star Wars action figures, one could compensate for the loss of his beloved by providing money – in sufficient quantities – which would allow Jack to better develop his Star Wars collection, which he values for its own sake. *If* substitution monism is true, i.e., if enough of one good can compensate for the loss of any other, we should accept that money can compensate for any preferentist disadvantage for Jack. However, looking carefully at premise two shows how implausible substitution monism is even for a version of Strong Strong Subjectivism. Though Jack might value his collection of Star Wars action figures there comes a point at which further compensation in terms of such action figures will not compensate for the loss of his beloved; once this point is reached, no further action figures or monetary compensation could compensate Jack for the loss of his preference for a loving relationship with Jill.[28] In Jack's case,

[28] This is to some degree complicated by a qualifier inserted by Wolff and De-Shalit in defining substitution monism: "at least before a 'saturation' point kicks in and additional units bring no further satisfaction." Indeed, Wolff and De-Shalit assume that the "saturation point" will not be reached in cases of cash compensation; money, after all, is widely fungible (ibid., 195n16, 196n20). But notice that *money*, here, does not reach saturation point. Money continues to satisfy Jack's

monetary compensation cannot make up for *any* loss of preference satisfaction. Of course, Jack is psychologically simplified. Real people are far more complex. But this complexity makes doubt rather than confidence a more appropriate attitude to take toward the suggestion that money could compensate for any failure of preference satisfaction. Though we should accept premise two, we should be strongly inclined to deny the antecedent, even if we accept a version of Strong Strong Subjectivism, which we shouldn't.

Premise two is therefore correct, but its antecedent is false. But just for the sake of argument, let's grant the antecedent of premise two, and say that welfarism *must* claim that *any* failure to satisfy a preference can be made up for by sufficient satisfaction of preferences in other areas, and that money will always allow one to fulfill this sufficient satisfaction of preferences. This leaves the third premise. Is it the case that, *given* the assumptions to which we have submitted for the sake of argument, there are disadvantages that could not be made up for by cash compensation?

> Consider, for example, support for people with disabilities. While it is true that people with disabilities sometimes seek support from the state in cash form, this, first, is only one of the many measures sought, and second is seemingly rarely if ever claimed as compensation for the special miseries of disability . . . Yet aside from cash transfers there are many other strategies that societies adopt for addressing disability. These include medical intervention, support by means of provision of equipment and paid careers, and technical, social, and cultural change.[29]

Should we accept that disability cannot properly be made up for by cash transfers? We must remember that for a preferentist *cash is of no* per se *value*. The only thing that could make up for a failure of preference-fulfillment is the further fulfillment of preferences. But this is significant. Given the assumptions we have allowed, to satisfy any preferentist criterion for adequate compensation, it must be the case that cash in sufficient amounts is at least indifferent to the disabled person in comparison to non-monetary compensation, i.e., by "medical intervention, support by means of provision of equipment and paid careers, and technical, social, and cultural change." For a preferentist to be happy with any form of cash compensation, the life in which A is compensated with cash, and the life

desire for a collection of Star Wars action figures. Rather, it's the *action figures* that reach saturation point. One might interpret substitution monism in a way that rules out all saturation points. But so doing strips the force of Wolff and De-Shalit's argument. There is an obvious and principled reason for rejecting cash compensation: saturation points, or points at which the satisfaction of additional preferences to ϕ do not compensate for the loss of one's preference to ψ.

29 Ibid., 25–6.

in which A is compensated by non-monetary means, is of at least equivalent rank in A's conception of the good.[30] But under this assumption, is it implausible to believe that disability *can* be compensated with cash? Absolutely not! After all, the person involved is, at worst, indifferent between a cash-compensated life and a non-monetarily compensated life. Wolff and De-Shalit's argument is thus unconvincing.

The next example betrays the same problem.

> Or consider cases of severe environmental injustice, in which people have to be evacuated from their homes, for example because of contamination caused by a chemical spill. These people often report that they lose not merely in financial terms, but also, and perhaps primarily, suffer profound feelings of dislocation (literally); the loss of a sense of place, which impacts upon their self-identity. Such loss, therefore, cannot be removed or properly "compensated" by cash transfers.[31]

Again, the example is a poor one. We must remember that for cash compensation to be adequate, it must be the case that the cash-compensated life and the non-monetarily compensated life (i.e., perhaps by means of cleaning up the environmental disaster) are of *at least* equivalent value according to the conception of the good of the person in question. But under this assumption, there is precisely *no* intuitive pull to the suggestion that cash is not a reasonable compensation for those who suffer disadvantage. It leads to lives they value living just as much.

6.5. OPERATIONALISM, PUBLICITY, AND AN ECUMENICAL PROPOSAL

Some hold that welfarism forms a poor basis for moral or political obligation given that welfarism is difficult to put into practice. Welfarism suffers from epistemic problems, in particular the inability to make interpersonal or intrapersonal comparisons of well-being. It is difficult for any given

[30] Some approaches to the welfare value of preferences may deny this; some might hold that the preference for that which could be obtained by non-cash compensation versus that which could be obtained by cash compensation is just one preference among many, which could be outweighed by the further satisfaction of preferences provided by cash compensation. Hence for a preferentist to prefer a life of cash compensation does not require the individual in question to prefer the life of cash compensation, so long as this person's preferences are satisfied to a greater extent *by* cash compensation. One might say, for instance, that the preference not to be a drug addict rather than to be a drug addict is outweighed by all the intense momentary preferences one satisfies *as* a drug addict. But this approach to the welfare value of preferences is surely a non-starter, as is illustrated by this very case. See Parfit (1984), 497.

[31] Wolff and De-Shalit (2007), 26.

individual to know what they prefer, let alone for any particular person to find out what someone else prefers. And it is even more difficult for any particular social policy to be assessed on the basis of welfare, given that, for any given individual person, the extent to which they achieve any particular level of well-being is difficult to determine and can be determined – if at all – only in the *ex post*.

David Braybrooke offers the following version of this critique. Referring to "utility" (by which he means the satisfaction of preferences), Braybrooke writes:

> Outside the theoretical discussions of economists and philosophers, the concept of utility is not in current use . . . If one grants (in spite of various difficulties) that the Neumann-Morgenstern technique can in principle give measures of utility valid for persons taken one by one, the fact remains that no one has drawn up anything like a full schedule of even a single person's utilities, and there is no prospect of anyone's ever doing so. Moreover, the problem of translating these measurements into interpersonal comparisons remains. The current suggestion that the problem of interpersonal comparisons be resolved by simply assuming that human beings are sufficiently alike for us to use any one person's scale as a basis for comparing all the rest, whatever its other merits or demerits, hardly gets to the starting gate in practical affairs. We do not and will not have the measurements for any one person, to say nothing of all the rest: 24 million in Canada; 240 million in the United States.[32]

If Braybrooke is correct, the situation for any preferentist view seems bleak.

But the problem gets even worse for my view. Because my view defends PC, it defends a theory that seems to have the unsettling consequence that no one could ever come to know how good a life they are leading. Because no one could ever experience anything like all metaphysically possible value data, no one could ever come to have a coherent and complete conception of the good which, according to my view, defines at least in part a given person's well-being. Faced with such problems, Braybrooke declares that welfarism is "up in the air, in Cloud Cuckooland."[33]

I confess to finding this objection less than compelling. My project here is to outline a conception of moral reasons that form the central moral structure of a basic minimum. As explained in the Introduction, it is not my project to offer a public policy in light of these reasons. To put this another way, my topic is moral reasons, not *policy* reasons.[34] Policy reasons,

[32] Braybrooke (1987), 171–2. [33] Ibid., 172. See also Rawls (1995), 182n11.

[34] The distinction between moral reasons and policy reasons should strike the reader as reminiscent of the distinction between objective reasons and subjective reasons; on my understanding, policy reasons just are the subjective moral reasons that apply to political institutions. For further discussion

which direct political institutions and other moral agents to adopt particular policies rather than others, are likely to be highly contextualized, and will reflect widely varying beliefs about how best to conform to genuine moral reasons. With this distinction in mind, however, it would be a disastrous mistake to provide a conception of moral reasons that is designed to ease operationalism, or ease the development of public policy. Imagine, for instance, that despite the fact that welfarism of the form I embrace here provides the best account of moral reasons, we accept an alternative to welfarism (call this "Theory O") because Theory O offers a more obvious set of policy reasons; Theory O could be better operationalized. Imagine now that it just so happens that we come to learn, through divine intervention, or luck, or whatever, that though our methods have so far been utter failures when it comes to the achievement of a view that best expressed our understanding of the basic minimum and its moral importance, they have been successful when it comes to Theory O. Leaving aside any evaluation of our past practices, what stance should we adopt toward our future practices? Should we be morally content to continue with our behavior as is? I contend that the answer is no: though, perhaps, we should not blame ourselves for the adoption of Theory O, we would regret having done so and seek to change our future behavior. Hence if our considered judgments when it comes to genuine moral reasons favor a welfarist approach – which I have so far argued they do – we cannot reject this approach simply on grounds of difficult operationalization.

Of course, the problems discussed here would be much more difficult if we had *no clue* how to construct a public policy on the basis of a welfarist approach to the basic minimum. Though this would not alter our commitment to welfarism as a theory of moral reasons, it would perhaps make our genuine moral reasons totally irrelevant from the standpoint of social policy. And though some uncertainty is certainly to be expected in any moral endeavor, total cluelessness is perhaps less than we want from a moral theory. But I think we are not simply fumbling in the dark. There is an important consilience between a welfarist approach and a *capabilities* approach at the level of public policy. If we accept a welfarist approach to objective moral reasons, there is good reason to believe that a capabilities approach is the best approach to *policy* reasons.

First, if we accept the welfarist approach, there is public policy reason to install the basic capabilities – or at least many of them. The capabilities

of the distinction between objective and subjective reasons, see Schroeder (2007), 13–14, and Brink (2003), 220.

approach as defended by Nussbaum, or as amended by Wolff and De-Shalit, maintains strong global support, especially from those who are worse-off. In other words, these capabilities *matter* to the disadvantaged.[35] If so, it is likely that granting these capabilities will have salutary effects on the development and achievement of long-term valued projects for individuals. The reason such capabilities are valued, one might expect, is that they are necessary means for the achievement of that which the disadvantaged value. If our goal, then, is to increase aggregate well-being, the widespread support of the capabilities approach seems to indicate that the capabilities approach is a good bet when it comes to public policy. This is especially true if, as Nussbaum supposes, establishing the central capabilities itself has the power to overcome adaptive preferences and "reveal" an individual's more genuine conception of the good.

Second, there will rarely be policy reason to go beyond the installation of such capabilities. In particular, as already noted, taking active steps to force people to achieve valued projects is often counter productive when it comes to the achievement of well-being. Direct involvement in people's lives is unlikely to advance the general goal of the achievement of valued projects. Being forced to be a sailor is very different than being a sailor of one's own choosing; most individuals will refuse, or will not value, the former. Hence, in terms of social policy, there is good reason to believe that the capabilities approach is a plausible way forward.[36]

Given these facts, I have no *per se* objection to a capabilities approach as a starting point for social policy or as a proper theory of policy reasons. Indeed, it may very well be that a capabilities approach is the best instrument that anyone can use to satisfy genuine moral reasons, especially given that the capabilities are widely prized.[37] Of course, if we can improve on the capabilities approach, we should. (For instance, one possible addendum to the capabilities approach might be to develop educational curricula to encourage the development of long-term achievements, goals, and projects. This proposal would go beyond provision of capabilities, but would actually seek to encourage individuals to use these capabilities in living better lives.) But there is good reason to believe that the capabilities approach is at least a solid beginning in leading us to promote overall life quality.

Though I believe the capabilities approach is a strong guide to social policy, perhaps with a few minor modifications, we should not confuse an inquiry into policy with a philosophical inquiry into the nature of the

[35] Wolff and De-Shalit (2007), 11–12; Nussbaum (2000), 76–7; Sen (1999), 227–48.
[36] Nussbaum (2000), 88–9.
[37] Cf. Wolff and De-Shalit (2007), app. 1.

moral requirements that serve as the ultimate *goal* of public policy. Insofar as we adopt a capabilities approach, it is only in the service of promotion of the basic minimum to the extent that *The Teleological View* directs us to do so. How close we come to conforming to our genuine moral requirements on the welfarist approach I outline here is likely to be subject to uncertainty. Despite our best evidence of success or failure, given the construction of my view, we will always be operating – and operationalizing – to some degree in the dark. But replacing a view that generates uncertainty with a view that provides certainty at the cost of plausibility is not good business, morally speaking. When faced with a choice between certain mistakes and uncertain successes, it is morally best to choose the latter.

6.6. RISK

The previous objection lays the groundwork for the final objection I discuss in this chapter. Wolff and De-Shalit argue that a welfarist approach fails not just on grounds of inappropriate cash compensation, but also on grounds that it makes no distinction between the achievement of well-being and the *secure* achievement of well-being. They write:

> [W]hat matters for an individual is not only the level of functionings he or she enjoys at a particular time, but also their prospects for sustaining that level. To put this another way, exceptional risk and vulnerability is itself a disadvantage, whether or not the feared event ever actually happens. A casual employee, who may be put out of work at any time, is in quite a different situation from someone on a permanent contract, even if she is in receipt of the same wages and never actually unemployed.[38]

WBM makes no provision for the security of one's achievement of a valued project. One could very sensibly maintain the basic minimum despite the fact that one's achievement of a valued project is or was insecure for very large portions (even the entirety) of one's life. If this sort of security is essential to the basic minimum, WBM must fail.[39]

I think we should reject the claim that an important feature of the basic minimum is a lack of susceptibility to risk. There are two reasons for this. First, we would not say that a person who maintains a valued project, but whose maintenance of this valued project is insecure, fails the basic minimum. Rather, it seems sensible to say that, of this person, though they

[38] Ibid., 8–9.

[39] Security is also important to Shue's conception of the basic minimum, as noted in Chapter 1; see note 19.

maintain the basic minimum, they do so in a way that is not secure; if matters do not change, one might expect them to lose the basic minimum. It seems right to say that some can maintain the basic minimum in a way that is subject to undue risk. But if avoidance of undue risk is an element of the basic minimum, it would appear that such a claim is nonsensical: no one who maintains the minimum can be subject to undue risk. But this claim is far too strong. (Of course, risk will be relevant to the achievement of the basic minimum for some: for those individuals who value projects only in conditions of security, or projects of which a central element is security or absence of risk. For these individuals, however, WBM adequately protects their interest in the avoidance of risk: it is part of their achievement of welfare.)

In addition, I think we should reject any sort of moral reason to reduce risk. Recall the distinction between moral reasons and policy reasons. It seems quite clear that we have policy reason to reduce risk. The greater the risk to the achievement of the basic minimum, the more likely it is that this basic minimum will be lost, losing the accompanying good (which we have moral reason to promote). Furthermore, undue risk can have a negative effect on our achievement of well-being. In particular, it can cause pain, frustration, and can lead to stress that might have an effect on the achievement of valued projects or other welfare goods. But this says nothing about the *per se* moral importance of risk. But there is no moral reason to reduce risk. Recall that in Chapter 1 I drew a distinction between a *mere* capability and a *substantive* capability. A mere capability is a capability that is never used to improve a life. Conversely, a substantive capability is a capability that *is* so used. With this distinction in mind, consider the distinction between *mere* risk and *substantive* risk. Mere risk is risk that never impacts the quality of a life. Substantive risk, on the other hand, does. My drive on the freeway today subjected me to mere risk. Had I crashed, that risk would have been substantive.

Any view that accepts a *per se* moral reason to reduce risk must hold that there is moral reason to reduce *mere* risk. But I find this position quite far-fetched, especially if the reduction of mere risk is in conflict with other potential moral goals – including the promotion of valued projects for those that don't yet obtain a life of valued, self-directed meaning. Of course, this does not mean there is no policy reason to reduce mere risk. The – dashed annoying! – thing about risk is that one can never tell whether it is mere or substantive in the *ex ante*. Given our position of uncertainty, there is surely policy reason to reduce the mere risk of failing the basic minimum. But there is no *per se moral* reason to do so. One would certainly not be willing to trade-off the achievement of valued states for others, no matter how small, for the reduction of *mere* risk.

Indeed, I think the claim that we have *policy* reason to reduce risk best explains Wolff and De-Shalit's position. In arguing for a moral reason to reduce risk, Wolff and De-Shalit write:

> North-eastern Israeli Negev is home to several Bedouin tribes. The Bedouins live in what may be described as a "town" of tents. North of this area – in occupied Judea, south of Hebron – lie settlements and industries whose sewage, including chemical waste, runs into the open gorge near the Bedouin village. The Bedouin understandably objected to the contamination of their wells. Furthermore their children were exposed to the chemicals in the open gorge, and to avoid crossing it were forced to take a different route to school. This meant negotiating a very busy road, with dangerous heavy traffic... [S]ince most of the Israeli Negev is either a military zone and off-limits to civilians, or else Israeli kibbutz lands or nature preserves, they literally had nowhere to go, even if they had been prepared to move... Thus, in order to avoid homelessness, the Bedouins were forced to take risks to their health and to their children's lives, and these risks were bigger, perhaps in all three senses identified above, than those faced by others. It seems natural to say that they were disadvantaged in one or more ways regardless of whether or not they were aware of the risks they were facing. This is also independent of their current level of achieved functioning.[40]

I think that Wolff and De-Shalit's case is important, but it, at best, shows that we have policy reason to reduce risk. I think it is natural to describe the Bedouin as disadvantaged. Surely the fact that they now have to deal with runoff of industrial waste, to navigate difficult roads, etc., are hardships when it comes to their achievement of well-being. For all we know, continued exposure to such risk will begin to affect the extent to which the Bedouin can genuinely engage their valued projects. Given that we are concerned about their achievement of the basic minimum not just now but in the future, there is *policy* reason to reduce risk that is independent of their *current* "functioning" or achievement of valued projects. But to claim that the achievement of the basic minimum requires reduction of risk seems to generate implausible trade-offs; one could imagine, for instance, that reducing mere risk of failure of a valued project for the Bedouins actually increases the *substantive* risk of non-minimum goods for others. It would appear, depending on the numbers involved, that any proposal that includes a lack of risk in its account of the basic minimum must justify the imposition of substantive risk – must justify making people's lives *worse* – for the sake of a reduction in *mere* risk. But this is untenable.

[40] Wolff and De-Shalit (2007), 67–8.

But if we assume that the well-being of the Bedouin is not affected *in any way* by the risk they face – in other words, if their risk is *mere* risk – it seems to me quite wrong to say that they are *thereby* genuinely disadvantaged, simply for facing greater risk. They may be disadvantaged with regard to that which we have *policy* reason to provide them. But if their well-being is precisely the same before their lands were contaminated as it was afterwards, it seems quite wrong to say that we now have *per se* moral reason to reduce risk or that the Bedouins – or anyone else – fail the basic minimum as a result of such risk.

6.7. CONCLUSION, AND UNFINISHED BUSINESS

I conclude this chapter by noting that WBM can avoid the more compelling objections I discuss here. Given the strength and flexibility of welfarism as a doctrine (and, indeed, the overall plausibility of the resulting view), I contend that those interested in the structure of the basic minimum, or in the structure of moral and political reasons more generally, have strong reason to take it seriously in disputes about the moral fundamentals of a basic moral or political threshold.

By way of a conclusion to this book, let me briefly sum up the theses I have so far advocated. First, I've argued that non-welfarist approaches to the basic minimum face serious problems that can be avoided by a welfarist alternative. In addition, I've argued that one such approach (WBM, combined with PC) can avoid the welfarist's dilemma. Also, I have offered a slightly weakened interpretation of the traditional overriding account of the moral structure of the basic minimum, represented by *The Teleological View* in combination with *Lexical* and *Prioritarianesque*. These propositions characterize my positive approach to the basic minimum.

It is also worth noting what I have not done. First on this list concerns the issue of political neutrality. For the most part, I have left discussion of the neutrality most associated with so-called "political liberalism" to the side here. However, though I have not argued that my view could achieve an overlapping consensus among comprehensive ethical doctrines, I have offered what I believe is a strong argument *immanent* to our own comprehensive doctrine. I hold that there is good reason, supported by substantive moral argument, for us – myself and the reader – to reject any political conception that is not sensitive to concerns about human well-being.[41]

[41] But if my view is vulnerable to an objection from political neutrality, it is not alone. Take, for instance, Nussbaum's list of ten basic capabilities. She claims that these capabilities are supported

Second, I have sought to show the flexibility of a welfarist approach by offering positions – without endorsement – for those who might find them attractive. For instance, one might accept that the welfarist approach I defend here should be "luckist," or should be sensitive to the moral quality of individual projects. One can accept either a subjective or objective substantive theory of welfare. Whether any or all of these positions are ultimately acceptable is beyond the scope of this inquiry. Nevertheless, nothing in this book requires a commitment on all or indeed any of these potential interpretations of a welfarist approach to the basic minimum.

Third, and connected with the point made in the previous paragraph, I have endorsed a number of views in this book that could be rejected without rejecting the spirit of a welfarist approach to the basic minimum. As I noted in the Introduction, the view I endorse is *modular*. Though I officially accept WBM rather than WBM* or WBM2, I accept that the basic minimum lexically dominates sub-minimum marginal welfare benefits and is weighted according to a prioritarianesque value curve in comparison to super-minimum project-improvements; I accept *The Teleological View*. These views could be tweaked without doing substantive damage to a robust and recognizable welfarist approach to the basic minimum. One can accept any particular module without accepting the others; the arguments are, for the most part anyway, freestanding.

Fourth, my approach to the basic minimum describes only one corner of morality, especially when it comes to the moral obligations of political institutions. I do not claim, for instance, to assess the plausibility, or the weight of the basic minimum against, considerations of *culture*, *community*, *democracy*, or other important values that may or may not hold of

by a conception of "human dignity" or "truly human functioning." But though Nussbaum's list of capabilities does not judge the justice of institutions by the extent to which individuals achieve this conception of life quality, it does much to organize political systems *based on* a fully-developed ethical comprehensive doctrine rooted in a substantive perfectionism (see §2.7). According to Nussbaum, "[t]he intuitive idea behind the approach is twofold: first, certain functions are particularly central in human life, in the sense that their presence on absence is typically understood to be a mark of the presence or absence of human life; and second – this is what Marx found in Aristotle – that there is something that it is to do these functions in a truly human way, not a merely animal way" (Nussbaum (2000), 71–2). Given her commitment to the substantive perfectionism of Marx and Aristotle, it is hard to see how Nussbaum's capabilities approach might avoid the complaint that her view overrides the "fact of reasonable pluralism." Nussbaum herself claims that her view *could* be supported by an overlapping consensus (see ibid., 5). It is beyond the scope of this book to consider whether it could. However, there are no grounds for believing that her view could be so supported *while mine could not*. If anything, WBM is "more" neutral (if this makes sense) than Nussbaum's view: my view holds that some forms of life may constitute the basic minimum in a way that Nussbaum's does not. With this, it seems to me sensible to leave the topic of political neutrality aside. I leave it up to readers to determine whether a rejection of any reference to moral reasons or to human well-being is acceptable in the face of my arguments for WBM, and the moral importance of the basic minimum, here.

the political domain. My topic is limited to the relative moral weight of the basic minimum in comparison to reasons to promote other valuable states of persons. It may very well be that an interest in, say, democratic institutions is in conflict with, and trumps, an interest in the promotion of the basic minimum. I leave this open for future inquiry.

Fifth, I have not, in this book, offered any argument that there should be a basic minimum. This, I think, is an important bit of unfinished business, but business that my approach to human well-being may help to finish. Insofar as there are independent reasons to accept *Lexical, Prioritarianesque* and *The Teleological View*, a robust basic minimum (a basic minimum that at least satisfies BM3), simply "pops out." I should note, however, that my intention in this book was not to argue that there should be a basic minimum, but rather to clarify, insofar as there should be such a minimum, its structure. I hope to have succeeded in this latter, more modest, task.

I should also mention a sixth and final bit of unfinished business. My approach to the basic minimum and its moral importance is abstracted from the genuine and pressing concerns of real-world individuals whose lives are in desperate need of moral attention. As stated in the Introduction, I conceive of my task as akin to the anatomist, rather than the surgeon. My view is a moral-philosophical investigation, not an investigation into social policy. As such, abstraction of the form I accept here is appropriate. But though I broach the topic of policy only very briefly, I do not regard such an inquiry to be less important philosophically. Understanding the nature of moral obligations to the worst-off is complex business, and must be taken in stages. This book is only the beginning: a more or less abstract account of the moral reasons that drive such an obligation. And though I have said a few words about how our moral obligations might best be fulfilled – including my endorsement of the capabilities approach as an approach to social policy – much work remains to be done. This book is but one part of the long and difficult project of best promoting the interests of the least-advantaged among us.

Bibliography

Annas, Julia (1993), *The Morality of Happiness* (Oxford University Press).

Aristotle (1999), *Nicomachean Ethics*, ed. and trans. T. Irwin, 2nd edn. (Indianapolis: Hackett Publishing Company).

Arneson, Richard (1989), "Equality and Equal Opportunity for Welfare" in *Philosophical Studies*, 56(1), 77–93.

(1992), "Property Rights in Persons" in *Social Philosophy and Policy*, 9(1), 201–30.

(1997), "The Priority of the Right over the Good Rides Again" in *Ethics*, 108(1), 169–96.

(1999), "Human Flourishing versus Desire Satisfaction" in *Social Philosophy and Policy*, 16(1), 113–42.

(2000a), "Perfectionism and Politics" in *Ethics*, 111(1), 37–63.

(2000b), "Welfare Should Be the Currency of Justice" in *Canadian Journal of Philosophy*, 30(4), 497–524.

(2000c), "Rawls versus Utilitarianism in Light of *Political Liberalism*" in Davion, et al. (2000), 231–52.

(2000d), "Luck Egalitarianism and Prioritarianism" in *Ethics*, 110(2), 339–49.

(2003), "Liberal Neutrality on the Good: An Autopsy" in Klosko and Wall (2003), 191–218.

(2004), "Luck Egalitarianism: An Interpretation and Defense" in *Philosophical Topics*, 32(1-2), 1–20.

Baker, John (1992), "An Egalitarian Case for Basic Income" in van Parijs, ed. (1992), 101–27.

Baron, Marcia, Philip Pettit, and Michael Slote (1997), *Three Methods of Ethics* (Oxford: Blackwell).

Barry, Brian (1992), *Justice as Impartiality* (Oxford University Press).

Beitz, Charles (2009), *The Idea of Human Rights* (Oxford University Press).

Benbaji, Yitzhak (2006), "Sufficiency or Priority?" in *European Journal of Philosophy*, 14(3), 327–48.

Braybrooke, David (1987), *Meeting Needs* (Princeton University Press).

Brighouse, Harry and Adam Swift (2006), "Equality, Priority, and Positional Goods" in *Ethics*, 116(3), 471–97.

Brink, David (1989), *Moral Realism and the Foundations of Ethics* (Cambridge University Press).

(2003), "Prudence and Authenticity: Intrapersonal Conflicts of Value" in *The Philosophical Review*, 112(2), 215–45.
(2008), "The Significance of Desire" in *Oxford Studies in Metaethics*, 3, 5–45.
Broome, John (2004), *Weighing Lives* (Oxford University Press).
Brown, Campbell (2005), "Equality, Sufficiency... or Both?" in *Economics and Philosophy*, 21(2), 199–220.
(MS), "How to Live a Life Worth Living."
Buchan, John (1915), *The Thirty-Nine Steps* (New York, NY: Penguin).
Buchanan, Allen (1984), "What's So Special About Rights" in *Social Philosophy and Policy*, 2(1), 61–83.
Casal, Paula (2007), "Why Sufficiency is Not Enough" in *Ethics*, 117(2), 296–326.
Crisp, Roger (2003), "Equality, Priority, and Compassion" in *Ethics*, 113(4), 745–63.
(2007), *Reasons and the Good* (Oxford University Press).
Davion, Victoria and Clark Wolf, eds. (2000), *The Idea of a Political Liberalism* (Lanham, MD: Rowman and Littlefield).
Dorsey, Dale (2005), "Global Justice and the Limits of Human Rights" in *The Philosophical Quarterly*, 55(221), 562–81.
(2006), "A Coherence Theory of Truth in Ethics" in *Philosophical Studies*, 125(3), 493–523.
(2009), "Headaches, Lives, and Value" in *Utilitas*, 21(1), 36–58.
(2010a), "Three Arguments for Perfectionism" in *Noûs*, 44(1), 59–79.
(2010b), "Truth and Error in Morality" in Wright, et al. (2010), 235–48.
(2011), "The Hedonist's Dilemma" in *Journal of Moral Philosophy*, 8(2), 173–96.
(MS), "Subjectivism without Desire."
Dworkin, Ronald (1984), "Rights as Trumps" in Waldron (1984), 153–67.
(2000), *Sovereign Virtue* (Cambridge, MA: Harvard University Press).
Elster, Jon (1982), "Sour Grapes: Utilitarianism and the Genesis of Wants" in Sen and Williams (1982), 219–38.
(1983), *Sour Grapes: Studies in the Subversion of Rationality* (Cambridge University Press).
Feinberg, Joel (1970), "On the Nature and Value of Rights" in *Journal of Value Inquiry*, 4(4), 243–60.
Frankfurt, Harry (1988), *The Importance of What We Care About* (Cambridge University Press).
Griffin, James (1989), *Well-Being: Its Meaning, Measurement, and Moral Importance* (Oxford University Press).
(1996), *Value Judgment* (Oxford University Press).
(2001), "First Steps in an Account of Human Rights" in *European Journal of Philosophy*, 9(3), 306–27.
(2007), *On Human Rights* (Oxford University Press).
Hanfling, Oswald (2006), "Rights and Human Rights" in O'Hear (2006), 57–93.
Harrington, Fred (MS), "The Rightholder as the Source of Duties."
Hassoun, Nicole (2008), "World Poverty and Individual Freedom" in *American Philosophical Quarterly*, 45(2), 191–8.

(2009), "Human Rights, Needs, and Autonomy" in *Proceedings for the 3rd International Conference on Philosophy*.
Hawkins, Jennifer (2008), "Well-Being, Autonomy, and the Horizon Problem" in *Utilitas*, 20(2), 143–68.
Herman, Barbara (1993), *The Practice of Moral Judgment* (Cambridge, MA: Harvard University Press).
Holtug, Nils (1998), "Egalitarianism and the Levelling Down Objection" in *Analysis*, 58(2), 166–74.
(2003), "Good for Whom?" in *Theoria*, 69(1-2), 4–20.
(2006), "A Note on Conditional Egalitarianism" in *Economics and Philosophy*, 23(1), 45–63.
(2007a), "Person-Affecting Moralities" in Ryberg, et al. (2007), 129–61.
(2007b), "Prioritarianism" in Holtug, et al. (2007), 125–56.
Holtug, Nils and Kaspar Lippert-Rasmussen, eds. (2007), *Egalitarianism: New Essays on the Value of Equality* (Oxford University Press).
Hume, David (1739), *A Treatise of Human Nature*, ed. D. and M. Norton (Oxford University Press, 2008).
Hurka, Thomas (1993), *Perfectionism* (Oxford University Press).
Hutcheson, Francis (1726), *An Inquiry into the Original of Our Ideas of Beauty and Virtue* (Indianapolis: Liberty Fund).
(1755), *A System of Moral Philosophy* (New York: Continuum).
Kamm, Frances (1993), *Morality, Mortality*, vol. 1 (Oxford University Press).
(2003), "Rescuing Ivan Illych: How We Live and How We Die" in *Ethics*, 113(2), 202–33.
Kaufman, Alexander, ed. (2008), *Capabilities Equality* (London: Routledge).
Keller, Simon (2004), "Welfare and the Achievement of Goals" in *Philosophical Studies*, 121(1), 27–41.
Kitcher, Philip (1999), "Essence and Perfection" in *Ethics*, 110(1), 59–83.
Klosko, George and Stephen Wall (2003), *Perfectionism and Neutrality: Essays in Liberal Theory* (New York: Rowman and Littlefield).
Kraut, Richard (1989), *Aristotle on the Human Good* (Princeton University Press).
(1994), "Desire and Human Good" in *Proceedings of the American Philosophical Association*, 68, 39–54.
Lippert-Rasmussen, Kaspar (2003), "Measuring the Disvalue of Equality Over Time" in *Theoria*, 69(1-2), 32–45.
Locke, John (1689), *First Treatise of Government* in *Two Treatises of Government*, ed. P. Laslett (Cambridge University Press, 1988).
Mason, Andrew (2001), "Egalitarianism and the Levelling Down Objection" in *Analysis*, 61(3), 246–54.
McIntyre, Alasdair (2007), *After Virtue*, 3rd edn. (Notre Dame University Press).
McKerlie, Dennis (2001), "Justice Between the Young and the Old" in *Philosophy and Public Affairs*, 30(2), 153–77.
Mendola, Joseph (2005), "Intuitive Maximin" in *Canadian Journal of Philosophy*, 35(3), 429–40.

Mill, John Stuart (1859), *On Liberty*, ed. E. Rapaport (Indianapolis: Hackett Publishing Company, 1978).
Miller, David (2007), *National Responsibility and Global Justice* (Oxford University Press).
Miller, Richard (2010), *Globalizing Justice* (Oxford University Press).
Nickel, James (2007), *Making Sense of Human Rights* (Oxford: Blackwell).
Norcross, Alastair (1997), "Comparing Harms: Headaches and Human Lives" in *Philosophy and Public Affairs*, 26(2), 135–67.
(2002), "Contractualism and Aggregation" in *Social Theory and Practice*, 28(2), 303–14.
Nussbaum, Martha (1999), *Sex and Social Justice* (Cambridge University Press).
(2000), *Women and Human Development* (Cambridge University Press).
(2006), *Frontiers of Justice* (Cambridge, MA: Harvard University Press).
O'Hear, Anthony, ed. (2006), *Political Philosophy* (Cambridge University Press).
Olsaretti, Serena, ed. (2006), *Preferences and Well-Being* (Cambridge University Press).
Parfit, Derek (1984), *Reasons and Persons* (Oxford University Press).
Pettit, Philip (1997), "The Consequentialist Perspective" in Baron, Pettit, and Slote (1997), 92–174.
Pogge, Thomas (2001), *World Poverty and Human Rights* (New York, NY: Polity).
Portmore, Douglas W. (2007), "Welfare, Achievement and Self-Sacrifice" in *Journal of Ethics and Social Philosophy*, 2(2), 1-28.
Qizilbash, Mozaffar (2006), "Well-Being, Adaptation, and Human Limitations" in Olsaretti (2006), 83–109.
Quine, W. V. (1981), *From a Logical Point of View*, 2nd edn. (Cambridge, MA: Harvard University Press).
Rachels, Stuart (1998), "Counterexamples to the Transitivity of 'Better Than'" in *Australasian Journal of Philosophy*, 76(1), 71–83.
Railton, Peter (2003), *Facts, Values and Norms* (Cambridge University Press).
Rawls, John (1971), *A Theory of Justice* (Cambridge, MA: Harvard University Press).
(1995), *Political Liberalism* (New York, NY: Columbia University Press).
(1999), *Collected Papers*, ed. Samuel Freeman (Cambridge, MA: Harvard University Press).
(2001), *Justice as Fairness: A Restatement*, ed. Erin Kelly (Cambridge, MA: Harvard University Press).
Raz, Joseph (1987), *The Morality of Freedom* (Oxford University Press).
Rickard, M. (1995), "Sour Grapes, Rational Desires, and Objective Consequentialism" in *Philosophical Studies*, 80(3), 277–303.
Roemer, John (2004), "Eclectic Distributional Ethics" in *Politics, Philosophy, and Economics*, 3(3), 267–81.
Rosati, Connie (2006), "Preference Formation and Personal Good" in Olsaretti (2006), 33–64.
Ryberg, Jesper and Torbjörn Tännsjö (2007), *The Repugnant Conclusion: Essays on Population Ethics* (Springer).

Scanlon, T. M. (1998), *What We Owe to Each Other* (Cambridge, MA: Harvard University Press).
Schroeder, Mark (2007), *Slaves of the Passions* (Oxford University Press).
Sen, Amartya (1979), "Utilitarianism and Welfarism" in *The Journal of Philosophy*, 76(9), 463–89.
(1980), "Equality of What?" in *Tanner Lectures on Human Values* (Cambridge University Press), vol. 1, 195–220.
(1983), "Poor, Relatively Speaking" in *Oxford Economic Papers*, 35(2), 153–69.
(1984), *Resources, Values and Development* (Cambridge, MA: Harvard University Press).
(1987), *On Ethics and Economics* (Oxford: Blackwell).
(1993), *Inequality Reexamined* (Cambridge, MA: Harvard University Press).
(1999), *Development as Freedom* (New York, NY: Anchor Books).
(2009), *The Idea of Justice* (Cambridge, MA: Harvard University Press).
Sen, Amartya and Bernard Williams eds. (1982), *Utilitarianism and Beyond* (Cambridge University Press).
Sher, George (1997), *Beyond Neutrality: Perfectionism and Politics* (Cambridge University Press).
Shue, Henry (1981), *Basic Rights: Subsistence, Affluence, and U.S. Foreign Policy* (Princeton University Press).
Sidgwick, Henry (1907), *The Methods of Ethics*, 7th edn. (Indianapolis, IN: Hackett Publishing Company).
Singer, Peter (1972), "Famine, Affluence, and Morality" in *Philosophy and Public Affairs*, 1(3), 229–43.
Smart, J. J. C. and Bernard Williams (1974), *Utilitarianism: For and Against* (Cambridge University Press).
Smith, Adam (1776), *An Inquiry into the Nature and Causes of the Wealth of Nations* (London: Home University Library).
Sobel, David (1994), "Full Information Theories of Well-Being" in *Ethics*, 104(4), 784–810.
Sreenivasan, Gopal (1995), *The Limits of Lockean Rights in Property* (Oxford University Press).
Streeten, Paul (1994), "Human Development Means and Ends" in *American Economic Association Papers and Proceedings*, 84(2), 232–7.
Streeten, Paul, et al., eds. (1981), *First Thing's First: Meeting Human Needs in Developing Countries* (London: Oxford University Press for the World Bank).
Sumner, L. W. (1996), *Welfare, Happiness, and Ethics* (Oxford University Press).
Temkin, Larry (1993), *Inequality* (Oxford University Press).
(1996), "A Continuum Argument for Intransitivity" in *Philosophy and Public Affairs*, 25(3), 175–210.
(2003a), "Determining the Scope of Egalitarian Concern: A Defense of Complete Lives Egalitarianism" in *Theoria*, 69(1-2), 46–59.
(2003b), "Egalitarianism Defended" in *Ethics*, 113(4), 764–82.
Thomson, Judith Jarvis (1990), *The Realm of Rights* (Cambridge, MA: Harvard University Press).

Townsend, Peter (1985), "A Sociological Approach to the Measurement of Poverty" in *Oxford Economic Papers*, 37(4), 659–68.
Tungodden, Bertil and Peter Vallentyne (2005), "On the Possibility of Paretian Egalitarianism" in *Journal of Philosophy*, 102(3), 126–54.
van Parijs, Philippe, ed. (1992), *Arguing for Basic Income* (New York, NY: Verso).
van Parijs, Philippe (1995), *Real Freedom for All: What (if anything) can Justify Capitalism?* (Oxford University Press).
Velleman, David (2000), *The Possibility of Practical Reason* (Oxford University Press).
Waldron, Jeremy, ed. (1984), *Theories of Rights* (Oxford University Press).
Weirich, Paul (1983), "Utility Tempered with Equality" in *Noûs*, 17(3), 423–39.
White, Stuart (2003), *The Civic Minimum: On the Rights and Obligations of Economic Citizenship* (Oxford University Press).
Whiting, Jennifer (1988), "Aristotle's Function Argument: A Defense" in *Ancient Philosophy*, 8(1), 33–48.
Williams, Bernard (1974), "A Critique of Utilitarianism" in Smart and Williams (2004), 75–150.
(1981), *Moral Luck* (Cambridge University Press).
(1993), *Morality*, Canto Edition (Cambridge University Press).
Wolff, Jonathan and Avner De-Shalit (2007), *Disadvantage* (Oxford University Press).
Wright, Cory and Nikolaj Pedersen, eds. (2010), *New Waves in Truth* (New York, NY: Palgrave Macmillan).

Index